Happy Face:
A Family of
Monsters

Nicole D. Phoenix; Keith H. Jesperson

Crimson Cult Media

Happy Face: A Family of Monsters

Copyright © 2025 CrimsonCultMedia. All rights reserved. Crimson Cult Media DBA Sinister Society supports the right to free expression and the value of copyright. The purpose of copyright is to encourage writers and artists to produce creative works that enrich our culture. The scanning, uploading, reproduction, and transmission in any form or by any means of distribution, electronic or mechanical, including photocopying, recording, or by any information storage or retrieval system of this book without written permission, is a theft of the authors' intellectual property. If you would like permission to use material from the book (other than for review purposes), please contact crimsoncultmedia@gmail.com. Thank you for your support of the authors' rights. For more information please visit https://crimsoncultbooks.com

This book is for educational purposes only. Please see the Publisher and Author notes included.

Library of Congress Control Number: 2024949603

Printed in the United States of America

Digital ISBN: 979-8-89467-019-5

Paperback ISBN: 979-8-89467-023-2

Hardback ISBN: 979-8-89467-017-1

Audiobook ISBN: 979-8-89467-018-8

Contents

Foreword	V
Letter	1
1. Introduction	2
2. Disclaimers	3
Letter 1.1	6
3. American Justice	7
Letter 1.2	15
4. A Killer's Life, Part One	16
Letter 1.3	27
5. Becoming Part American	28
Letter 2.1	37
6. Damaged Goods	38
Letter 2.2	49
7. My Resume	50
8. A New World	62
9. Self Destruct	72
10. Taunja Bennett	87
Bennett by KHJ	102

11. Daun Slagle	103
12. The Learning Curve	119
13. The Letters	139
KHJ Hand Tracing	151
14. Friday the 13th	152
15. Checkmate	162
Columbia River by KHJ	175
16. Saving Face	176
17. Killer Kit	191
18. Wyoming	197
19. Postscript Clutter	205
Art by Keith H. Jesperson	209
20. MORE Postscript Clutter	210
21. Even More Postscript Clutter	212
Art by Keith H. Jesperson	213
22. Tale of Two Tales	214
23. One Last Story	217
Art by Keith H. Jesperson	219
Letter 3.1	220
24. Afterword	221
25. Resources	223
26. Forensic Psychology Study Questions	225

Foreword

By John Borowski, Filmmaker/Author

Being a filmmaker and author on the subject of serial killers, I meet and work with a wide range of people. Having communication with forensic psychologists, investigators, sheriffs, corrections officers, attorneys, prosecutors, judges, and even correspondence with serial killers. I crossed paths with Keith Jesperson when I was attending a true crime convention in Indianapolis, Indiana.

I arrived at the convention on May 23, 2011. As soon as I walked in, the owners of the establishment wanted to speak with me. They showed me an envelope that was sent to the establishment but sent to the attention of the convention. I filmed the opening of the envelope. It was a letter from Keith Jesperson, who I knew of from murderabilia circles. The letter read that Jesperson knew of the convention and others there. Then he stated he was interested in me making a film about his life. My heart stopped as I was filming. I was in disbelief. Trying to think of how Jesperson knew of me and how he knew we were having the convention. I didn't write him back immediately. I wasn't intensely interested in his story as I am more fascinated by serial killers who are complex in their psychology and murders. Like the case of Albert Fish, which is one of the most psychologically complex serial killers. Fish had a deep religious psyche and twisted the stories of the Bible as reason for his murders.

Eventually, I did write Jesperson back and we began corresponding. I became more interested in his story as we spoke. The most fascinating part of his case doesn't even include Jesperson himself! What is most interesting to me is how Laverne Pavlinac and John Sosnovske were arrested and convicted for one of the murders. Pavlinac went to the police and accused Sosnovske of murdering Taunja Bennett. There was no proof whatsoever that either had committed the crime. In what was a total miscarriage of justice, they were sent to prison. After five years, they were released when Jesperson admitted to murdering Bennett. I am always interested in human rights and injustices committed by both sides of the coin: the murderer and those involved in investigating the murder. Many times, innocent people are sent to prison because states want to bring a close to the case and garner a successful feather in their hat.

Jesperson told me to send him a New York Times article, and he would put it in the correct order and write more about it. I sent him the article, and he cut parts up and numbered them in sequence. This was fascinating to me. Eventually, I felt I had a great miniseries on my hands. Receiving the letter from Jesperson as the springboard, I could have also gone to visit and interview Jesperson, then interview the people involved in the conviction of Pavlinac and Sosnovske, weaving both of these stories together and exposing the injustice of the system. After writing to Jesperson for a year, I approached him and told him I was ready to create a miniseries on his case and that I wanted him to commit to the project. He then refused me, saying that he was working with someone else on a book and that "it is all about timing." I was shocked at first. But then I realized that, of course, he was going to manipulate me. He is a serial killer! That is what they do. They are masters of the con and expert narcissists. Jesperson conned me for a year. Serial killers crave constant attention. They enjoy reading stories about themselves in the newspapers and on the internet, constantly hoping to see even a tiny glimpse of a mention of their name. They always want something from you. Sometimes, it is just writing letters, and other times, it is money. Whoever caters to these serial killers are victims themselves because they are being manipulated to give them what they want in exchange for something the person writing them may want, like an autograph to display, collect, sell, or trade.

In 2014, I created the term "serial killer culture" when I released my film of the same name. The term encompasses a broad spectrum of people involved in the serial killer culture. Artists, friends of killers, murderabilia collectors, forensic psychologists, survivors, and many more fall under the umbrella of serial killer culture. Part of the culture is art and the killers who make it. Some killers con the public by creating so called "art". Like John Wayne Gacy, whose paintings look like they were painted by a five-year-old. Actually, a child could probably do a better painting than Gacy. This is just another way to gain attention. But there are some killers and other prisoners who actually exhibit talent when creating their art. This talent may have been hidden within them and because of their time in incarceration, their artistic talent is released. Elmer Wayne Henley of the Houston Mass Murders is a talented artist. Like Jesperson is, his landscapes and portraits, especially his self-portrait, show definitive talent.

Serial killers corresponding from prison and writing their autobiographies is nothing new. The most famous correspondence case was between hate-filled Carl Panzram and corrections officer Henry Lesser in 1928. H.H. Holmes wrote his autobiography, *Holmes' Own Story*, in prison BEFORE his trial, attempting to convince the public he was innocent of nearly obliterating the entire Pietzel family. Gacy wrote a book on his trial called "A Question of Doubt", which is nearly unreadable. When writing to Dennis Rader, he nor I could use the letters B.T.K as a prison rule. Which is where we get into the truth. How can anyone decipher whether writing by serial killers is fact or fiction? Are parts fact and other parts fiction? This can be difficult to figure out, but if one is immersed in the serial killer culture and an expert in their field, there are ways to tell. Gacy made admissions when he was finally apprehended, but then, once in prison, he stated that he never killed anyone and twelve other people had keys to his house. Like twelve people really came into his house and buried bodies in his crawlspace. Sometimes, serial killers can be laughably absurd. It is my belief that Carl Panzram lied about some of his evil deeds because he knew he was being sent to a scary Penitentiary, Leavenworth. But there was also a lot of truth in Panzram's autobiography, like the scar behind his left ear from an operation. I doubted his stories of traveling the world, but then, after I completed my documentary, *Carl Panzram: The Spirit of Hatred and Vengeance*, I came across his passport photos from traveling the world. So he was telling the truth. The truth is important. Urban myths are created, and people believe them. When producing my miniseries, *The John Wayne Gacy Murders: Life and Death in Chicago*, I uncovered numerous myths about the case. The biggest was that there was not a smell of death in the house when police were invited in. The investigators needed a reason for the second search warrant, and the smell was the perfect ruse. The lesson here is to be careful when communicating with serial killers. Never lose focus of what they have done and who they are—predators seeking victims.

Is this a truthful autobiography by Jesperson? It is up to you, dear reader, to judge it for yourself.

902

While I was killing them all, I gave no thought to what my actions would do to my family. Why? Because getting caught never entered my mind. But sitting in a 6'x8' foot cell for the rest of my life hits home. What life I have left is defined by how I lived it outside these walls. I killed myself being a murderer. We only have one life to live and we have to make it a quality life. Not toss it off like trash. Am I boring you with me feeling sorry for myself? Boohoo!! Getting caught as a serial killer will do that to you. Poor poor

Introduction

By Author Nicole D. Phoenix

Humans have always been fascinated by the darker side of human nature– what drives people to commit horrific acts? Serial killers, in particular, are some of the most intriguing when looking into this darkness. What makes them tick? Were there any signs that could have helped prevent such atrocities? These questions and many others are asked by numerous people who seek to understand how someone can turn into a cold-blooded killer.

In pursuit of understanding the complexities of serial crime, I initiated a correspondence with Keith Jesperson, infamously known as the Happy Face Killer. Through his unedited words, I present a candid and unsettling glimpse into the mind of a notorious killer. This raw, firsthand account offers a unique opportunity to explore the thoughts, emotions, and experiences that shaped Jesperson's actions. By examining his inner world, can we uncover valuable insights to prevent future tragedies? This is my hope.

Disclaimers

On April 6th, 2024, I turned 69 years old. Two days before, on April 4th, I sat in a hearing room here at Oregon State Penitentiary, talking over a Zoom meeting with a judge in Florida about my conviction of murder in the second degree, a life sentence to run concurrent to my Oregon prison time. Six minutes to settle my Florida murder case at a court cost of 100.00. Twenty-nine years after turning myself in for the murder of Julie Ann Cunningham of Clark County, Washington state. Finally, all of my cases are on record as being solved in court. For the past 29 years, I had to maintain a certain story-line in order to get things done without landing on death row in Florida.

Every murder is different, and yet every murder has to appear to be the same. The blame goes to the victim for something they did, causing me to kill them.

The legal system demands this! Yes, the American justice system is flawed. When lawyers get a hold of suspects, details will fit the story told in order to achieve the perfect outcome. Consider it a game of chance, like chess. Each player trying to outsmart the other.

In this game, you have the police chasing suspects and gathering up evidence so their prosecutor boss can win at trial versus lawyers and suspects trying to avoid a conviction or at least being convicted of a lesser crime. When the prosecutors have what they feel is a winning case, they present it in a trial and hope that the jury agrees with them and the suspect's guilt.

The prosecutor's job is to seek the truth, not just seek a conviction. Most follow their jobs seriously; some steer off their path and will convict, knowing they do not have the real suspect. It becomes a numbers game. Convictions are all they are after.

My first murder was one of those cases.

Two totally innocent people are arrested and later convicted in a chain of events documented by Jim McIntyre, the prosecutor in the case, told to the *Los Angeles Times* news magazine. The story was published on September 1st, 1996, 'A Question of Guilt' by writer Barry Siegel. He outlined the story of evidence gathering and a trial leading to their convictions. It would also tell a story about me. How I was able to win their freedom from prison. Too bad, though that the story left out lots of reading between the lines material that will help to explain things.

A few years ago, I received a letter from a Ms. Maria Dilorenzo of Staton Island, New York, asking me if I'd like to use her blog at *beyondthecrime.com* to tell my story. We talked, and I began writing out my story titled 'Guilt Details' Parts 1, 2, 3, and 4. Maria placed my material on her blog for all to view. There were also about five hours of Question and Answer audio.

Everyone that wrote me would be sent to her blog to cut through all of the bullshit told by other writers and investigators willing to hide facts to protect certain people's retirements.

Over the past 29 years, there have been many books and TV shows trying to tell my story. Bill Kurtis of American Justice told it with a gleam in his eye. Showtime did a movie starring Ann Margaret as Laverne Pavlinac. The movie flopped because the storyline was a cover-up. Crime writer Jack Olson wrote his version of events to make me out to be worse than I was. As he told me on a visit, he had to juice it up a bit to capture his audience's desire for evil. David Arquette played me in a movie shown on the Lifetime channel. It flopped as hard as Showtime's.

My father decided he wanted to do a book and contacted Lionel Dahmer, Jeffrey Dahmer's father, hoping to do a joint book. Thank God it didn't work out.

Around 2006, my own daughter, Melissa Moore, went on the Dr. Phil show, and all of a sudden, she became an item in true crime. Her book called 'Shattered Silence' written by M. Bridget Cook, is a bunch of lies told to create her daddy as a monster. TV shows came after the book. A series called 'Monster in my Family' kept me in the news as Melissa is introduced as my daughter at the start of every episode. At every turn, someone new is providing a book or news story.

In 2011, crime writer Matthew William Phelps asked me to be Raven, the call-in serial killer to his hit series on Discovery channel called *Dark Minds*. I'm Raven in seasons two and three. He goes on to write his book called 'Dangerous Ground,' a book about me and mostly about him. How writing books on killers makes him visibly ill. Personally, I think he's full of shit.

Go to the internet for answers about me. I've read Wikipedia and all what they made up. I'm sure all over the net. In here, I have no access except what is copied and allowed through the mail.

In 2010, while I sat in the Riverside County Jail, I received a book written by Christopher Berry Dee called 'Dead Men Talking' in the chapter about me, he committed fraud when he wrote I had been convicted of first-degree sexual assault in the case of Daun Slagle in Shasta, California. Rape...claims to have seen documents providing all this information. Truth be known, the Daun Slagle case was dismissed in April 1992. I contacted John Blake Publishing in the United Kingdom to report Berry Dee's fraud and threatened a lawsuit. I'd later get a letter from the pissed-off writer telling me I'm a convicted person and open game to writers like himself. I'm sure the book took a hit when it was pulled and changed.

In these past few years, I have been on two podcasts—#1 Brutal Nation and #2 The Lighter Side of Serial Killers. I told a story-line to keep me off of death row in Florida. Now that Florida has sentenced me to no more time, I can finally write a book to tell all my life's stories.

- Chapter Two: American Justice
    The early fog had burned off by 10:00 am and two bicycle riders were riding the Scenic Columbia River Gorge Scenic Highway when they noticed something odd in a ravine just east of the Vista House monument. Upon close inspection, one stayed
- at the scene while the other raced to make a phone call to police. Sunday morning, January 22, 1990. Multnomah County Sheriffs Responded to see a partially nude young woman laying face up, what was left of her face, in a ravine, dead with a rope tied around her neck. Soon the crime scene
- was crawling with investigators trying to secure evidence to catch whomever was

American Justice

The early fog had burned off by 10.00 am, and two bicycle riders were riding the scenic Columbia River Gorge Scenic Highway when they noticed something odd on a ravine just east of the Vista house monument. Upon closer inspection, one stayed at the scene while the other raced to make a phone call to the police.

Sunday morning, January 22, 1990. Multnomah County Sheriffs responded to see a partially nude young woman lying face up, what was left of her face, in a ravine, dead with a rope tied around her neck.

Soon, the crime scene was crawling with investigators trying to secure evidence to catch whomever was her killer.

Her face looked as though her killer had beat her with a hammer. Her jeans were down by her ankles. A half-inch diameter nylon rope around her neck. Her body was removed to the coroner's office to confirm her death was by more than just strangulation.

Detective John Ingram of the Multnomah County Sheriff's Office and Detective Alan Corson of the Oregon State Police Office in Multnomah County were assigned the case.

In every investigation in Oregon, a State Police Officer is assigned to allow the investigators to keep going should it cross over the county line's jurisdiction. This would play into this case. Both detectives settled in to try to come up with answers.

Eight days after her daughter went missing, Mrs. Bennett of Gresham, Oregon, saw photos in the news and identified her at the coroner's office as Taunja Ann Bennett, 23, of Gresham, Oregon. Taunja, a mildly ~~retarded~~ woman, frequented bars and taverns in the area. It didn't take long to locate the B and I Tavern on State Avenue, as it was the last place Ms. Bennett was seen alive.

On the afternoon of Saturday, Tuesday 21st, 1990, she had been drinking beer and playing pool with two men. The bartender, a woman, remembered it wrong when she claimed it had been raining and Taunja was soaking wet when she entered the bar about noon. She could not recall when Taunja left but guessed it to be at least by 3:00 pm.

No one knew the two men with Taunja, and a wide search turned up nothing.

It had been about two weeks since learning who was murdered, and nothing was being found out when detectives went to their bosses at the Multnomah County District Attorney's Office to talk it over with Assistant District Attorney Jim McIntyre.

District Attorney Michael Schrunk assigned the Bennett murder case to Jim McIntrye and Keith Meisenheimer, his second chair. A decision was made to use the press to look for answers in the investigation.

They contacted the Oregon Newspaper and placed a well thought out ad looking for the public's help to help solve the Bennett murder. The story told the basics: Looking for two men last seen at B and I Tavern on State Avenue Saturday afternoon, January 21st, 1990, in the company of Ms. Bennett.

They had to be careful when placing the ad not to include certain facts. There are people who will confess to any crime for attention or other reasons. There will be crank calls coming in. they needed to be able to weed out the crazies.

At first, not many calls came in. Those two men never came forward. Then, one afternoon, a call came in from the Clackamas County Sheriff's Office, reporting to Multnomah County. Strange. The actual phone number on the ad would go directly to the office of Multnomah County Sheriffs. The woman calling in 'anonymously' had called Clackamas County Sheriff to report hearing John Sosnovske was the killer of Taunja Ann Bennett, found with a rope tied around her neck in the Columbia River Gorge. Detective John Ingram took the call. When the anonymous woman hung up, he typed in John Sosnovske's name into his computer and his name popped up in the system as being on county probation. Nothing serious, mostly petty things. He followed the man's trail to talk to John Sosnovske's probation officer.

Why was an anonymous woman calling in to point at Sosnovske?

Right off, John's probation officer said, *"That has to be Laverne Palvlinac calling you!"*

For the past three years, Laverne had called the police whenever she and John were fighting to try to get rid of him by sending him back to jail. Once, she even reported to the F.B.I. to say Sosnovske robbed the bank in Tigard, Oregon. Several times reported that Sosnovske was violating his probation by drinking alcohol. Each time, her reports to the police came up empty. John Sosnovske is legally blind, has no driver's license or car, and has to be driven by someone to work or anywhere.

Laverne's second husband died of cancer. Sosnovske had been working at their farm and climbed into her bed soon after and became a future husband-to-be to Laverne, eighteen years older than John, real love-hate relationship with frequent calls to the police. It was safe to say Detective Ingram was getting the full picture of who Laverne Palvlinac was from county probation you can bet county probation sent a copy of Sosnovske's file over to prosecutor John McIntrye to review.

Regardless of Palvlinac's lies to police in previous complaints about Sosnovske, both detectives Corson and Ingram went out to meet Laverne Palvlinac to hear what she had to say for herself.

She opened her door and invited them in for cookies and fresh coffee. It didn't take long for Ingram to get Laverne to confess to making the anonymous call to him. She tells a story about hearing Sosnovske talking to another man she doesn't know about taking a woman into the gorge and killing her. But by this time, after talking to county probation, they knew Sosnovske couldn't drive a car and could not have done what Pavlinac suggested he did. Easy, really easy to cut to the meat of her claims is to hook her up to a polygraph machine to see if she is capable of telling the truth. Do they test her? No! Instead, they meet with the DA's office to request a search warrant to search Pavlinac and Sosnovske's home. They show up to a Grandma-looking woman offering coffee and cupcakes as they tear apart their home, looking for any evidence in the Bennett case. All they found was a box with a piece of paper and the words written in pencils: T. Bennett, great piece! Eventually, this note would be proven to be written by Laverne Pavlinac.

At this time I'd like to ask the cops, *what were they thinking here?* County probation told them Pavlinac was a liar and Sosnovske had to be driven everywhere. Could they be considering using her to frame Sosnovske for the murder? Or, maybe they just were bored and wanted to see how far Laverne could be pushed in the case just for giggles. If they were to talk to Sosnovske, they needed probable cause to do so, and since the search didn't produce anything, Laverne needed to obtain a pick-up order to talk to Sosnovske.

In the days that followed the search of her home, Laverne kept calling Detective Ingram to voice her concerns about how her life had been and where it was heading. I'm sure Detective Ingram told her things to create probable cause in another search of their home. Four days later, searching Laverne's car trunk, they locate a small purse like the one Taunja had and newspaper clippings about the murder. And one very important thing more: a cut-out piece of women's jeans where the fly was. Taunja's jeans had the fly area cut out of them. This fact had never been disclosed to the public or the press. Only the killer could know this.

The police showed up at the lumber mill where Sosnovske worked and took him into custody for questioning. The evidence in the car went to the Oregon crime lab. For the next ten hours, Detectives Corson and Ingram drill Sosnovske for answers. Eventually, they hooked him up to a polygraph machine to test him, and Sosnovske failed.

The polygraph claimed Sosnovske was the killer of Bennett. Unequivocally!

Faced with the results of the test and the fact he felt the detectives believed Laverne's lies, he decided to tell his lies.

Being on probation with the law has taught him a few things. Tell the police a story to send them after someone else. Use the story being pushed and put a twist to it. Laverne's story begins with her overhearing Sosnovske talking to a man at the JB's Lounge off Interstate 5 at exit 286, Wilsonville, Oregon, over 25 miles from the B and I Tavern in NE Portland. No one at JB's remembers Taunja Bennett being there. No matter, because all stories are to include exit 286 off I-5 as where the story begins.

Both Sosnovske and Bennett have no car or driver's license. Someone had to push them there.

The bicycle riders who found Bennett's body on Sunday morning, January 22, 1990, were Bennett's first suspects in her murder. That is how the evidence trail is established. After they were clear that their alibis checked out, the family looked at them. Then, after cleaning them, the circle grows to places she went to and people she hung out with. When all of that didn't find them a suspect, they contacted the public using the press, hoping to weed out any crazy person from lying about murder and sending detectives down a preferable rabbit hole of wrong ideas of how it should end.

And we might ask: Is Detective Corson and Ingram that gullible to believe a known liar sending them down a rabbit hole after an innocent man? Apparently so!

And then again, there is their suspect, John Sosnovske. His problem is he believes the detectives believe Laverne's lies this time. I don't think he could conclude that the detectives were aware of Pavlinac's lies and were using her to frame him because they just wanted to see how far she was willing to take it.

Either way, he needed to send the detectives in another direction away from him.

After his failed lie detector test, Sosnovske tells how he got a ride from JB's Lounge in Wilsonville with his friend Chuck Riley. As Chuck drove, he looked to the back seat and saw the body of a dead woman. He doesn't ask Chuck about it at all. Dropped off at home, Chuck Riley must have taken the woman into the gorge to dispose of her in the ravine.

Way to go, Sosnovske! Send them after your friend!

And, of course, the detectives had to track down this Chuck Riley character. Days later, Chuck's alibi checks out, and the crime lab reports all of the evidence found in Pavlinac's car is planted there by Pavlinac and her bogus. The note found is in Pavlinac's hand.

When Corson and Ingram return to talk to Pavlinac, again she invites them in for pastry and lemonade this time. Confronted with the fact that she lied about the evidence, she decided to tell another bigger lie.

In this new lie, she knows Sosnovske killed Bennett because she was the one to drive him and her dead body from Wilsonville and to her resting place.

I know, test this time! But they don't.

Hook, line, and sinker, they swallow her lies and turn on their tape recorder.

What if Detective Ingram is schooling Laverne Pavlinac to tell a certain story to fit facts she could not comprehend? When they took Laverne Pavlinac's car in to look at it for evidence, they found no trace evidence to conclude Bennett had been in her car. This point has to be explained away in her next lie to the police.

What if Ingram schools Laverne Pavlinac, and after they get their story straight, he calls Detective Corson, and they both go over to see Pavlinac to hear it; only Corson is hearing it for the first time and believing it is all on Laverne?

Detective Corson isn't in on this frame-up? However, he brings credibility to her story and is on the stand claiming it.

Pavlinac starts her story by saying she was at home when Sosnovske called for a ride. He tells her to bring something plastic and meet him in the parking lot of the Burns Brothers truck stop behind JB's Lounge. When she pulls into the busy truck-stop lot, she sees Sosnovske standing over what appears to be the body of a dead woman.

(Now, this would have been a good time to call the police to get him arrested and out of her life for good.)

She pulls next to them, and Sosnovske takes the plastic shower curtain from her car, wraps Bennett's body in it, and places it in the back seat of her car. They get in and he tells her to drive toward the Columbia River Gorge up to the Vista House monument.

She tells how it was pouring rain that night. About twelve miles later, Sosnovske climbed into the back seat and cut Bennett's fly from her jeans as a memento of the act. They drove east of the Vista House monument, and at the ravine, Sosnovske carried Bennett's body into it, depositing her face up on the cold, wet ground.

Driving back home, he tossed the plastic shower curtain out the window. Then threatened Laverne that if she told anyone, he would kill her whole family.

But here she was telling anyway.

In a murder case, it matters where the person was killed. Where the murder took place is who has jurisdiction in the outcome of the case. An overlooked fact in this made-up story by Pavlinac (And Detective Ingram).

However, this fact didn't get past Detective Al Corson. He won his argument over Ingram, and they arrested Sosnovske and placed him in Washington County jail because Wilsonville is in Washington County. Because this case is now Washington County's case, a whole new group of investigators and prosecutors will re-examine the evidence for trial. This means that Pavlinac's story-telling fell on someone else's ears other than Detective John Ingram. And he just could not let that happen, especially since they had staged a drive-around with Pavlinac.

Imagine this: Detective Ingram picks up Laverne and drives her to where Bennett's body was found. Points to the ravine. Let her read about the clothes Bennett had been wearing. After it sinks in, he drops her off and calls up Detective Corson. Corson and Ingram go over to pick up Pavlinac and drive her, at her instruction, to the exact place where Bennett's body was found. They take photos of her pointing to the ravine.

As they drive, she is able to tell Detective Corson what Taunja was wearing, getting every detail right. Case Closed!

With this new development that will soon have Pavlinac talking to new people in Washington County, Ingram knew he had to see Pavlinac to get her to change her story again.

Years later, Pavlinac was asked why she had changed her story, and she told detectives that she was visited by Multnomah County Sheriff Detective John Ingram and was told he would have to release Sosnovske into her home if she didn't change her story. That they just didn't have enough to convict him. So, a new story was fabricated.

In this new story, Sosnovske calls Pavlinac at home, asking for a ride. She shows up and finds Sosnovske standing next to a live Taunja Bennett. Both of them get into the back seat and make out as Laverne follows John's instructions to drive to the Vista House Monument's parking lot at Crown Point.

They park, and both Bennett and Sosnovske exit the car and have sex in the doorway of the building. A few minutes into this great consensual sexual act, John returns to the car to get a length of rope and to tell Laverne to follow him to watch him have sex with Bennett.

Pavlinac takes the rope and ties it around Taunja's neck, and squeezes it tightly as John gets done with his sexual experience.

In the aftermath of the event, Laverne realizes she has just killed Taunja Bennett. John carries Bennett's dead body to Pavlinac's car and places her in the back seat. They leave the lot and find the ravine and deposit her on the cold, hard ground.

For hours, Detective Ingram went over this story with Pavlinac before calling up Detective Corson.

When Corson met Ingram, they both went to see Pavlinac, and as always, she opened the door and offered coffee and cake.

Then tells Corson, "It's correction time!"

The tape recorder turned on to record her confession to murder. After it is taped, do they arrest her? Do they give her a lie detector test? NO! They leave the confessed murderer at her home and go see the boss Jim McIntrye to let him make up his own mind on if this new story is what he wants to sell a jury.

Adding up what they had, he tells them to move Sosnovske from Washington County jail to Multnomah's jail. Then go out and arrest Pavlinac and put her in their jail.

At the booking counter, something strange took place.

Pavlinac hugged both detectives.

What did they have? They didn't have the shower curtain added to her new story to explain away no trace of Bennett in her car. They had no explanation for the battered face of Taunja. They didn't have a confirmed crime scene investigation.

Imagine having sex on hard, cold concrete, and it left no marks on Bennett's backside. No one saw this act taking place when the parking lot was filled with cars.

They had John's failed polygraph test and Laverne's taped confession of the murder and knew exactly everything Bennett had been wearing.

What they had was both Pavlinac and Sosnovske in places they could control.

By Pavlinac's reaction to being arrested, it is safe to say she was sold the idea of not going to prison if she testified against Sosnovske.

So why do I say this? Later in the year, near November, Wendell Birkland, Laverne's lawyer, came to her with a deal to do ten years. This kind of made her aware of the wrong deal she felt she made. All of a sudden, she recants her confession, and her defense team gives her a lie detector test, and she passes it, proving she made it all up.

They didn't kill anyone! But too little too late!

The damage had been done. It would be her own words on tape that would eventually convict her of killing Taunja Ann Bennett of capital murder.

In January of 1991, her trial began, and she had one hiccup. A note found on a wall in a Livingston, Montana bus station claimed to have killed Bennett on January 21, 1990.

Two people took the blame so he could kill again.

He offered the fact that he had cut off Bennett's jeans's fly area. The prosecutor simply said, 'It must have been one of Pavlinac's family members who wrote the message.'

Nine out of the twelve jurors wanted Pavlinac to be put to death.

Sosnovske would be threatened with the death penalty, and he caved in to accept a life sentence of fifteen years to life. What he should've done is go to trial to face them to give him a death sentence that comes with an automatic appeal.

However, the problems of the shady evidence in the case, chances are the DA would not go for the death penalty to avoid the automatic appeals.

In March 1991, a second message was found on a bathroom wall at a truck stop in Umatilla, Oregon, claiming to be Bennett's killer. Again, DA's sidelined the notion of being wrong.

At some point, you can bet that the prosecutors felt a need to drop the case against Laverne Pavlinac and John Sosnovske. But because they had invested so much time into it, it just didn't fit their narrative.

Their only real act in the case was to provide it all to a jury and let the jury decide. If acquitted, they would say we tried and move on to the real killer. A guilty verdict turned out to be maybe not what they had hoped for.

Too many people were asking too many questions.

Those messages on the walls were pulling at them.

Something bad was coming.

her killer. Her face looked as though her killer had beat her with a hammer. Her jeans were down by her ankles. A ½ inch diameter Nylon Rope around her neck. Her body Removed to The coroner's office to confirm her death by just how. Strangulation. Detective John Ingram of The Multnomah County Sheriff's office and Detective Allen "Al" Corson of The Oregon State Police office in Multnomah county were assigned The case. In every investigation in Oregon, a State police officer is assigned to allow The investigation to keep going should it cross over county lines jurisdictions. This would play into This case. Both detectives settled in to try to come up with answers.

A Killer's Life, Part One

People always want to know...How does a person become a murderer?

There has to be some driving force in the universe to create us. Most will go back to our childhood to try to discover an answer. Try to pinpoint the angry child because of his or her parents' influences. Most of the information out there about me has been talked about and diagnosed to form opinions, and not necessarily correct. What they don't know, they make up.

And I am tired of it.

I will not tell you everything that went on in my life because most things are not important. Tear apart someone else's life if you have to. Most want to provide a sort of history lesson to understand me to your own crowd and don't bother to listen to what really happened to me.

I was born Wednesday, April 6th, 1955, to Gladys and Leslie Jesperson in Chilliwack, British Columbia, Canada. I'm the middle child of five. I have an older sister named Sharon, an older brother named Bruce, a younger brother named Brad, and a younger sister named Jill. None of them turned out to be killers. We all grew up in the same household under the same rules and experiences. Our parents stayed together all through our upbringing. However, we all chose different paths to live by.

The first sign that most psychologists point to as a warning sign that someone will go down the path of murder is bed-wetting.

Bed-wetting? No, not me! My brother Bruce had a problem with it himself up until his early school years. Mother would find soiled underwear under his bed. He was forced to wear a diaper until he was ten or so. I remember Bruce would go to school and take the diaper off before getting to school and put it back on before returning home. I think it was the shame of having to wear it that finally made Bruce make an effort to control himself.

Fire starting? I do like to sit around a campfire roasting smores. Our homes all had fireplaces, and my father made sure we always had enough firewood to keep the home warm in winter. Come to think of it, there was this one time when I climbed into a neighbor's old house used to store firewood and newspaper. He had just built a new home not far from his old, smaller house. That Saturday afternoon, five of us kids, including my brother Brad and myself, climbed into an open window and built a fire in the fireplace. The fire grew hot, and the cedar wood began to explode with pops here and there, sending out sparks of embers into the stacked newspapers. We all noticed at once how a blaze started behind us. We panicked at seeing it and stomped out the flames, pulled apart the fire in the fireplace, and climbed out the window to escape in several directions.

Apparently we didn't do a good enough job at putting out the fire because an hour later, firemen were finishing up the job.

Word went out to find out who set the fire; my brother Brad was quick to point at me. So were his three friends.

My father had me take my life's savings out and give it to the man for the damage caused. He asked who else was included, and I could not point back at Brad or his friends even though people reported seeing all five of us exiting the home. Maybe not telling on the others is why I wasn't bent over his bed and whipped with his belt.

Animal cruelty? I was around four years old when Dad brought home two brown lab puppies we named Duke and Diamond. They were all of ours, not just mine, but try telling the dogs that! Animals sense those people they want to be around.

Duke picked me.

We became buddies and played together all of the time. At night, Duke would sleep on my bed. When he needed to do his business, he would run downstairs and scratch on the front door until Mom opened it for him. Minutes later, scratch on the door to be let back in and get up to my bed, he would come. At suppertime, Duke had his place between Dad and myself. Mother could be heard telling us not to feed the dog at the table. And when she thought we were not looking, she would toss Duke some things.

Diamond had a different idea.

He liked to run off for days and come back all beat up from fighting other dogs. Dad gave Diamond to a friend of his who drove logging trucks. Heard that Diamond died when he backed up his truck and ran over Diamond.

I once found a crow with a broken wing and tried to nurse it back to health. Had it for several days when my brother Bruce decided it was time to kill it. He took it over to his friend Billy Robinson, and they tortured it to death, injecting it with bleach.

The Robinson boys were all crazy when it came to messing with animals that just happened to wander onto their property. Billy, Bruce's friend, and Danny- well, Danny was evil with his throwing knives. For many reasons, Duke and I never went over there together. There are only so many kids our age in the neighborhood. We all tried to get along. For years, we all tried. It was a great day when the Robinson's moved to Kamloops. Mr. Robinson worked for Finning Caterpillar of Chilliwack before he was transferred to Kamloops.

I have often wondered, where are they now? Did those evil boys end up in prison?

My father was a design engineer who ran Chilliwack Welding and Machine Shop. Back in those days, it wasn't uncommon for old homes to be moved to new foundations elsewhere. Our first home was a ranch style home on Henley Avenue built by our father. He even dug a swimming pool into the backyard. Something he regretted later when people kept dropping off their kids to swim there, not asking if they could.

He built a fence to stop them, but they just jumped the fences. So, one day, he filled the pool with dirt. Across the street from the Henley home was a playground park full of slides, swings, and teeter-totters built by Les Jesperson and Company. I was too young to remember living there.

When I was four, Dad moved home to our property and Lickman Road, several miles from town in the rural countryside. The property was five acres divided by a creek on the east side of Lickman Road south of Keith Wilson Road.

If you ever want to visit my home, as you drive east out of Vancouver, BC, on Hwy 1, turn south on Lickman Road. You'll pass Atcheletc School to the left, my first year of school had been there, pass over a set of railroad tracks that are raised, the farm just south of the tracks is where we bought milk by the gallon, then there is the Keith Wilson Crossing, at the corner of Lickman and Keith Wilson is where Bruce and I picked up our newspaper to deliver to our customers, south on Keith Wilson, we were the second house on the left before the wooden bridge across our creek where twice a year, salmon swam up into to spawn if you were to keep driving on the left was Remple's Raspberry Farm and then a quarter mile further the Redder River, one of the best salmon and steelhead rivers of the world.

Our father had cleared the land and poured a new foundation to park our older house on. Damned up the creek at the back of the property, adding a waterwheel for effect. Large maple trees provided a rope swing so we kids could swing out over a deepened part of the creek to let go and swim in.

An island had a bridge over to it with a sitting bench to just sit and reflect on things. Another bigger bridge connected both sides of our property, allowing our horses and other animals to cross into the south half of our land. Eventually, he built a two-car garage and a small barn for stalls and hay storage. We had sheep, chickens, ducks, horses, and a steer. When we moved into the two-story home, we had to get rid of thousands of garter snakes. We tried everything to make them leave, and then one day, we came up with a solution: capture a few buckets full and relocate them to a few ponds full of millions of frogs.

Some snakes must have returned to tell the rest to follow them to their new feeding station because, within a few days, it was hard to find a garter snake.

Our spring-fed creek grew bigger as it ran west through several pieces of property full of beaver dams before emptying into the Vedder River a mile or so downstream. Us kids could always go fishing for trout in the creek. Always careful to watch for bears, especially during the salmon spawn. Our mother called us back from wherever we were with a whistle she blew. If we didn't hear it, Duke certainly let us know it was time to go.

Bruce delivered the Vancouver Sun newspaper after school. He had maybe fifty customers in all. My paper route was with the Province. The paper had to be delivered by 7:00 AM every morning. Because Bruce sometimes had school activities, I had to learn his route to be sure papers were delivered. He didn't have to learn my route. Fair? When bad weather hit, my mother could drive me to deliver my seven-mile course. Even though my delivery numbers were half as many as Bruce's route, at Christmas, I'd end up getting more money in tips. One customer at the end of my route would have a cup of hot chocolate waiting for me in the mailbox.

My second year in school was spent in the new Unsworth Elementary School on Unsworth Road, about a mile from our home. A three-room school covering grades one to six. To get there, head east on Keith Wilson to the next road and head north a short way.

My time there seemed uneventful. A few fights with the locals is all. No big deal!

However, one fight I had with Brain made it to other books.

We punched each other, and he ran home to Mommy; Mommy came outside and, using foul language, defended her son. I simply yelled back at her the same language she used on me. Got on my bike and began to ride home.

About halfway home, my bike was bumped off the road by Brain's older brother's car, bending my rear wheel. The twice-my-age boy jumped out of his car and commenced to kick the shit out of me with his pointed boots. The mommy had called the police to file a complaint against me for swearing at her.

As it turns out, that evening, there was a Chilliwack City Council meeting, and police showed up to pull my father from the meeting to tell him of my behavior, which didn't go over well. He was always trying to keep our family name to a higher standard. Having his boss, the chair lady, hear of my altercation offended my father.

By the time I had limped home, dragging my destroyed bike with me, Dad showed up and didn't want to hear excuses. Before he could grab me and use his belt to solve his anger, mother pulled him aside to explain things.

Things were talked about, and Brain's parents bought me a new bike. I must admit that alcohol played a major part in how angry my father became over that event.

I know as you read these stories there is a randomness to them. No definite timeline, as some stories cross over into later years. You try to remember back sixty years or so. Let's just say these incidents started or happened while I was living in Canada before 1967.

Being a kid growing up is hard enough without the drama of having been born on the same day as my older brother Bruce. Every birthday party became Bruce's party. He was allowed as many friends as he wanted to come to it. I had limits to just two or three.

My mother created an Easter cake with wax paper holding coins inside. Nickels, dimes, and quarters. If my guests got the quarters, an argument took place that I ruined his party. Most of my friends were also Indians. We call them now Native Canadians or Native Americans. My father hated my friend Joe Smoker. He spied the cute green-eyed strawberry-blonde girl named Josie and commented how I should have more friends like her.

'What's her name?' he asked.

'Josie Watikta.'

"That's an Indian name!' he said, and I explained she is Joe's half-sister. Frowning at me, he left the party.

Off of Unsworth Road sits a sort of amusement park down a long driveway. The owner lived in a large white home at the beginning of the entrance road. The place had an indoor swimming pool with a concession room selling hot dogs, soda, and candy. Behind the pool there was a pond with bumper boats we could play in. The pond was also stocked with trout to fish for at a price per inch.

On this one late morning, the owner had not opened up his store, and several of us boys wanted to get something to eat. I was nominated to go to the home and talk to him.

There was one big problem with this.

He had a large German Shepherd dog tied to a chain guarding his home, and we just didn't know how it would react.

I walked up to the door to knock, and all of a sudden, the dog flew at me and bit down hard on my left arm at the elbow and just held on to me. The owner came out and used his broom to try to beat his dog into letting go.

I fought back tears and yelled at the owner to stop hitting the dog. 'He's doing what he's supposed to,' I yelled.

He asked why I was there and I told him to open up his store. He reached down and told the dog, 'Good boy.' The dog let go of my arm.

He bandaged my arm and we went to the pond so he could open up the store. Fed all of us kids and called my mom to get me to the doctor.

A funny thing happened after that. Me and his dogs became friends. In fact every strange dog I'd meet after being bit by that dog were my friends too. I can't explain it.

Boys will be boys, right? My brother Brad and I were tossed together at birth. We would share the same bedroom for the next eighteen years. We played together and got into trouble together as well. The house fire was just one incident. We were always looking for ways to occupy our time.

And we had even convinced our father to make us two slingshots that look a lot like the wrist rockets of today. When he handed us the weapons, he warned us not to shoot each other in the face and sent us off to explore our new toys.

We soon found out that glass marbles flew better than rocks. And as it was berry season next door at Remple's Raspberry Farm, some of the local people were bust picking berries. We both climbed an old maple tree next to the fence that bordered the rows of raspberries. We spotted an old lady bending over and thought what a big target she made for us.

Our first shot went low, and she stood up and saw no one around.

Our second shots found their target!

Each marble hit a butt cheek, and we heard her scream in pain. She looked around and finally spotted Brad laughing. I had hidden behind the tree trunk. She had Brad climb down. Because Brad got caught, I couldn't help but laugh too. We were both taken over to see our father for punishment.

Our father, upon hearing what we had done, made us boys bend over to receive a belting. He could hardly hit us because he was holding back his own laughter. She didn't think it was that funny. He took our toys away until she went back to work. Giving them back, he told us not to shoot at anyone or any animal that was possibly someone's pet.

It didn't take long before the novelty of having a slingshot wore off, and we went on to other toys like spears, bows, and arrows.

We never owned BB guns or pellet rifles. Several of our neighbors did, and they conducted wars with them. Different rules applied. We could shoot at each other, but not in the face. All was going well until one of the kids shot at a boy peeing, and that too became not allowed. Our parents eventually heard of the war games and put a stop to it.

Our father hunted to keep meat in our freezer. Moose, deer, and elk were harvested every year. Eventually, we would have three horses, and on some weekends, he would pick one of us boys to go horse riding trails in search of meat.

When it came to my turn, we rode up to a mountain lake to catch trout at the river coming into the lake on the opposite shore from the cabin we would stay in. An old rowboat would be turned over. We tied the horse in a meadow and left Duke guarding the cabin.

Big mistake!

We were about halfway across the lake when my father let out, 'That crazy dog!' and turned around to get to Duke before the dog drowned.

Duke feared we were leaving him, and he was swimming after us. We pulled alongside Duke, and Dad reached down and pulled him on board. He certainly was a happy dog. We fished the river and caught dinner. Then spent the night in the old cabin.

The next morning, I grabbed the poles and turned over the boat. Duke didn't want to be asked and jumped in the boat. Normally my father would be drinking alcohol on these trips. He had brought a bottle of rye whiskey only to have it fall out of a saddle bag when he pulled out the lunch that Mother had made for us.

The bottle landed on some rocks and broke. I saw it happen and said, 'Poor Dad, you dropped your whiskey.' years later, in telling this story, he laughed at it, but back then, he wasn't laughing. He wasn't mad at me. He was mad at himself. The next time we went, or he went horseback trail riding, he exchanged the glass bottles with plastic bottles to protect his alcoholic beverages. The learning curve.

I was about six years old when our grandfather Ray Bellamy decided to include his grandchildren in his hobby of fishing. He would take all of us to the rivers and streams and try to teach us how to catch salmon and trout. As he soon found out, I was the only one who could sit and be quiet and not have to complain about everything. Soon, he just took me fishing. He had a fourteen foot long boat on a trailer he named '*Little Coho*'.

He would show up at our home early every Saturday to pick me up and head over to fish the Frazer River's backwaters, including where the Vedder River entered the Frazer for salmon and steelhead. He taught me how to troll for them. We always caught salmon. Sometimes, I'd catch them all. Sometimes, he would. Mostly, we both scored. When it wasn't in season for salmon, we checked out creeks and small rivers using bait and spinners.

All was going well when, one morning, we got a call telling us my grandfather had suffered a heart attack and died.

We went to the funeral to say goodbye. The Supreme's song 'I Hear A Symphony' played at the funeral. I walked up to the open coffin to say goodbye. Feeling more sorry for myself because this meant no more weekends fishing with Grandpa Ray.

I think I was about eight when he passed. Two weeks later, we were called over to Grandma's home. Dad drove me over to be told by her that Grandpa Ray would have wanted me to have his boat, trailer, and motor. I'd also get all of his fishing poles, reels, and a large green metal tackle box. In the box were smells of resin and other fishing smells that would, and still do, remind me of Grandpa Ray.

We drove home, pulling our new boat and fishing supplies. Dad told me that even though it was given to me, it would be mine to protect and allow all our family to use it. Telling me this created a curse on me. Most of the lures were to catch salmon, and now that Grandpa Ray was gone, I became limited to trout fishing mostly. So I began to fill the box with my own gear that I bought.

As it turned out, the rest of the family counted on me to share my large green metal tackle box full of lures with them. They came to me to use my trout poles and not the old ceramic reels and salmon poles used for trolling.

This angered me.

When I complained to Dad, he yelled back at me, telling me, 'Grandpa Ray gave it to all of us, not just you.'

I realized at that moment that to protect my property; I had to buy a smaller tackle box to put my own personal fishing gear in. I had to build a lock box to slide under my bed away from prying eyes. The next time someone needed to use fishing gear, they would get just what Grandpa Ray had given us.

Fast forward to when we lived in Selah, Washington, and I was around sixteen years old. Dad came to me asking if I had enough fishing lures and gear to go on a two-week trip into the Blackwater region of British Columbia. I told him that I did. Hoping I'd be going that year to Canada. But as it turned out, he took several of his friends from business and tried to impress them with the great fishing trip. I remember him pulling into the driveway with his pickup truck loaded with camping supplies. He ran inside to the closet holding Grandpa's fishing gear and grabbed it all. I laughed to myself as they drove away. Boy, will Dad ever be surprised! There is no store near our camp in the Black Water to buy fishing lures. I just giggled at the prospect of him telling his people he had everything they needed to catch trout and opening the metal box to find it empty.

Two weeks later, Dad drove into the drive, got out, and ran in to confront me.

'Where' is all of Grandpa Ray's fishing supplies? You told me you had enough for a trip! Where is it?'

I explained to him that everything Grandpa left us is there in the box minus every lure lost by people- including yourself and never replaced. I keep my personal fishing poles and equipment locked up. Had I gone with him, yes, we would have had enough to cover the two-week vacation.

Soon after that, no one went to the box to see if there were things to use. And hearing 'no' from me sent them to buy their own equipment. As for my '*Little Coho*' boat, Dad felt it best to trade it in for a ski boat we all could use. A boat we never went fishing in.

My father would take all of us kids camping for at least two weeks every summer. His pickup truck would be loaded with a camper. His friend, Ralf Clark of Chilliwack, also had his pickup camper combo. We traveled all over British Columbia, checking out old gold towns like Barkerville up by Quesnel. Some trips were just moving from one campsite to another to check out the scenery. Do a little fishing and watch our campfire glow. Eat marshmallows and hot dogs. The adults divided us kids up into the two campers as we traveled. As it ran out one year, we kids were hearing a crude poem/song about sex. I was around ten years old when I first heard 'God Dammit Mr. Murphy.' Most would hear it sung and never remember the words. With my great memory had the song down to every word. As we traveled up the roadway in Ralf's camper several of the other kids talked me into singing it for Mr. Clark as we drove. They told him we had a crude-dirty poem to tell him, and he had to promise not to get mad at me for singing it. He agreed. So I sang it to him, and he was laughing so much that he had to pull over and hear it again before resuming up the road.

Later that evening, sitting around our campfire, Mr. Clark pulled my father aside to talk to him about not being mad at me when I sang the poem to him. He, too, agreed not to yell. So, like a cranked-up organ monkey, I began to sing 'God Dammit, Mr. Murphy!' When I finished, he had me sing it again and again—then told me never to sing it to Mother. We had a great vacation that year.

Later that year, when my parents were hosting a monthly party of twelve couples, their own made up club called 'The 24 Hat Club'. I would be awakened by Dad at about midnight. They were all drunk by then, and my song was mentioned. I was escorted down to our living room and everyone turned their ears to me, Mother included.

I sang:

Goddamn it, Mr. Murphy!

God bless your heart and soul
Last night I fucked your daughter
But couldn't find her hole
I finally found her hole, Sir!
It was underneath her frock
Goddamn it, Mr. Murphy!
I couldn't find my cock!
I finally found my cock, Sir!
It was underneath my pants.
Goddamn it, Mr. Murphy!
I couldn't make it dance.
I finally made it dance, sir!
It became straight as a pin.
Goddamn it, Mr. Murphy!
I couldn't get it in!
I finally got it, Sir!
And wiggled it about
Goddamn it, Mr. Murphy!
I couldn't get it out.
I finally got it out, Sir!
It was red, black, and blue.
Goddamn it, Mr. Murphy,
next time, I'll butt-fuck you!!

Again and again, I was asked to sing it over and over. Hours passed before the party broke up. You would think hearing it would get old, but as their '24 Hat Club' kept coming back to our home, every night around midnight when they were all drunk enough to laugh at me, I was asked to sing it again.

Then we left Canada, and I hoped not to be asked to sing it again. However, new friends came into the picture, and it kept being sung at Dad's drunken requests.

In 1966, my father began making plans to move the family to the Yakima Valley in Washington state. Why? He designed equipment that was changing the Hop industry.

The frozen valley had about 1,200 acres of hops. The Yakima Valley had 25,000 acres of hops. Best go where most of the business is. He invented the W shaped chip that is used to secure the twine to the ground that the hop plant climbed up on. A punch press would punch out over 24 million of them, ten at a time, 2,000 every two and a half minutes. He needed to move his operation south.

We made several trips down to look at property, settling on a home north of Selah, Washington. I gave my paper route to my friend Donald. I said goodbye to my friends Reg Rouley and Joe Smoker, and in April 1967, we moved south across the border into the United States of America.

I didn't want to leave Canada. I vowed to return when I could. So every trip back to Canada my parents made, I asked to go to see my friends and keep in touch.

It was really hard to let go of how simple a life we had up there.

Eight days after her daughter went missing Mrs Bennett of Gresham, Oregon saw photos in the news and identified her at the coroner's office as Tanya Ann Bennett, 23, of Gresham, Oregon. Tanya, a mildly retarded woman frequented bars and taverns in the area. It didn't take long to locate the B+I Tavern on Stark Avenue as being the last place Ms Bennett was seen alive. On the afternoon of Saturday, January 21st 1990, she had been drinking beer and playing pool with two men. The bartender, a woman, remembered it wrong when she claimed it had been raining and Tanya was soaking wet when she entered the bar about noon. She could not recall when Tanya left, but

Becoming Part American

Chapter Four: Becoming Part American

Many of you are wondering about the punishments my parents came up with when they disciplined us kids.

Mother used a wooden spoon to spank our butts with.

Father used his leather belt to strap our backsides.

I can't remember my mother ever hitting me. I saw her hit Bruce and Brad a couple of times. Not hard. Just to get their attention. And I can only remember Dad using his belt on me four times.

If I were to get into trouble at school, I'd get it at home, too. Had fights with Joe and Brain once for getting caught jugging salmon by the local game warden. Once, for getting caught shoplifting when I was thirteen years old. At sixteen, we fought like adults. He used his fist, and I won only because he was drunk at the time.

I've read material that had suggested he beat on me repeatedly. That is simply not the case. Using the belt came as a last resort to something really bad happening. Now, I don't agree with it. In fact, when I had children, I made it a policy never to hit them at all. Wanted to stop the cycle of abuse. I know I did wrong. Getting beaten, as I saw it, solved nothing. It just made me hate my father for doing it to me. If anything, it made me hide my actions better so as not to get caught and beaten. I'd still get into school fights and do things that were not okay. The only difference was nobody told Dad.

America is a country of immigrants. You would think we Canadians would be welcomed with open arms and accepted as one of them for immigrating to the United States legally. We were outcasts!

The moment we showed up in Selah Dad had purchased one of the largest homes in the area. People believed we were millionaires. Hardly! Sure, Dad had a high-paying job, and the thoughts of the locals did create a monster, putting his head into the clouds, being maybe better than most were. He decided to buy toys to add to the gossip: new cars every year, speed boats to go skiing on weekends. He helped to create the appearance that we were rich.

I left a three-room elementary school in Canada and was tossed into a class of two hundred sixth graders in Selah, Washington. Most of them followed along with me to graduate high school in 1973.

Spring break was over, and my parents enrolled us kids in school. I went to Sunset Elementary and landed in room 12, Mrs. Hoode's class of thirty students. Canada's education program had us kids over a year ahead of the kids in Selah. The school year in Canada is ten months long. In the United States it was only nine months. So, my last two months in sixth grade had me coasting through it. In Canada, all my friends called me Keith Jesperson; no nicknames were given to each other. We were respectful of our feelings. Not in the U.S.A. as soon as I showed up in room 12, other students started coming up with nicknames to call me. Why? I was a big boy at twelve, I was around five foot-eight inches tall. At fourteen, six foot tall, at eighteen, I was six foot three inches, and at my tenth year high school reunion I was six foot-six inches tall and weighed in at 210 lbs. Something just had to be done.

Sandra Smith, a very beautiful girl, came up with 'Tiny', and it stuck like glue to paper. I argued with her not to call me it, but the more I rejected it, the more everyone else climbed on board to call me 'Tiny'. Probably even today, if you were to show my photo around Selah from when I was in school, few would be able to name me 'Keith Jesperson'; most would definitely identify me as 'Tiny.'

Even today, as I do time in prison, I still get letters from people from the Yakima Valley who remember me as 'Tiny.'

Our home is located one and a half miles north of the signal light of Main Street in Selah on the west side of Selah Loop Road. A pond in front of the home with an island and a pole with seven dwarfs walking around highlights the area. The next driveway is for the Silver Spur Mobile Home Park. There was no park back in 1967, just our big home and twenty acres behind it to hold our horses. Every weekday, a school bus picked up us kids in front of our home and bussed us off to school while Duke waited for our return that afternoon, watching from the porch step in front of the front door. On Lickman Road, Duke would chase cars where we lived, but now cars sped by at over 50 mph; the dog knew his limitations, and so he waited on the porch for my return.

June came, and with it, summer vacation. Dad took us all to Disneyland in his convertible car. Later that August, we took a two-week fishing trip to the Black Water west of Quesnel, BC. All the while, he had a building built next to our home to relocate his punch press to the building was thirty feet wide, twenty feet high, and maybe seventy feet long. Father had gone to the Yakima County building to apply for an industrial permit to build his manufacturing plant next to his home. Back then no permit was needed, however, he demanded the planning department issue him a permit anyways and get one. In Canada, our father had been in politics and understood how things changed over time. Member of City Council, Charter member of the Chilliwack Lions Club, his company sponsored the Chilliwack City boxing and hockey teams. His intentions were projected to the future as he asked for permits to be issued for all his new projects.

I bring this up for a good reason.

Years later, the actual use of the building would come into question when neighbors tried to stop work on what would be made inside it. Presenting a permit issued by the zoning department dated 1967 settled the dispute in court.

By late summer or early fall, the punch press was up and running. My brother Bruce became a helper and would eventually run the press and have myself, and Brad do the grunt work. We would be paid real wages, a minimum wage of $1.50 an hour to keep the press punching out 22 to 26 million clips a year.

After school and weekends were filled with running the press as long as we had steel wire to run.

Back home on Lickman Road, we rode our bikes everywhere, hiked trails into the woods, and fished the creeks and rivers. The Frozen Valley got lots of rain and snow. Moving to the Yakima Valley surely was a cultural shock. It is a semi-dry desert area full of sagebrush, few trees, and very little rain. We found friends our age close by and listened to what they had to say about what they did for fun to pass the time.

Everyone we met was a monster. Each one had shotguns and 22-caliber rifles to kill anything that moved in the open sage brush-filled landscape. The local farmers endorsed this behavior by even supplying ammunition to kill robins in cherry season. Weekends spent in High Valley Ranch shooting sage rats and jackrabbits and coyotes and anything else that wandered in their rifle sights.

Our home had just one 22-caliber rifle and Bruce always seemed to have it. Brad had friends that allowed him to borrow one. I had my 35 lb fiberglass bow and arrows. I remember when we first were invited out with our friends next door. They felt sorry for me, having brought my bow and arrows. They spotted a rabbit and offered me the Rast shot. That was the last time they felt sorry for me when my arrow killed the cottontail. They would have left it there. I butchered it and ate it that night after cooking it over a campfire.

The boys' other pastimes consisted of motorcycles. We had the Selah hill climb a few miles from our home, reachable, riding through orchards. Keeping up with the Jones was a reality! Keith, Steve and Marc raced motorcycles and snowmobiles, they were sponsored and very good riders.

I asked Dad about getting a bike and showed him a brochure of a Honda 90 Trail Cycle. 'You meet the nicest people on a Honda.'

my efforts made an impression on him. He had a job for me to do and if done, he would buy me the motorcycle.

The following year, our twenty-acre pasture was being watered by the ditch system using gravity to let water flow over the fields. Dad gave me the job of working the ditches, to keep our fields green, allowing our horses to eat. From the moment we made the deal, my job became easy, and no one had to watch over me to be sure the job was done.

For two years, I watered the pasture, waiting for the day Dad bought me my Honda, which cost 3100.00 new.

There had been a hiccup, though.

In the fall of 1968, my neighbor classmate named Lester Hunt and I got caught shoplifting at Mead's Thriftway in Selah. He told me he had never been caught and I followed along and sleeved several candy bars I had money to pay for. We were leaving the store when Mr. Mead himself nabbed us.

We were placed in a room and waited for the Selah police to show up. Soon, Officer McGuire arrived and placed Lester and myself in the back seat of his patrol car.

He drove us to the Selah Middle School, where we both went to seventh grade, slowly drove around the school, allowing our classmates to see us in his car, then drove us to the police station and had us fingerprinted and photographed before letting us go with a stern warning to tell our parents what we had done.

When I got home that Friday afternoon, my siblings already knew what we had done. Our parents were not home. They were in Canada again and wouldn't be home until Sunday night. All of my brothers and sisters threatened me to tell Mom and Dad that if I didn't, they would.

I just don't get it. Every time I got into trouble, they just couldn't help themselves and had to tell me. I reminded Bruce of his shoplifting toys at a store, and he emphasized how he hadn't gotten caught. So, that was off-limits for me to even think of talking about it.

Huh! One hell of a concept, huh?

It was okay as long as you don't get caught, like driving fast in a car and no cop to see you do it.

Our parents came home and packed their 1968 Ford Thunderbird in the four-car garage. As they exited the car, I looked over my shoulder at Bruce and Sharon to see them pointing to Mom and Dad- 'Tell them or we will!'

Hearing me tell Mom and Dad what I had been caught doing Friday angered Father told me to go up to his bedroom and expect an ass whipping. I was prepared for the belt and placed magazines into my clothes, hoping he wouldn't notice and his belting wouldn't hurt so much. But after just a couple of his hits, he realized something was not correct and had me drop my pants to see magazines and continued to swing his belt. Now, with no clothes to cover my skin, the belting hurt worse.

Being spanked wasn't the end of it. On Monday morning, Dad called up Mr. Mead to tell him we would be there after I got out of school to make things right.

After school, my father marched me in to see Bob Mead. It is all about the perception of the Jesperson's name. I had tarnished our name in the place where we live. Dad needed Bob to know that he needed our name and reputation to be in good standing in the community.

'You must have a job for Keith to do to pay you back for what he stole.'

I don't think Bob expected such a reaction to me stealing two dollars worth of candy that he took off of me. He grabbed a couple of garbage bags, and we walked to the back alley behind the store, pointing to the trash lying everywhere. 'Pick it up, and we'll be square,' Bob tells us.

Then my father told me and Bob that for the next two weeks after school, I was to come to the store to pick up the trash and run home in time for supper. He left me there to pick up the trash.

And so, every night before running home for supper, I stopped at the grocery store, picked up several garbage bags, and spent a couple of hours picking up the trash in the back of the store.

I think Mr. Mead was getting used to having me around. He might even have felt sorry for me being punished so much for stealing so little amount. I actually looked forward to the task and continued to pick up the trash for two weeks longer than required.

I'd run the two miles home to get the dinner table for supper just in time every time. But the worst of this experience came when Dad greeted me at the table, 'How is my little thief doing today?'

Everyone stared at me, waiting for my response, 'No, Dad, I didn't steal anything today.' a ritual that went on for months.

When Dad heard I hadn't acted alone, he called Lester's parents to try to set up a meeting. But they told him it was me who had corrupted their son, not the other way around. Lester and I would still meet, but not at his house. I wasn't welcome.

In the early spring of 1969, Dad took Brad and me to Paulin's Honda in Yakima to buy my Honda 90 Trailcycle.

I picked out a yellow one and then saw Brad pick out a red one. I had worked to get mine, and Brad didn't have to do anything except ask for his. Damn right, I was pissed off! And to make things worse, Dad licensed my motorcycle so he could ride it on the street. What it meant to me was Dad could now keep me from riding my own bike whenever I wanted to. He often took it with him on trips.

Our summer vacation in 1969 was epic. We loaded both bikes onto our new twenty-five-foot Explorer motor home and headed across the United States for the next ten weeks.

We visited Mount Rushmore, Kellogg's Cereal plant, the Mustang Ford car plant in Detroit, took a ride in the maiden of the mist at Niagara Falls, climbed the Empire State Building in New York, walked through the Smithsonian Institute in Washington DC, stayed two weeks with Uncle Ivan on Fogo Island, Newfoundland, watched a man walk on the moon on TV while we sat in a park next to the Mississippi River. We were parked at Idaho Falls and bumped into one of our friends from Selah. Small world! At fourteen, I met eighteen-year-old Betty Ford on Fogo Island, and for ten days, we made out at every single chance we could. I discovered sex and the figure of a woman holding onto me, hoping I'd take her off of the small island. But I was a kid.

We returned home to find Duke waiting for me to return.

When we first moved to Selah, I looked for a paper route to deliver the Yakima Herald Newspaper. They gave me a phone number to call another boy who had a large route in Selah. Maybe I could work out a deal with him. Jeff's papers arrived at Helm's Hardware, and all three hundred-plus papers had to be delivered after school over a two-mile area. He told me that if I helped to deliver his route three days a week, he'd pay me $30.00 a month. That was a lot of money in 1967. took me just a few days to learn the route and soon I was doing it all by myself and not just three days a week.

Collections were over, and he didn't pay me anything. Jeff's word wasn't worth a thing!

So, I didn't deliver for him the following day, and I'd get a call, 'Not my problem!' I wasn't in Canada anymore. These Americans were scammers! I would run into several of these types before my life ends. The prison I'm in is full of these kinds of people.

In the late fall of 1969, my brother Brad, along with Lester's brother Dan Hunt and another boy, would enter a garage of a home in Selah and steal three motorcycles. They brought them to our garage and repainted them. Then rode them at the Selah hill climbs once too often.

People who were friends of the man who owned the stolen cycles reported back to him, who now had them.

I was riding our lawn mower mowing our yard when a pickup pulled into our driveway. The man walked over to me and asked my name. I told him, 'Keith.' He told me to tell my brother Brad to get his three motorcycles back into his garage by 10:00 pm that very night or tomorrow he'd be back with the police. I told the man I wondered where those bikes had come from.

Part of me wanted to keep silent and not warn them to let them find out how bad their actions were and deal with Dad's wrath. I also knew that if Dad found out that I knew about the deadline and didn't tell Brad to warn him, I'd be in worse trouble for not protecting my brother, and *especially* my father's reputation.

So when Brad came home on one of those cycles, I told him what the man said.

By 10:00 pm that evening all three stolen motorcycles were back in the owner's garage. No charges were ever filed.

By the fall of 1968, all three of us boys were running the punch press in our factory. We all had bank accounts and checkbooks. $1.50 doesn't sound like a lot of money now, but in 1968, families were being raised on the minimum $1.50 an hour wage. We got home from school, got into our work clothes, and ran the press until supper time. Then, back at it until 10:00 pm on school days and on weekends, we started up at 8:00 AM and put in at least eight hours, punching out one hundred and sixty-eight boxes if it all ran okay.

Bruce ran the press—the easy part, except when a lock-up happened to a dye or ejector. Brad and I did the grunt work. Cut the burlap off the steel wire reels and change boxes every two minutes. When Bruce wasn't running the press, Brad took over, and when both were off doing whatever they were doing, I ran the whole show.

We were paid real wages with taxes taken out. When I ran it myself, I'd also include which brother wanted the money the most as a co-worker. We learned early on that the company paid out three dollars an hour to produce the 'W' shaped chips. There is no way Dad would pay me the whole three dollars an hour to run the press by myself. Learning early on to manipulate how we were to get paid, this job became how we were able to afford to buy motorcycles, horses, and cars.

In 1970, both Brad and I sold our Honda 90 Trail Cycles and bought Yamaha 175cc Enduros. Before Dad could license one of them, we removed the lights and mufflers and replaced them with expansion chambers, which were illegal on roads. Dad would have to buy his own damn motorcycle and ended up getting a Yamaha 80cc, street legal, and everything.

When we moved to Selah, we owned three horses: Star, Dynamite, and Flicka. I would buy a registered quarter horse named Dawn. All of us kids joined 4H, and we rode in parades and showed them off at the Yakima County Fair. Selah's Red Hot Riders 4H club.

Dad had a large horse truck we loaded up on weekend trail rides like we had done up in Canada. We used our horses to go hunting for deer and elk in the fall. We did not have enough horses for everyone to ride on hunts, so some of us hunted on foot. We took turns. In the fall of 1970, Brad was on Dawn when an accident happened, causing Dawn to be shot. That was the end of the 4H experience. It wasn't Brad's fault.

At Christmas 1967, our father created a game for us children on Christmas Eve. The Christmas Tree sat in the formal living room of our home. The challenge was to get somehow our name hung on the tree without getting caught. Have it on the tree by Christmas morning, and Dad gave up $20.00. when we went to bed, he would use fishing lines to create traps with cans, pots, and pans. Mother hated this game. She would hardly get any sleep on Christmas Eve. It would be quiet, and all of a sudden, pots and pans would be pulled over, and the scamper of feet back upstairs.

When Christmas morning came, no names were on the tree. Dad won, and he rubbed it in all year until the next Christmas, 1968.

Christmas morning 1968 came, and I smiled at Dad. 'I got my name on the tree.' I told him, and sure enough, there it was, hanging on the tree. He paid me the $20.00 and asked me how I did it, and that was my secret. Of course, I rubbed it in right up until Christmas of 1969.

Dad raised the prize to $50.00 should each or anyone come Christmas morning to have their names on the tree. He gave us cards with our names on them, signed with his name, after we were sent upstairs to bed. He spent hours setting up a maze of lines and traps to capture us. Come the morning of another mostly sleepless night for Mother, and I again claimed to be successful in putting my name on the tree.

And sure enough, there it was on the tree. Reluctantly Dad pulled out fifty dollars and gave it to me. He kept asking me how I was able to do so and no one else. Our mother was laughing at the results. My brothers and sisters were angry at me for not also taking their name tags and putting them on the tree. However, I turned it back at them for not offering to take my name tag with them when they tried to get past the maze.

Everyone wanted to know how I had been able to beat his traps. Anger-filled Christmas, so I told them all. 'Remember Dad,' I told them as I had all of their attention, 'the aspect of the game was to get my name on the tree without getting caught. Right?' Mom agreed. So I told them that the night before he chased us upstairs, I unlocked the window next to the tree. During the night, all I had to do was to slip out my window, walk around the house, open the window next to the tree and, reach in and, hang my name tag, close the window that automatically locked when I closed it all of the ways.

Dad yelled that I had cheated. Mother countered that I had followed the rules. There would be no more Christmas Eve games, and Mother got her much-needed sleep.

Somehow, this made Dad angry at me. Often, when we were alone, he kept at me to return the $70.00 I had won from him. At the Yakima Valley County Fair in 1970, I took a friend of mine named Roger to the fair and treated him to a good time, spending $80.00. Dad didn't approve of my wild spending on someone he didn't like. He decided to punish me by charging me room and board out of my paycheck to the sum of $80.00 per month to teach me a lesson. For the next six months, my paycheck was $80.00 light. Bruce and Brad didn't have to pay for room and board. I believe it was really payback for not giving back his Christmas game money. He told me he was teaching me a lesson in money management. Mother put a stop to it.

Of all of my friends that I have ever had, my father only approved one, just one. Royce Kenoyer. I first met him in 1970. I bought a ten-speed bike from him and rode it to school. When Royce went to work after high school, he learned to be a machinist. Spent time in the army and married a nice woman in Germany. They are my children's Godparents. Their son Steve is now my daughter Melissa's husband—small world.

#43

Chapter Three: A Killer's life, Part one

People always want to know how does a person become a murderer. There has to be some driving force in the Universe to create us. Most will go back to our childhood to try to discover an answer. Pinpoint the angry child because of his or her parents influences. Most of the information out there about me has been talked about and diagnosed to form opinions not necessarily correct. What they don't know, they make up. And I'm tired of it.

I will not tell you everything that went on in my life because most is not important. Tear apart someone else's

Damaged Goods

While in 8th grade and Brad in 7th grade, we saw too much of each other. He felt the need to call me new nicknames like 'Igor' and 'IG', short for Igor. Sticks and stones can hurt you, not names some people say. But names do hurt.

We both have been sharing a bedroom since we were very little. I felt a need to get away from him and decided to camp out on a cot on the covered porch of our home next to our father's office. Sleeping in a sleeping bag and Duke laying at my feet, radio playing music all night long, I was in another world. I got to like it so much that even in winter, I stayed on the porch.

While I was sleeping outside one night, my sister Jill came to me asking me to join her and our neighbor, Debbie Ward, in a tent in our backyard. They were having a sleepover and invited me to join them for a sexual experience. Debbie got undressed, exposing everything to me, and so did my sister, and of course, I got undressed as well. They groped me, jacking me off, and I fingered their vaginas. Jill and Debbie were like twelve years old and I was close to fifteen. The whole episode was harmless. I didn't have sex with either girl with my penis. Things changed after that night with Jill. I'd sneak into her bedroom while she slept and kiss her, trying to get her to touch me some more. She never again experimented sexually with me.

However, some nights, Debbie would leave her bed at home and crawl into my sleeping bag to play. Then not long after we had been screwing each other, they moved away, and I wondered if I had gotten her pregnant. Or she had gotten herself pregnant using me? And just maybe nothing that dramatic took place in their moving away.

As I mentioned before, our father drank a lot of alcohol. He told us he wasn't an alcoholic, even though he consumed a lot of alcohol. He laid his foot down on us kids learning to drink alcohol. As long as we did our drinking at home, it would be okay. Our parents would go to Canada several times a year, spending whole weekends away. Our home became party central on those weekends. My brothers organized Kegger parties with hundreds of kids showing up.

Come Sunday, there was a major cleanup before Mom and Dad came home. When I had my license and drove my car, I became the one sober enough to drive the drunken kids home, especially the girls. Often, I'd get them making advancements on me as I took them home. Kissing and even fucking happened. At school, not many remembered what we did in my car. I certainly remembered cleaning up puke and pee that some just had to leave me for my help to get them home safe.

Maybe they would just rather forget that we did the wild thing. Not to have to admit that maybe I had taken advantage of them while they lay there, not fully awake. They certainly didn't say 'No!'.

At one party, a boy passed out behind a car, and the driver backed over him, dislocating his shoulder. My father even hosted my brother Bruce's senior class party, providing much of the alcohol to them. I never had to organize a Kegger at home. Every time our home was empty of adults, either Bruce or Brad had it covered. At one of Bruce's Keggers, I grabbed his girlfriend's breast as she walked by, and Bruce quickly defended her by punching me hard. Later that night, when they were both drunk, I drove her home, and she allowed me to touch her.

Those were the days! And maybe the precursor of me landing in here.

My brother Bruce and I had issues. We still do. Upon my arrest for murder, he has taken the stand that I no longer belong to his world. My name is never mentioned in his home. A well-known fact is most family members of convicted murderers abandon them in prison. Very few ever talk to or support family members convicted of murder. My brother is no exception, to him I don't exist. And sadly enough, neither do my children.

When Bruce entered high school, I heard all about how the upper classmates hazed the newcomers entering high school. They forced freshmen to drop their pants to expose their underwear. Sick bastards! Bruce went through it and survived. Don't know how many boys made him drop his pants to check out his underwear. A good thing he had quit shitting himself or wearing diapers, seeing that might have been big news in school!

In the fall of 1969, my time to enter high school had come. And I wasn't going for it. Because of my size, most of my friends were juniors and seniors. None of them were going to force me to drop my pants.

For weeks after school started I kept seeing other classmates being asked or forced to drop their pants and I got warned by Bruce that my turn was coming. Sooner or later, it was going to happen. And he should know because I found myself surrounded in a hallway of the old building by at least ten of the juniors, my brother Bruce in the middle, and the fight was on. I tossed a couple down the stairs and hit and kicked past most of them. They finally pulled my pants off of my hips without undoing them. Satisfied, some left limping away, and I told Bruce we were not done. He seemed to think we were.

Several days later, several of my friends and I caught one of Bruce's partners and took him into the school's lunch room just before the noon meal started.

We ripped off his clothes and held him on top of a table so everyone could see him- especially the girls, that he was completely naked. Taking his clothes with us, we left him there crying to trying to cover up as the girls laughed at his tiny penis.

Several days later, we heard he killed himself.

Found hung up in a tree.

At home, Bruce gave me a look, and I said, 'What? You're next!' Our father sensed there were problems afloat, but I wasn't telling him anything, and certainly Bruce knew the rules about telling. And no one came looking to talk to me.

The school believed it to be about the hazing problem they had let happen and did nothing to stop it. So, kids kill themselves all the time for various reasons. Why try to explain it? And as the school year ran along, most just moved away from the early hazing and concentrated on school activities.

Then, there was one of my class's biggest scammers named Terry Nalley. He borrowed $6.00 from me so he could buy his student body card, allowing him cheaper access to school functions. He promised to pay me back in a couple of weeks. At our ten year high school reunion party, Terry asked me to make a beer run to the store. He handed me a hundred-dollar bill and stayed in the car, expecting me to do all of the work. I came out with a six-pack of beer and handed it to him. He looked puzzled. Told him, 'Remember borrowing the $6.00 for your student body card? Well, I just got paid back with interest!'

Back at the reunion party, he complained that I had taken his money. I explained why, and he found no sympathy from several classmates he still owed money to. He left, and I never saw him at our twenty-year reunion. I'm sure he would be the one to tell all when I was arrested that I could be generous and then very stingy with my money.

At seventeen, my sister Sharon would get married to her twenty something boyfriend named Chuck Folk. Nowadays, Chunk would have been charged with statutory rape. Back then, a baby on the way meant marriage. And our father forced the issue. A very large wedding took place, and all of our relatives were invited. Dad gave them his new 1968 Ford Thunderbird as a wedding present.

I bring this up for two reasons. Our uncle Russel came down from Canada with his wife and children. He was a highly-ranked member of the Royal Canadian Mounted Police. He talked to me about maybe one day I join the force, should I ever decide to return to Canada. When they returned home, I soon got a recruiting package to go over.

For years, I entertained the idea of becoming a Canadian cop. Then, in 1972, I learned to run a backhoe and drive a dump truck. My career soon shifted elsewhere. Upon my arrest in 1995, my father was interviewed, and he brought up the story that I once wanted to join the force but could not due to a school accident.

Reading Wikipedia's account of this story it is said I got injured at the RCMP boot camp and had to quit. I had even taken French at school for a couple of years, and it never stayed with me because I could not find anyone to talk to about it. Use it or lose it.

About a year after they were married, our father pushed them apart to get a divorce. Now that the wedding was over and the child was born, Dad wanted the ex-marine out of our family.

Maybe Chuck wasn't all there in his head. He had two photo albums full of violence in Vietnam. Photos of all of the men, women, and children he had killed. Each photo had a story to tell about how they were killed. I found them interesting and asked to see them whenever I was at their home. He would eventually burn them to free his soul of the memories of war. You would think the U.S. Military would destroy all types of photos showing death when releasing men into public. Defuse the whole situation and leave the war behind. Chuck would die in a gun battle with cops years later.

On April 6th, 1971, I took and passed my driver's license, and later that day, Dad took me to Pingrey Motors in Selah to have me buy my first car. His lessons on money management left me with not much to spend. For just $400.00, I bought a 1961 Oldsmobile Super 88 with a 394 V8 and automatic transmission. White with red interior. I also paid for a year's insurance, and now I was really mobile. Like Bruce, I now drove my car to school and soon had girls wanting to know me just because I had a car.

Our summer vacation in 1971 took us to the lodge at Culta Lake, about seven miles from our old home on Lickman Road. I was told to leave my car behind. Bruce would show up late in his Willy's Jeep. He knew how to drive his vehicle to Canada even though Dad didn't want us to. It is a control thing. I drove the 1970 Chevy pickup truck, pulling our eighteen-foot fiberform ski boat. The rest were in Mom's 1971 Mercury Royal Brougham Town car. For the next three weeks, we enjoyed water skiing and other activities. I'd meet a girl at one of the concession stands and we planned a date to the Chilliwack Drive Inn Theater. I had gotten it cleared with our parents that I could take the truck without the horse rack on it on my date.

I really was looking forward to being with Lucy at the drive-in theater/ even though it has been over 53 years later as I write this out, it still pisses me off reliving the events of that night in the summer of 1971.

Lucy, a petite blonde, blue-eyed beauty, lived in Walla Walla, Washington, and was visiting her grandmother in Chilliwack for the summer. She worked at the Trampoline, a miniature golf course concession across from the Pavilion building at Cultas Lake. We had met in our mutual flirting and agreed to go on a date that Friday night. At first, she mentioned who was asking her grandmother. Hearing I'm a Jesperson sealed the deal. Her grandmother saw us Jesperson's as Royalty in the Chilliwack area. Back in the 1800's the Jesperson family immigrated from Denmark to New York. Drove across America in a covered wagon to San Francisco and north to the Frazer Valley, settling on Fairfield Island, just north of Chilliwack's city center.

They built a dairy farm and constructed a large rock quarry home with gardens and statues from Italy. Once, the Queen of England visited the estate. Every year, there was a story in the local paper showing off the Jesperson Farms Rose Gardens. The home cost $11,000.00 back in 1909 to build. Les Jesperson's city welding and machine shop had helped to build up many of the city's buildings. As a member of city politics, we were royalty in the eyes of most residents in the area. Lucy's grandmother approved of her dating a Jesperson. What could go wrong?

Before leaving Selah to come to Cultas Lake Lodge, my parents invited another family from Selah to join us if they could. The Hayes decided to take them up on the invitation and showed up at the lodge in the late afternoon that very Friday. Seeing the Hayes pull into the lodge parking lot and seeing it was the whole family, I knew I better leave real soon so as not to be summoned to help Dad fix a problem of what to do with the Hayes' children.

I jumped into the pickup and headed for the exit. Traffic was heavy and it forced me to have to wait before leaving. There was a knock on the window, and I turned to see Father staring at me. He ordered me to park the truck. My plans to be alone with Lucy just got dumped on.

I was still able to go on my date. Only now, I had four other faces to take. Both my brother Brad and sister Jill and now the Hayes two children who were friends of Brad's. The cattle/horse rack would be placed on the pickup so we could carry legally or hidden children in the back. And with the rack on the truck, I'd have to park in the back row so as not to ruin the viewing of other moviegoers.

Dad and Mom were going to entertain the Hayes downtown at the local bars and nightclubs. Maybe take in a meal of Chinese food at the Empress Hotel and an all-night of getting drunk and doing what grown-ups do. They would drive off in Mom's Mercury, and I drove to Chilliwack with all four of my responsibilities in the back.

No one sat up front with me. At Grandma's house, Lucy came to the door and saw the truck had the rack on it and the other four faces pointing and making gestures at us. I explained being dumped on. She wanted to go out and have fun, not babysit other people's kids. We decided, or should I say Lucy decided, not to be part of the problem and stayed home. Royalty only goes so far.

I drove to the Chilliwack drive-in and rolled up to the booth to pay. Jim, a friend of our family, waved us through without paying, only telling me to park in the back row. Parked, I stayed with the truck to watch the two movies. The others walked to the outside covered area to have their own fun time.

It was past eleven when they came back complaining they were hungry, telling me to drive to the "Dog n' Suds" burger drive-in. Once we got there, everyone ordered burgers and drinks. "Dogs n' Suds" copied the 'A+W Root Beer Family' family burger restaurant concept. Soon a girl marched over with a tray and we were handed our food and drinks. My four passengers all claimed to have no money, and I had to buy the food, which pissed me off even more. I decided to teach them all a lesson. I drove to Lickman Road and sped down it towards the raised railroad tracks on the radio played 'Magic Carpet Ride' by Steppenwolf as I planned to race over the tracks and hopefully get some air. I swerved side to side several times to force them to hang on. I'm sure they must have felt I had lost my senses by the radical driving I was doing.

I was floored when I hit the top of the tracks and almost lost control when the truck had movement under its tires again. At Keith Wilson I headed east to Vedder Crossing and raced up to the lodge and parked.

I walked to the back of the truck to find no one there.

Panic set in!

I raced back to the railroad crossing, expecting to see bodies scattered all over the roadway. Nothing! So I retraced the path I had taken and saw nothing. A couple of times I thought I saw people walking along the road but when I got close they were gone. Not knowing what to do next, I drove back to the lodge.

Around midnight, the adults came home and asked where everyone was. I was sitting in the cab of the truck trying to come up with a plausible story to explain my actions. I was just about to spin a lie when two cop cars showed up, and all four of them got out of the cars, along with the two policemen. You guessed it! Brad was quick to tell me about my radical driving and how they had jumped out of the truck at the stop sign, a road before the railroad tracks. What they didn't know was that Chiliwack had a 10:00 pm curfew. That is why the police pulled over and gave them a ride back to the lodge. Both officers recognized the former council member Les Jesperson and gave him the proper language to take care of it himself.

There would be no police report filed.

Royalty.

It is all about image.

Everyone walked up the stairs to their rooms, leaving my drunken father there in the parking lot to deal with me. He had graduated from using his belt on me to fist fights, and first, there was a lot of yelling, then he threw the first punch and missed. He told me to quit moving. The drunken bastard couldn't hit a moving target. I stood next to a metal support pole when he punched at me again. I ducked, and he hit the pole. It made a 'ping!' and he cried out in pain.

At that moment, I felt it was time to leave and run off into the woods, finding a hidden area to spend the night.

Morning came, and I stood there watching the lodge. Our boat was gone, so I tried to sneak into the lodge to get to my suitcase. I planned to run away. Leave royalty and get to my car in Selah and not be there when everyone returned home.

Yes, I was really feeling feeling sorry for myself.

I picked it up and turned to go out the door and Mother blocked me. She told me that all four of them had come clean and what they had done to ruin my date with Lucy. Dad had listened to them spin their stories; I'm sure they were downplayed and promised he would not fight me anymore. She asked me not to leave. I set down my suitcase and gave Mom a hug, then walked back out to the woods, making my way around the lake to the concessions to hopefully see Lucy gain. We exchanged phone numbers but never saw each other when she returned to Walla Walla.

As far as the rest of our story there I kept to myself as much as possible. I had to laugh when I saw Dad with a cast on his right hand. He had broken it, hitting the pole. A gift that kept on giving! Those four had money and could have paid for their food and had to give it to me to make things right. And I never told them about the railroad tracks. They must have been doing over seventy and punched down on the gas peddle, kicking in the four-barrel carb and passing gear when the truck crested the top of the tracks. The truck flew as I listened to the song, 'Bad to the Bone.'

For the past few years, Dad had taken us deer hunting near Bickleton, a small town near Goldendale, Washington. We had been invited to the canyon by employees of our father's business in Moxee, Washington. They would show us how to get there and where we could camp. We used horses sometimes. That was where my horse Dawn had been shot. Hunting, as it turned out, was just one more place for men to get drunk. The men stayed in camp drinking and telling stories while we kids went looking for deer.

In the early deer season of 1971, I was heading to that canyon with my brother Brad and one of his friends. We made it down into the large canyon and found a great place to set up camp. Found lots of firewood and built a fire. At about ten that evening, we saw headlights coming down the road. Three pickup trucks parked behind my car, and six men walked into the light of our fire. They were pointing their rifles at us and telling us we had their camping spot.

Standing my ground, I told them we were there first, and they would have to leave and go somewhere else. That was when one cocked me with his rifle and pointed at me. We were kids. We got the message. I loaded up my car, drove about half a mile back up the road, and built another fire to sit around. We were pissed at them. We knew who they were. Drunken assholes that didn't know they were pointing guns at their boss's sons.

After Brad and his friend went to sleep, I couldn't sleep and walked back to our former camp to listen to them brag about chasing us off of a nice fire.

Honestly, that was the first time I thought of killing men.

My knife at the ready, I could have slipped in and cut their throats and rob them had I been alone I believe I would have done it. But knowing my brother Brad just could never keep quiet about men pointing guns at us, I figured it best to walk away and try to ignore the problem.

The next morning I had hiked up above their camp and aimed my rifle, my 30-06 with 9 power scope at their heads as they got ready to hunt. It would have been really easy to kill at least two of them before the rest got wise.

As I had predicted, when we got home, Brad ran to Dad to report what had happened. The story made it back to Moxee, and everyone said they were sorry.

Big changes were coming to the Jesperson Family in the spring of 1972. father sold his clip-making punch press to Hop Growers Supply in Toppenish. He moved the machinery to a building and promised Ken, the owner of Hop Growers Supply, that his two sons, Keith and Brad, would run the next two years of production.

That is when they exited the business and trained their replacements. When he told us about what he promised Ken, we were surprised to hear he committed us to seal his deal. 'What are you bitching about?' he asked. 'You will be making fifty cents a box. That's $10.00 an hour operating fees.'

Brad and I drove the twenty miles to work every day. We had steel to run. When I ran the press by myself, I made ten dollars an hour. As I go through my life with you reading this, you will see me coming back to the press time and time again to help me make ends meet when my other jobs were not doing it.

Father made the clip building into horse stables and bought a John Deere 310 Backhoe and Wittenburge 10 Yard Dump truck so we could start to build what would be the Silver Spur Mobile Home Park in the acreage behind our home. Fifty-two lots were in plans to create.

Neither of us knew how to run a backhoe. So Father asked us to see if anyone had any interest in learning how, along with him. It is called multitasking! Brad and I ran the press, and when we were home, I'd be out in the field digging with the backhoe. You can say all of my time was taken by work. Dad didn't pay me to learn how to run the backhoe. We learned together as we completed the jobs. And before long a new business was formed called 'Jesperson's Contracting'. We hired out to do jobs for other people installing sewer systems and digging all kinds of projects. Working for other people, Dad paid me $2.50 an hour. The backhoe was rented out for $25.00 an hour with the operator. That was the going rate for the business in 1972. we both got truck driver's licenses and also hauled dirt and gravel to customers as well.

Soon, the contracting business took over everything, and only on weekends was work being done on the mobile home park. As lots were completed, homes were moved in, charging $75.00 a month rent.

When school started in the fall of 1972, Brad and I would drive to Toppenish after school and on weekends to run the press. Dad had to hire men to replace me on the backhoe and dump truck. Of course, Brad played football during football season, and I wrestled during the basketball and wrestling season. School sports were important.

During a wrestling practice in the late fall of 1972, I climbed the newly installed rope to the ceiling of the high school gym while my friend Ted pulled on the rope, keeping it tight as I went up hand over hand to the top. I slapped the wooden beam, and all of a sudden, I fell to the hardwood floor below. The rope had pulled out of the bracket designed to keep it secure. The problem was that the janitor who installed the rope used a two-inch diameter rope with a bracket designed to have a two-and-a-half-inch rope. He made the end of the rope bigger, wrapping it with electrical tape. He didn't even push the rope through the bracket and tie a knot in it so it couldn't pull free. With over 400 pounds on the rope, the tape simply let go, and there I was, coming fast at Ted.

My right foot pushed Ted out of the way as I crashed onto the floor. Some have said I laid there a good couple of minutes without moving. Knocked out by the impact to the hardwood floor. Over twenty feet, I had fallen. Then my piece of shit wrestling coach named Wayne Lalley walked over and yelled at me, 'You're not hurt! Get your ass up and hit the showers!' my foot was swelling fast. Several wrestlers helped me to my good foot and balanced me as I hopped to the dressing room. No way was he going to allow me to cut off the sweaty uniform. Lalley had me pull my suit off of my injured leg, make me take a shower, and get into my regular clothes before allowing me to get into his car. He drove me to the school's doctor's office a few blocks away and left me on the doorstep of the closed office. He told me he called my mother to come to get me and take me to the Memorial Hospital in Yakima. The school doctor was called and would meet us there.

X-rays were taken and the doctor told us it was just a bad sprain, nothing to worry about. And for the next four months of walking on a sore swollen left foot, working on it, the doctor kept telling us there was nothing to worry about. Eventually, the swelling will go away. And then, one day, he just told us never to see him again. He was wiping us off of his client list. The school doctor was another piece of shit. Why? As it turns out, they were all in it together. Conspiracy to defraud us. To fuck me over! And the law as it stood then was on their side. Just as long as they kept me in the dark so as not to be a lawsuit in the 126 days from the date of the accident. After 126 days, as the law stated, I could no longer sue them for damages.

As soon as the school doctor canceled on us, we sought out a doctor who specifically handles foot problems. We went to see Dr. Jack Irwin of Yakima. X-rays were taken, and he told me I had been walking and working on torn ligaments. That surgery would be needed to fix it. My father contacted Ted Roy and Associates to start legal action against the Selah School district. That is when we found out about the 126-day time limit. It was going to be a very long battle in court to get to an end in the case—certainly, no guarantee of a positive outcome.

I had sold my 1961 Oldsmobile in the fall of 1972 and bought a 1947 CJ2A Willy's Jeep. I met a friend of mine at the end of the school year last spring named Jerome 'Jerry' Day. Jerry had a 1946 Willy's Jeep, and I introduced him to a friend named Bob, who was in the Yakima Valley Mountaineers Jeep Club. The same club my brother Bruce had been in while he owned his Jeep. Jerry and I hung out a lot, and I saw how much fun Jeeps were and just had to have one. We even raced our Jeeps in local mud races. I entered the obstacle course at the Granger Cherry Festival Jeep Jamboree and took home the third-place trophy.

I would graduate from Selah High School in June 1973 with a general course of study. I was told no college for me, Dad had his plans for me in his business future. So why try hard in school to pass at the top of the class? And with my leg injury, I wasn't going anywhere until it was fixed. Brad and I continued to run the press in Toppenish, and when there wasn't any steel to run, we spent time on Dad's backhoe finishing up the mobile home park.

life if you have to. Provide a sort of history lesson to understand me to your own crowd and don't bother to listen to what really happened with me.

    I was born Wednesday April 6th, 1955 to Gladys and Leslie Tespersen at Chilliwack, British Columbia, Canada. I'm The middle child of five. Have an older sister named Sharon, an older brother named Bruce, a younger brother named Brad and younger sister named Jill. None of them turned out to be killers. We all grew up in The same household under the same rules and experiences. Our parents stayed together all through our upbringing. However, we all chose different paths to live by.

My Resume

Have you ever seen the movie *Harry and the* Hendersons? About a family that hit a Sasquatch with their car and brought 'Harry' home to live with them. A kind gentle beast. Not the monster everyone believed a Sasquatch to be. You don't have to look like a monster to be one.

People who have dealt with my father, Les Jesperson, have often reported how when he entered a room, he sucked all of the oxygen out of the room.

Everything was all about him!

Les Jesperson is the monster, and I am the son of that monster.

Dan Bowers called me over to talk to him about my dog Duke. I don't know or remember when exactly. It was when Duke was fourteen years old, and I was eighteen, so 1973. He told me Duke was dead. That my father had to kill him. No details. Just to tell me to break the ice before I could talk to him.

My father took the coward's way out and made up a story about why he had to put a bullet in Duke's head. He had taken the dog on an overnight trip to Cascade Park, northwest of Selah, past Wenas Lake. He claimed Duke must have gotten into coyote poison set out by the forest department, so to put the dog out of its misery, he shot him and buried Duke in a hole. Dad seemed to be broken up over the whole situation.

A week later, I drove to Cascade Park to try to find where Dad said he buried Duke—asked some people who were camping in the park if they had seen the grave. A young boy told me to follow him. We crossed the creek and soon smelled rotting flesh. There was Duke on top of the ground, flies buzzing everywhere. My father had lied to me. It would be my secret. I wouldn't ever tell him or suggest I knew the truth.

A little over a month later, my father and I were in East Valley, stopping at home. The people there were showing us a litter of white poodle puppies. He told me then that he was promised the pick of the litter so I asked the woman when the promise had been made. A month before Duke had died.

Okay, I get it! Duke was old and could hardly get around; I had to help him on my bed or into the pickup. Death was not far away, not long after Duke had been killed a close friend gave me a male German Sheppard puppy to love, to help me move on. When Father came home and saw my new dog, he blew up, telling me I had to get rid of him. Now, hearing of a promised puppy made sense.

I made my mind up not to like this new bitch of Dad's. And a I turns out, his dog felt my anger and would run from me when I looked at it, it would squat and pee. How his new dog reacted when I was there made him ask if I was beating his dog. I was not. About a year later, his dog named Gypsy had tumors and needed to be put down. He handed me a $75.00 check to give to the vet. I cashed the check and put a bullet in the dog. I gave it a running start before shooting it with Dad's 30-30.

His next dog, a white Sheppard bitch acted the same way around me. He named it Pepsi. I yelled at it one day, and it ran out into the road and was killed by a passing car. He had to clean it off of the road. His next dog, named Blacky was killed by a car over at Bruce's home. He had me dispose of it. The last dog I saw with him was a cat that barked named Scamper. Scamper tried to be my friend, but again, I pushed it off. What happened to my German Shepherd puppy? I gave the dog to my close friend Morris. He worked at a dairy farm and even the owner of the farm loved the dog. I stopped in to spend time with him. I was probably the only person that could walk into the property, and the dog would not bark. We called him Dog.

My first real job out of high school was working for Larson Fruit Company in Selah, building one thousand apple bins, and I was paid $2.34 an hour. Five of us made up the crew, and we punched them out in less than a month. Vern Larson kept us around for another month, loading trucks and boxcars before letting us go.

I went to work next for John Alder Chevron gas station by Terrance Heights not far from Yakima. I pumped gas and helped with oil changes, changed tires, and generally everything to do there. He was great to work with and to work for. I worked for him up to when I went into surgery in November of 1973.

Dr. Jack Irwin took bone from my hip and put it into the arch of my left foot, held by pins. Two months later, another surgery to pull the pins and fix what didn't heal. Two months later, with the cast removed, I could go to work.

In those four months, my father had me in our garage painting name signs for the stable's horses and board signs for the Silver Spur Mobile Home Park, which had been completed to fifty-two total lots. I had sold my Jeep and needed to get something to get around with.

In late March 1974, I went to work for my father again, running his backhoe and dump truck. I would buy a new 1974 Honda CB750 motorcycle in April. Just before I bought the bike, I broke my right hand's little finger. I was clearing rock from the dump box when the tailgate slammed on my hand at about seven that morning. I wiggled the tip, and yes, it was broken! Not wanting to have me lose a full day of work, Dad found a Popsicle stick, taped up my finger, and told me to wait until late afternoon to see the doctor.

Dr. Haven did the x-ray of my finger and told me I needed surgery. A week later, Dr. Haven used two pins to fix me. That afternoon, I picked up my motorcycle. I had a cast on my right wrist and was able to ride with little problem.

State Industrial Insurance paid for it all, and because I was not to work, I paid three-fourths of my salary while I healed up. This, of course, didn't fit well with my boss. He had me still operating the backhoe and driving the truck. Even though I was working full time, I only got the checks from State Industrial Insurance. The balance could have been paid under the table to make it right. But it wasn't! I was living at home that was about to change.

Watson Paving came to town and needed someone to take out the concrete curbs along the path of re-paving Interstate 82 between Selah and Union Gap. My father bid on the job and actually needed my help or else. But before I'd work for him, things needed to change as far as paying me for my services. Real wages! I compared his need for me so I could always go run the press and get ten dollars an hour. Watson Paving is a union shop. The man standing by my backhoe holding a shovel made more than I did. Dad made three times as much per hour and could afford to pay me more, but didn't.

Regardless getting a real paycheck afforded me to move out of Dad's home and freed up my weekends. I was no longer there at his summoned call.

A high school friend of mine joined me in renting a two-bedroom apartment at the Selah Apartments. Brad Tidrick, back then, was trying to break into the oval racing scene. Often, I'd come home to find a sheet of plastic on the living room floor, and either an engine or transmission piece was on it. Today, in 2024, I'm sure most of Yakima's racing culture has heard of him. Heard he has a transmission repair shop in town. Back then, Brad and I rode our bikes to watch Evil Knievel jump the Snake River Canyon. We were at the gate about to pay $7.00 each to enter when we saw the rocket ship hit the end of the ramp and deploy its parachute. Oh shit! And that was it! We didn't enter the disappointed crowd and rode home.

Brad Tadrick had moved to Selah from Kalama, Washington. He kept after me to borrow the company four-wheel drive pickup so we could go deer hunting that fall of 1974 over at Kalama. I made the request for the weekend, and my father required one thing from me. He wanted the keys to my Honda CB750. He promised not to ride it drunk, but as we all know, Drunks will promise everything to be able to get what they want. And we needed his truck. My mother hated the idea of me leaving him my bike. She knew him best!

Brad and I drove to Kalama and shot nothing. Returned by Sunday night and early Monday morning, I drove to where we parked our equipment and started them up, and waited for Dad. Twenty minutes late

I walked to their home and walked in, 'Where's Dad?' I asked. It would be the first time I'd hear my mother swear.

'That damn motorcycle! I told you it was a bad idea to leave it with him! He's in the hospital! You have to go and see him!'

First, I called up the people we were supposed to be at to dig a swimming pool that morning to explain what was holding us up. Then I went to visit my dad, the drunk, in the hospital. I walked into his room, and right off, he demanded I destroy the evidence of alcohol on the bike so he didn't lose his license or insurance. He didn't want to talk. He chased me out to fulfill his plan to erase guilt.

I picked up my mother, and we went to the scene of the crime to pick up my motorcycle at the farm. The farmer was very nice and used his tractor to lift my broken motorcycle into the bed of our pickup truck. Then he walked us over to where the drunk crashed my bike—a sweeping curve on Wenas Road by Dobey Hill. I saw how he had drifted off the road, and the bike had come to a sudden stop in the ditch. Walking ahead of the crash site, I spotted the pop bottle with coke still in it. I reached down and picked it up, and smelled the contents. Rye and cola! Mother smelled it to.

'He didn't want to let the bottle go,' I told Mom.

Back at home, I dropped Mother off and poured gasoline all over my bike to cancel the whiskey smell. I removed what was left of the fifth hidden in the Vetter Fairing pocket and headed to the car wash in Selah. After washing all evidence of alcohol off of my bike, I drove over to our insurance agent and got permission to get my bike fixed. Dropped it off at Pavlin's Honda of Yakima and went back to talk to the drunk.

At the hospital, the drunk asked if I had destroyed the evidence, and I told him I had and failed to mention that my mother had witnessed it all.

'You promised not to be drinking, Dad!' I remember his response like it happened yesterday.

'I wasn't drinking son.'

'What about the alcohol I found?' I asked

'What alcohol, son?' he barked back. 'there is no evidence of alcohol. Let this be the last time we talk about this!'

And then it was; 'Denial of anything wrong!' a new story would come out to explain the accident. He tells how someone in a 1968 Ford Thunderbird car ran him off the road. How convenient! A 1968 Ford Thunderbird! Just like the one he used to own in 1968, he gave it to Sharon as a wedding present.

Let me explain his story to you about the use of a 1968 Ford Thunderbird car to explain away everything bad that happens. Ever since our camping trip in the late summer of 1968, while we sat around the campfire telling stories, Dad would tell his prediction story. He had driven down a road and felt something bad had happened there and pulled over, got out, and had been investigating the area when a cop pulled over and asked him why he was there. He just felt a strange feeling. The cop tells how a man changing a flat tire the night before had been run over and killed by a hit-and-run. The police officer told Les Jesperson to vacate the area, and that was his story every year around our yearly camping trip.

One night in late 1973 when we were camping at Ash Valley Ranch on the Durr Road by Umtanum Creek, drunken father admitted he had been driving his 1968 Ford Thunderbird down that road and ran over something. He found a place to park to sober up and returned the next day to see if what he thought had happened was real. A police officer later confirmed what he had done, not knowing Les Jesperson was the one who hit and killed the man.

The sober drunk told me the next morning to forget what had been talked about the night before. Sure, dad! And now, in 1974, to cover up his accident, he blames the car. Nothing is his fault!

The accident really fucked him up! Several operations were done to save his life. His vision would be affected so much that he had to wear a patch over one eye. His stomach had major problems. He developed hyperglycemia, and the medication he was required to take forced him to stop drinking and consuming any kind of alcohol. The hospital bills not covered by insurance needed to be paid. More changes were made.

I had to pay the deductible to get my bike fixed. My uninsured motorist insurance would pay Dad's bills. He never touched his homeowner's insurance. Why? Because he also blamed the bike. Since I owned the motorcycle, the whole accident was my fault for leaving him the bike to ride.

Because Dad could no longer work for months, he could not afford to pay me wages. All monies had to go to keep his business afloat. Not being paid meant I had to move back home also to be there to talk to future people's digging jobs.

My father would tell people later that I had to move back home because I couldn't make it on my own. That I needed his help of support. When he was finally able to return to work, anything he broke became my fault.

On one job, he was operating the backhoe and struck the side of the house, causing a lot of damage. He got off the machine and told me to take over. He went to talk to the homeowners, pointing at me, and told them he was sorry for what his son had done to their home. He was on his way to talk to our insurance adjuster to get it fixed. The homeowners had seen him damage their home and asked me why he told them I had done it. I explained to them that Father always blamed other people. It was all about his image of the boss is always right.

To add insult to injury, Dad didn't want to see my motorcycle. He told me I could not live there and own a motorcycle. I had to sell it, and the money went to pay more of dad's bills. I was told if I needed to drive someplace, I could use the company truck.

More problems were heading my way! I needed a third surgery to fix my foot finally. Scheduled for November 1974.

Since the mobile home park was nearly full, Father decided to sell his contracting business to Randy Johnson, a former employee of the Yakima County Health Department.

It would be my job to teach Randy how to run the backhoe and dump truck. Father had offered the business to me and was very pissed off when I refused to agree to take it over. I heard his rant, 'You're no son of mine! If you were, you'd take this offer! If you refuse, you're no son of mine!'. He tried to talk me out of my surgery to keep it all in the family. But the buyout price and contract were too high and too much in Les Jesperson's favor.

In the fall of 1974, I met and began dating Rose Pernick of Yakima. It seemed kind of odd how my father pushed us two to settle down. In April 1975 I'd just be twenty years old, and Rose turned eighteen in May. What's the hurry? In March 1975, I bought a 1967 Plymouth Barracuda and found a job running a case 780 backhoe for Alpine Lumber of Yakima. Driving the GMC truck pulling a lowboy became my first truck driving job working for someone else. My father's first request was to bring my equipment home for the weekends so he could steal from my boss hours of service.

'That's stealing, Dad!' I told him.

'Not if he doesn't find out about it!' was his reply. 'You'll be helping me get things done here.'

Five days a week, I worked for Alpine Lumber. On weekends I worked for the Jesperson Family units. Not having my own apartment sucked! On Rose's eighteenth birthday, she announced we were getting married.

Rose came from east Chicago. Her brother and mother moved into a house in Yakima owned by her mom's sister, my English teacher from high school, Mrs. Shoemaker. Money was tight, and I would have to pay for the whole wedding, which almost didn't happen. When I met Rose Pernick in 1974, she worked at a burger place and it was her co-worker named Pam that I wanted to date. Pam told me to take Rose out because she was new to Yakima and needed to have fun. At the wedding rehearsal, Pam and I kissed. I almost talked myself into going fishing and not make it to the funeral, I mean wedding. However, on August 2nd, 1975, we were married in Moxee, Washington.

We had a very short honeymoon to Canada and returned to our twenty-two-foot-long Terry Travel Trailer parked on space #47 next to the pump house in the Silver Spur mobile home park, in sight of my father's house. It wasn't a bright move on my part! Dad could look out his back window to see if we were home to be bothered. Rose and I had problems. She could not drive a car with no driver's license. We fixed that and I bought her a car, a 1971 AMC Javelin. The jobs she got hardly paid anything. Her paycheck went to her, not our mutual home. While dating, I had bought her a gold and ruby friendship ring and she returned it to the store and kept the money. She claimed she had lost it. I went to replace it and was told then by the store owner what she did.

Red flags kept popping up about who Rose Pernick, now Jesperson, was. At every turn, my mother was there telling me to work it out. She had been the one to try to get us to wait a year or two before we married to discover each other. When Rose demanded we get married soon, mom expected to hear Rose say she was pregnant. We had gone through that with my older sister. People kept looking at her belly. Years went by, and she asked when Rose would get pregnant—never satisfied!

My job with Alpine Lumber ended in November 1975 when snow and the cold shut down work. What was I to do? Run to Toppenish to run the press.

My father had plans to increase our lots to include six more. So, I used my influence to borrow a case 580 from Selah Septic Service for a time. He discounted us the operator fees because I'd be operating his machine. It took just a few weeks to finish lost numbers 53, 54, 55, 56, 57 and 58. number 56 would be reserved for my new home I'd soon get.

In the spring of 1976, I put up for sale our Terry Travel Trailer for $2,000.00. Just as someone called to buy it, Dad stepped in demanding I sell it to him so we both could enjoy it. I used the money to make a down payment on a Bendix 14 x 70 three-bedroom mobile home and put it in space #56. Dad helped me build a large deck and stairs.

I kept running the punch press and looking for a job running a backhoe. Alpine Lumber didn't want me. I must have figured out I had been using it on the weekends to help with my father's projects. Then, in June 1976, my lawsuit against the Selah school district came to a head when my lawyer, Ted Roy, presented my case to this nation's supreme court, and they agreed with us that the law needed to change.

The Fourteenth Amendment states all of us are equal under every law. A civilian's 126 days to file a case compared to a government person's seven-year time limit was not hired!

Winning the decision forced the lawyers to want to settle my case, accepting all of my medical expenses paid for and fifty thousand tax-free dollars to me. Ted Roy got a third, leaving me roughly $32,500.00.

Boy, did my father have a plan for me!

Probably why he pushed me to settle own, he hated running the park. There was always lots to do, and he was always looking for ways to leave. He had even considered selling the whole mobile home park and his home to be rid of the responsibility of being a landlord. Now that I had money to buy into the business, he, or should I say both my mother and father, hatched a plan for early retirement. My mother was afraid he would sell it. She liked the fact that owning the park brought stability to her family. Taking me aside, Mother begged me to stay there to be the manager of the park and allow them to coast. But we both knew that Les Jesperson could never sit still for long.

Here is the proposal: I would invest my $32,500 into the park for 10% ownership based on how much they had invested.

The bank owned most of our property due to bank loans to be able to build the mobile home park. They would collect $1,000 a month in income. I would collect $600 a month. The company would pick up all of our bills. Right off, we would develop the north property to include forty-six new lots, making a total of one hundred and four lots. The company would buy me a new pick up truck. He even enticed the deal to say we will go to the Blackwater Camp every year. In winter, they would retire down south and leave me alone. I'd be my own boss to run the park as I saw fit. Sounds good, but in reality, it was harder to do.

We agreed to the deal and hoped for the best.

I bought a 1976 ¾ ton Chevrolet Four Wheel drive long box pickup and put a 12,000 lb winch on it. I built a snow plow for winter to attach to any truck. We went to work building the forty-six new lots, and right off, our neighbors filed a stop work order in court. However, the court mostly sided with us, only requiring us to build a six foot high sight obscuring fence completely around our property.

Another job for me to do is 2,500 feet of chain link fence with posts every ten feet.

My muscles got big, using a pole driver to drive the ten-foot, ten-inch pipes into the ground. I got some help from Father. The whole project took just six weeks to complete as the first home moved in. With every new lot filled came a new driveway that had to be poured. Of course it was also my job to pour the concrete and work it.

We had some lots that were too small for larger homes. So, Dad made a deal with my lawyer, Ted Roy, to buy smaller homes and put them on the small lots to rent. Of course, these rentals became my responsibility, too, along with rentals my father was buying.

I can't expect the renters to mow their lot's lawns. It didn't take take long before all of my time was killed looking after the park and other people's rentals. In the winter, Dad had promised businesses that their parking lots would be plowed when it snowed. They sprung on me when they were packing up their pickup, pulling my old Terry Trailer to southern Arizona for the winter.

Twelve-hour days became the norm. and every month I collected the rents and paid the bills. Rose got a job at the Memorial Hospital as a unit secretary for four hours a day. I traded her car in for a new 1976 Ford Granada Ghia Coupe. Red on red.

There is just too much I can talk about with what went on in this job. There were suicides and people pointing guns at me when they tried to leave with my home furnishings. We had roaming animals that tore into the many trash cans. My father's solution was to chase them down and shoot them with BB guns. Not a good idea! We paid for a few vet bills. Once a year, I set out poison to kill off the population of roaming pets. Yes, it was illegal to do it. But as long as I didn't get caught, all was okay!

Some dogs and cats I took to High Valley Ranch to shoot and kill them. Thinning the herd. Some I took to the pound. I even took Rose's dog to the pound to be put down or adopted. She never looked after Sisco, never cleaned up poop or anything. She didn't miss her dog or knew it was even gone for several days. I had killed only one cat with my bare hands. Wasn't into torturing animals at all. Shoot them in the head and get it over quickly.

My father's nickname in the park was 'Nasty Landlord,' and he was proud of it. He tried to recruit kids to shoot the unleashed pets and strays. Even set up targets so kids could practice with BB guns. When some of the parents caught on to what he was doing, he was talked to badly. My father was a prick!

I tried to smooth things over when he was gone, but he was rubbing off on me. I was becoming him as a landlord. As long as you don't get caught, it is legal! It is like being a dictator or king of your city/country. What I say is it! To hold the power over my renters on my property. A mobile home is a lot harder just to move. There has to be another lot to go to. And not too many were available and I knew this. 'Pick up your trash or else!' Or else!

A mobile home park is a city in itself with city problems. A gang of boys got together to pay tribute to me- the government. Every night my pickup and home were their targets to toss eggs at.

One night, I hid in the shadows and caught a kid named Marc tossing eggs at my truck. The others ran. I took Marc over to see his parents in Space #93. His parents looked at me and claimed their son would never do what I was claiming I caught him doing. 'Well, okay then!'

Later that week, I bought a case of eggs, and at two in the morning, I threw eggs at everyone's homes in the park but Marc's. The other boys in his gang broke Marc's throwing arm. His parents claimed I must be behind it. 'But my house got hit too.' I told them.

Marc became an outcast to everyone and eventually set fire to his bedroom, which gutted their home and forced them to move. No more eggs were tossed at my home.

At Christmas 1976, Rose sent for her friend Janet from a little town in Ireland to vist us. Janet, a tall, slender beauty with long, straight hair, would sleep in the bedroom down the hall. As soon as I saw her, I wanted her. We set her up to have a date with my friend Jerry Day on New Year's. They hit it off and would eventually get married. More on Jerry and Janet later. Funny how the actions of one little something will change things for you years down the road.

While my parents were down south vacationing, our water well started to suck sand. So off to the bank, I went to borrow $25,000 to get another deeper well done. This loan had a $200.00 monthly payment to make.

When my father returned from down south, he was bored and decided to fuck up everything. He planned to build on an idea he had in his shop. His old shop was horse stables that brought in about $2,000.00 a month. He went to the bank and borrowed another $100,00.00 to buy equipment to manufacture his 'Wilderness Dry and Grill, ' an idea hatched up in the Blackwater the previous fall. He didn't ask me what I thought. I just argued that when it made millions, I'd get 10% of it.

Of course, any free time I could have had was now taken up rebuilding the plant. Our neighbors didn't like it to be changed to a manufacturing plant and filed an order to stop him. They claimed we lived in an agriculture zoning area, but Les Jesperson showed off his 1967 permit he had obtained just in case something like this stop order came. The plant was up and running by mid-summer 1977. sales of his idea didn't match what his expectations were, and by early 1978, he closed up the plant.

The Wilderness Dry and Grill was a bust!

We owed another thousand a month in back payments. Our business took a major hit, and when our bills added up, there was no way two households could be supported at that time. I told my parents to buy me out and run the park themselves. I also told Dad the new sewer system with the forty-six new lots was failing and needed an upgrade that was an estimated cost of another $50,000.00 to complete.

Before he ventured off with his Dry and Grill idea, the park and stables revenue was close to $10,000.00 a month. We took a loss of $3,000.00 and with the failing sewer estimated costs, we would lose another $1,000.00 to payments.

Since my father didn't want to be stuck in a rut looking after his park, a decision was made to sell the mobile home park. Before we put it on the market, Dad removed his own home from the park's total property. He sold his home and pocketed the money, not giving me my 10%. He argued it was his money. I argued that when I bought into the park, his house and property were included in the overall value of the property. Certainly, his home was mortgaged through the bank to cover loans for building up the mobile home park. As far as he was concerned, no contract was in writing, and therefore, 'fuck you, Keith!'

In around September 1978 our mobile home park was being sold to the Carlyle Group. A group of business people, including the Bush family of Texas, for an undisclosed amount of money. My guess is about one and a half to two million dollars. Sounds like a lot in 1978, however we take into account the money owed to the bank was a lot. What capital that would be left over would be what the increased value over the past few years was.

As soon as earnest money was handed over, Les Jesperson wanted to cut me out of the profit I could make in his deal with Carlyle. He proposed I be bought out. I'd get my pickup truck and my original $32,500.00. When I argued that 10% of the value increase should net me at least $70,000.00, he reminded me I was not in a written contract. It was a take-it-or-leave-it deal.

Before the sale was final, Carlyle required us to create three more lots which included a front lot to house the home of the new park manager.

Dad looked to me to help do this before he paid me off, and I soon learned it was going to get more interesting involving me. He told Carlyle that I would stay there to train the new manager for at least six months. Why? He needed me to keep the failed sewer problems secret so Les Jesperson could move away and to be around to be questioned when it was discovered. Something I never agreed to do!

As soon as I was paid off, I made arrangements to have my home moved to space #52 at the mobile home park behind the East Valley market by Moxee. Dad had already moved to an adult mobile home park nearer to Yakima when I bought a large double-wide home already set up in the park. He had left town and couldn't be reached for comment. Until my home was moved, the new manager came to see me every day to ask where things were. I didn't say stay six months—more like six weeks. Before long, management soon became aware of the failing sewer system, and Carlyle filed a fraud case against me and Dad for $250,000.00. I was the first to respond to Carlyle to tell them I should not be sued because at the time of the purchase, I had been bought out by Les Jesperson. They revised their lawsuit and named me as a witness only.

When my father called me, he told me I would be responsible for 10% of my money awarded to Carlyle, should Carlyle win. That was when I reminded him of no contract between us and he paid me off before he sold the park.

At court, Les Jesperson took the stand and couldn't remember his name, let alone anything to do with the operations of the Silver Spur Mobile Home Park. His common answer was, 'You'll have to ask Keith.'

Before I took the stand, Dad asked me what I was going to tell them. I said, ' I'm going to tell them the truth, Dad.'

Quickly, he barked, 'Don't tell them the truth! The truth will cost us plenty! Lie to them! If you pull this off, I'll make it up to you.'

Make it up to me?

I went on the stand and lied to them. Every story I told was a lie. If I had told the truth, Les Jesperson would have paid out a lot of money. There I was, destroying their case. I came across as a believable young man put in charge of a big project. The jury was all farmers who had to deal with companies wanting to steal their land. They handed down a settlement to say Les Jesperson owed only $5,000.00. Carlyle had even to cover our lawyer's fees. And no, I didn't have to pay 10%.

How did Dad make it up to me? I'm still waiting for that now at 69 years old.

A New World

For a short time I drove to Toppenish to make ends meet by again running the punch press. I'd look to the want ads for jobs I could do, noticed an equipment operator needed at Muffett and Sons by Buena. It was located between Wapato and Toppenish. I drove into their lot and parked, saw a female German Sheppard watchdog, and went over to introduce myself. I noticed her dish out of the water and filled it. I heard a scream, 'Don't touch the dog!' A man came to me at a run. Another came from the other direction, and we met there as I petted the dog.

'What are you doing here?' asked the first man named Pat.

I told them I was there to apply for the operator job.

The second man, named Mike, said, 'You're hired!'

Pat said to Mike that he hadn't seen me operate a backhoe yet, and Mike said, 'The dog like him!'

Sheba hired me! Especially to seal the deal, growled at Pat. Apparently, Sheba was a hard dog to know. Ex-sheriff's K-9 unit that was hard to control. More like unpredictable! So instead of putting the dog down, the police officer that trained Sheba, gave her to the Muffetts to guard their yard.

I'd make it my job to keep her comfortable and happy. I gave her butcher bones to snack on, and when I came to work, no matter what time it was, I spent time with her to let her know she was loved by at least me.

Muffett and Sons ran a plastic pipe business installing irrigation systems for orchards. I ran Case Backhoes, Buckeye, and Cleveland Wheel Trenchers and drove a freight liner, pulling a lowboy to move machinery and pip to job sites.

In the winter, I worked rebuilding equipment and this consisted of later work and lots of welding. The money wasn't the greatest. I started at $5.00 an hour back in 1978, and when I quit in April of 1981, my wages were only $7.00 an hour.

But I stayed very busy and got lots of overtime every month. Besides work, what made working for them great was that they treated their whole workforce like family. Every month we had a dinner at a buffet restaurant called 'The Royal Fork'.

Rose and I celebrated the birth of our first daughter in July 1979, Melissa Grace Jesperson. While Rose was pregnant in the summer of 1980 with our son Jason Roy, we traveled to Canada to visit my old friend Reg Routley living in Sparwood, British Columbia.

We met his family at a Christian retreat near Fernis Reg worked at that time for B.C. Coal. I asked about the wages and found out I wanted to make what he was making and inquired about a possible job. We took a day to investigate jobs and I was accepted to work at Fording Coat at Elkford when I would be able to get my social insurance number given to me.

This was my hope to be able to return to Canada. We would be leaving Yakima Valley's low wages and our parents. It was exciting to move away from my father and his bullshit.

Back in 1976, I bought a canopy to fit my pickup truck. Dad asked to borrow it in 1977, and I never got it back. He sold his truck with my canopy still on it! What was mine was his! He sold my boat. Grandpa left me back in 1970 when he wanted a ski boat. Then in 1978, I bought a twelve-foot-long Fiberglass 'V' hull boat with a seven-horse Elgin outboard motor so I could go fishing. He borrowed the boat and came back with a new Mercury motor after selling my antique Elgin motor. The next time he borrowed my boat, he traded it off for a nine-foot-long Livingston Twin hull boat, which was easier to put on his truck.

He didn't ask me. He just did it.

He told me I could borrow his boat and motor whenever he wasn't using it. I went to the Marina to recover my boat, complaining to the salespeople that the deal wasn't right. I wanted my property back. Too bad! It had already been sold!

Fucking thief!

Our son, Jason Roy Jesperson, was born in September 1980. my social insurance card came in the mail in March 1981 and I gave notice I'd be leaving to work in Canada after first confirming I still had a job at Fording Coal, A.K.A. The Elk River Mine, by the town of Elkford.

On April 10th, I drove to Elkford and started work on the 11th. Fording has a work camp I could live at until an apartment becomes available to move Rose and my children into at a cost of $160.00 a month- meals included!

As I drove my car along Interstate 90 near George, Washington I spotted a beautiful woman needing a ride. So I pulled over, and she got in. Her car had broken down by Moses Lake, and she made the mistake of getting a ride in the wrong direction. To help her out, we drove to her car, and I troubleshooted her problem and discovered the points her distributor had broken. A quick run to a Napa parts store and back to her car, we soon had her car running.

She is a hairdresser out of Spokane on her way to Wenatchee for a seminar about her job. She didn't drive to Wenatchee after I got her car fixed. Instead, I followed her back to Spokane. At that time, in 1981, I was loyal to my wife and family. I probably could have gotten lucky with her had I pushed for that kind of a thank you. But I was in a hurry to get to Canada. A very pretty woman my age.

Work at the mine was being regulated by Union help. I became number 901680 with the United Steel Workers of America Union. When I went to work, my name wasn't aboard; my number was. I'd check the board to find out what placement in the open pit mine was assigned for the day or night to my number. At shift change, my number came off the board. They operated on seniority. The longer you worked there meant the more access to different work you could apply to. My first job was laborer even though I knew how to run large equipment. A month or two in as a laborer, I could bid to being a dump truck driver. I drove Halpac 120's and Wabco 170's mine trucks.

Eventually I'd bid into being a welder. Maintenance is where the money is at! Twelve hours a day, every day for months on end, produced big payments.

It was a whole new world for me in Canada. Away from my wife and, more importantly, my father. He always injected himself into every job I had. Tried to influence every decision to offer the sale of the park. In 1979, he called me up to his new home and announced he was buying a motorcycle and felt I should as well so we could ride on trips together. He bought a CB750 Honda like the one he wrecked of mine back in 1974. he made the argument to his mother that he no longer was drinking and, therefore, okay to ride. No one could ever control Les Jesperson. He was going to do what he wanted to do, and no one, not even his wife, could stop him. I bought the Honda CBX, a six-cylinder, 1047 cc rocket on rails. Outfitted it with Vetter Fairly and backrest and universal saddlebags to carry stuff and extra helmet in. I took my wife for a ride and she refused to get on it again. It scared her badly. The bike could break the highway speed limit at 55 mph in first gear. The kind of motorcycle that would kill you if you didn't respect its power. My baby!

When the roads in Canada were free of ice and snow, I rode my bike to work from Moxee, Washington. It was only 500 miles to Elkford, at a ten-hour ride including fuel stops.

To move my family to Canada, I needed to have nothing left for me in the United States. Liquidate my assets, find someone to buy my mobile home, and settle all debts. When we sold the park, my brother Bruce borrowed $5,000.00 from me to pay a down payment on a home in Ellensburg, Washington. He paid me back in two years. My sister Sharon borrowed $10,000.00 from me at 10 ½ % interest, which the bank charged me. She complained about having to pay any interest, and every month, she didn't want to make her small payments. Most months, she didn't pay. In 1981, she still owed me almost all of it. I feared that if I went to Canada, she would never pay me. So I asked our father if he would take over the loan to her so I could get my money.

He explained to me, 'Business is business, right Keith? I can't do this for nothing. I have to make something on this.'

We were dealing with family here, and my father was going to fuck me. So much for making it up to me!

Les Jesperson charged me $2,000.00 to take over the loan to his daughter, my sister, at 10.5% interest. He gave me $7,000.00 so I could leave Sharon's problem behind. As for my house, a friend of his took over the payments at the bank. I make nothing in my home. And as it all turned out, I would have been ahead if I had just stayed in Moxee.

In late June 1981, an apartment became available for me to move Rose and our two children to Elkford. A new two-bedroom apartment for $983.00 a month, including heat and water. I know it sounds like a lot. But the amount I was making covered it and lots more. This was a small city that was created by the coal mine. You know the song 'I owe my soul to the company store'? As I say it, all was great being away from family. Rose loved the bigger payloads. What I cleared in a week at the mine was more than I'd gross in a month working for Muffett and Sons. All good things come to an end.

In March 1982, my parents told us they would be coming to visit soon. Dad and I talked about my job as a welder and I told him about the nice leathers we wore when welding. He told me to get him a set. And there it was! He was giving me an order to steal a set of leathers from where I worked, jeopardizing my job if caught. To please my dominating father, I always felt a need to satisfy his demands to win his favor. Even though he seemed to always screw me over, am I that gullible? Apparently so! Because I was going to do what he told me to do. And when I tried to leave the mine with a box full of leathers, the mine security stopped me and I was charged with suspicion of the attempt to the unauthorized removal of company property. I wanted to settle with keeping my job and in some kind of probation but the Union rep had other plans. A three-day wild cat strike took place to argue the suspicion claim. In the end, I lost my job. I lost the argument in arbitration. Now, mine management offered me my job back with years of probation if I admitted guilt. And what did father tell me? 'Deny everything! Make them prove it!' I had left him in the States, and here I was, listening to him again. I had no job and no apartment, and I had to sell my bike to feed us and move.

We moved to Hardieville, a small community north of Lethbridge, Alberta. I'd secured a driver's license to drive semi trucks and was hired on to Brighton Trucking. I made trips to Calgary and back every day, pulling flatbed trailers. Then, one day, my boss asked me to weld a store tire rack back onto a trailer. He decided then to make me work in his shop repairing trucks and trailers. I'd work all day in the shop and still take a load to Calgary and back. The money was good, but I grew tired of trucking at night after eight hours in the shop. I would hire Drain Brothers of Blairmore, Alberta, to run all kinds of excavators. The first one is a John Deere 690B. The machine would have an extension to where the bucket had been. Basically, we turned the digging machine into a crane sitting on a flat rail car. Our job was to pick up old railroad rail and place them into half-car trailers to be stacked elsewhere. There were the two of us, me on the 690B and the other on a CAT 215. My next job was to replace wooden culverts with steel ones under the tracks throughout Alberta for the Canadian Pacific Railroad. A few months later, our jobs were done.

Before Drain Brothers could settle a new contract, I hired on to GetKate construction of Lethbridge, running excavators and cat dozers and delivering equipment supplies to jobs using their 1976 Peterbilt and lowboy trailer. The Peterbilt had a 12-ton sixty-foot long stinger crane on it, as well as a 30-ton winch. In Canada, more work is done in the wintertime while the ground is solid. I worked for GetKite until the spring of 1983. Then, I went to work for Dueck Construction of Lethbridge welding and running their Bantam 166 excavator. We handled smaller jobs.

In March 1983, our third child was born, Carrie Marie on March 17th. With a new face in our family, my mother wanted to visit to see her grandchildren. They showed up with their motorhome and invited us to go with them to a relative's farm in Maple Creek, Saskatchewan, for a day of killing prairie dogs with rifles. I used my Jennings compound bow and arrows. There was a lot of talking going on between my mother and my wife while we men killed gophers. My mother suffered from cancer and missed her babies and her grandchildren. She hoped to convince Rose to move back to Yakima so she could be around our family more in the time she had to live. Going back to Yakima, Yakima's wages are going backward. I explained to Rose we would be leaving twenty dollars an hour to be getting, at best, eight.

I didn't want to leave. I couldn't leave until I could secure a legal green card to live in the U.S. We spent the day with Mom and Dad, and back home, Rose began to pack. She was tired of Canada. She told me she missed her family. Then she tossed at me an ultimatum, 'Come back with me, or you'll never see your children again!'

In late June 1983, Rose moved with my three children into a home her aunt Shoemaker owned in Yakima. I stayed behind in Lethbridge, working for Dueck Construction, waiting for me to get a legal green card. I had actually thought of returning to Fording Coal and admitting my guilt to get my job back and live in the work camp, sending to Yakima what I would have made in Yakima, $8.00 an hour.

As my life turned out, looking back from my prison cell now, it would have been a better solution than to follow my wife back to Yakima. Hindsight is 20-20 always.

By August 1983 I had my card and moved back to Yakima. My first job was welding for Russell Crane service for, you guessed it- $8.00 an hour. And when I handed Rose my paycheck, she asked, 'Where is the rest of it?' I heard her telling me, 'You need to get a better-paying job.'

So what did I do? Drove to Toppenish and ran the press on weekends for double shifts to bring in extra cash to cover what Rose had become used to.

In late September 1983, I landed a job driving an old 1964 Kenworth for Jerry's Steel Supply of Yakima and Sunnyside. I drove scrap steel and other recyclables to Seattle and Portland and came back with new steel for their customers. I got paid $150.00 a day per trip to the coast and $100.00 to haul old newspapers to Keye's Fiber of Wenatchee. Each week I grossed $850.00, clearing about $2,700.00 a month. It was more suitable to Rose's needs.

Trucking is a hard life. It isn't family-friendly.

My weeks started Sunday night and ended Sunday mornings. Just like the song, 'Six days on the Road and I'm gonna make it home tonight.' for three years, I worked for Jerry's Steel Supply to get ahead. But did I? Sure, I learned how to manipulate my log books, and I was driving around areas in the Seattle/Kent areas where the notorious Green River dumped his bodies. In fact, several of my favorite places to park to catch some sleep turned out to be where the Green River Killer parked when he dropped off his victims. I read the book by writer Ann Rule. Shocking! Coincidences? Some believed he could be a truck driver who worked around the area. On November 7th, 1986, my boss told me I was done. His son would be their truck driver. No notice! Just a 'Don't let the door hit you on the way out' sort of send-off!

Because Rose believed we were making enough money we needed to buy a large mobile home and put it in a park off of Wena Road, north of Selah. The four-bedroom home cost us

$30,000.00. Our mortgage was almost $500.00 a month. All set up in 1984. Mobile homes don't have basements, my daughter Melissa tells stories now to say in 1984 I went into our basement to get her box of kittens. Children say the craziest things!

In early 1986, Rose's mother went to the Peace Corps and left Kathy, Rose's sister, to look after. One day I made phone calls to home to get no answer. So I stopped in later in the afternoon to discover everyone was home. Why were they not answering the phone? Rose had unplugged it! Plugging it back in, the phone rang. At the other end was Ken Hudson, the bank manager. Ken and I were friends. Back in 1977, he came with us to the Blackwater for two weeks of fishing. Now, he was telling me Rose wouldn't talk to him. We were three months behind in our mortgage payments. Why? Rose and Kathy were fast food junkies! Every meal for them and my kids was at restaurants like McDonald's! Our mortgage went to their bellies!

Once before I had to take the check books away from Rose. She loved to write checks and not mark it down in the ledger. I had over $600.00 in service charges for one month. More than the amount she wrote the checks for. For months, when I got home, I'd have to take her to the store and use my account to pay for it. That got old! Came down to a trust thing and follow through thing to teach her about balancing money. Eventually I gave her back the money to pay bills with.

When Kathy came into our home, Rose had promised to get a full-time job, and Kathy was supposed to babysit our kids. That just didn't happen! Rose's solution was always, 'You need a better job, Keith!'

So I asked her, 'Are you going to get a job to help pay for our home?'

I called Ken back and told him to repossess our home. Rose wasn't going to help. And weeks later, we rented a home closer to Selah next to a feedlot behind the Elks Golf Course. And this time, I opened a new bank account to put my cheks into that Rose had no access to. I handed out cash to her to use at any store. No more McDonald's for regular meals! There is nothing wrong with mac and cheese at home or Ramen noodles. To cut down on costs, we had just one car. I rode my bicycle to work or jogged eight miles to Jerry's Steel in Yakima. When my job ended with Jerry's Steel, I didn't go out looking for another truck driver's job. I wanted to stay close to family. I applied to the Holiday Motor Inn's nightclub called 'The Owl's Nest' for a security job at night and got it. My hours were around nine at night to three in the morning. The pay wasn't very good, but it filled the time. At the end of the night, I was able to bring home bar sandwiches my kids loved to eat. All of my other spare time was spent running the press in Toppenish.

Around February 1987, I ran into Mike Muffett at a store, and he asked what I was doing. He had a job for me if I wanted it. Driving semis to haul pipe from Oregon to his/their many stores. Nothing like filling in all of my time with more work. Off work at the Inn at three, I'd go to Buena and drive to Beaverton, Oregon to get plastic pipe from Pacific Pipe, their business end make up to three deliveries before calling it a day at five pm. Just in time to put in a few hours at the punch press. Between Royce and myself, we ran the press 24 hours a day on the weekends.

When it got warmer outside, Mike's brother Pat had me digging on his job. Sheba was still there and seemed glad I was back spending time with her. My first night-early morning back, she didn't bark at the bicycle rider entering the property at 4:00 pm. I called her name, and while the Freightliner warmed up, I spent time with her. What a great dog!

Working three jobs suck! I was too spread out. Ralph, a man working for Muffett and Sons, had an older home in the Toppenish area and offered it to me as a purchase home. I'd be closer to two of my jobs.

In June 1987, we moved into the home on Germantown Road. My wife hated it there! Kids will adapt to just about everything. They made friends quickly and settled in.

Soon I quit being security at the Owl's Nest, spending more time at the punch press. As long as there was Steel to run, money flowed in. but the press is only about four months a year, and Muffett and Sons pay was- you guessed it- unchanged from when I left them six years before- $7.00 an hour.

Thinking it all over, had I just stayed working at Muffett and Sons back in 1981, I'd have my home paid for in Moxee, still have my motorcycle, still be happily married, and not stressed out like I was trying to catch back up to where I had been.

It seems like I was spinning my wheels where I was at Rose complained about the old house, the low wages, and where we lived. All of her family was again miles away. Her mother was back in Spokane, Washinton, over 200 miles from us. Do you want to know what is funny? Rose wanted to get married in 1975 to get away from her mother. Now, all she wants is to be near her. Where did some of my money go? Rose gave $8,500.00 to her mother to help her buy her home in Spokane. I remember one time when we visited, she had started to thank me when Rose spoke out, 'He knows nothing about this!' It took some real investigation into our money to finally solve what I wasn't supposed to know about.

Here I was, working my ass off to get ahead, and Rose was funneling some of it to her mother. Having learned of the money given to her mother, I confronted Rose about how she was being cheap to us while she stole from me/us. It made it sting more remembering her telling me to get a better-paying job.

To pay my bills, I needed a better-paying full-time job. I also knew that trucking offered more money to be made, but it wasn't a better-paying job by just itself. There were ways to manipulate work so I could make more. I would just have to drive a long-haul truck. Again, being away from home like I had with Jerry's Steel Supply. But as we saw it, working two jobs had me away from home, too. Looking for a job, I found it in Toppenish driving for Mid Valley Equipment, driving a 1984 conventional Freightliner pulling a refrigerated trailer to all points in the western eleven states. Thwenty-two cents a mile, $11.00 an hour based on 50 miles per hour on the log book. I'm allowed 70 hours of service in eight days. Not all of those 70 hours are driving. There are fuel stops and inspections, loading and unloading times. When trucking, we get very creative in how we turn in our legal logbooks.

Now, our boss will not pay us to unload our trucks. He will, however, pay an outside service to unload it. What I did was turn in a lumper's slip for $60.00 as an unloading fee and collect it from my boss. I would unload my load myself. Being I had driven for Jerry's Steel Supply, I learned what was valuable to sell as scrap. I'd rob truck stops of scrap metal trash and turn in broken aluminum wheels for serious cash—even unload other trailers for lumper's fees. My regular pay doesn't include overtime pay. It is all $11.00 an hour. In a month's time, I could drive 14,500 miles legally. However, that is hard to do. Most trucking companies pay McNalley miles, post office to post office miles. This means they cheat us all 25% of the actual miles driven. They do not pay odometer miles. And back then, all we could legally write in our log books was 50 miles per hour driven. Now, in 2024 I'm not sure how much is allowed. Probably don't even use log books, maybe this will make sense to you: Bend, Oregon is 200 miles from Yakima, Washingto. I can legally log it as 4 hours in my log book. I can in no way drive a loaded semi to Bend in 4 hours. It can't be done! There are too many hills and valleys along the way. More like 5 hours or more.

Have you ever watched the movie *Smokey and the Bandit*? They are going to do what can't be done. Drive 900 miles in eighteen hours. Loading time and fueling time, let alone stopping to eat, cuts into driving time. Now, it would be difficult enough to do it on an interstate highway. Worse when they are mostly on two-lane roads dealing with traffic. I figured they averaged 65 miles per hour in the time they had to drive. It is impossible to do 65 mph very long on a two-lane road dealing with traffic, let alone having to go faster to make it the average speed. So how to manipulate our log books in order to get loads to, say Los Angeles time? We are allowed ten hours of driving before we have to show eight hours off work or in the sleeper berth. A total of fifteen hours working each 24-hour period. Midnight to midnight. We run two books; one is current location, and one is backlogged to gather up hours we accumulate over time. Not actual times, but the log books we turn in to our boss at the end of every trip. We also have to have our fueling and loading and unloading dates properly into the log book we turn in. It is complicated, to say the least. Most of our meal times are used to keep proper logs.

In trucking, we work too hard for our money. A real love/hate relationship to be a truck driver trying to make a living. No wonder so many marriages end in divorce when one is a truck driver. It's 30 hours to drive to Los Angeles's produce market from Yakima legally. Most bosses want the loads there in 20 hours. They want you to do it non-stop, which is illegal. And if you were to get caught by the police, your boss would deny telling you to get it there non-stop. Remember it is the driver's responsibility for everything that happens to their loads and driving. Sometimes you just have to tell the boss to fuck off.

Self Destruct

Christmas 1986 became an eventful period of time. One night, a few days before I was called to go over to visit Jerry and Janet Day in Yakima, I brought my son Jason with me. When we arrived, Jerry told me he had to go to the store and he took my son with him. Odd?

As soon as they were out of the apartment driveway, Janet came to me sexually. She began to kiss me and requested we go to her bed to play. Sure, back in 1976, when I saw her, I wanted to bed her, but she was my friend's wife. Call me naive! I could not move on her that way and told her 'no'

we sat there and waited for Jerry to get back with my son. All the while I was trying to figure out how to tell him Janet made a play on me. I have to admit that I really found the situation stimulating. I could have fucked her, and who would be the wiser, but something just didn't feel right, like it was a setup. I just felt like Jerry was going to come home, find us in the bed, pull out his shotgun, and blow me away. They returned and when Jerry walked in the door, Janet moved her head to say,' No.' the head movement of them both said a lot. It was a setup. It was explanation time!

Jerry told me they had an open relationship. They were swingers, 'Go ahead and take my wife into our bedroom and fuck her!' I tried to explain how he/they were allowing a fox into their pen. That to allow me access to his wife certainly would turn out bad at some point in our relationship. There could be no going back once she allows me to have her. Well, a man has to do what a man has to do. I took him up on his offer and met Janet in her room and made love to her. She is a very beautiful woman—the very first woman to have sex with me since being married to Rose.

Not having to work the next day, I went back to see Janet for round two while Jerry was at work. I felt more at ease with the place all to ourselves. Sex with her was far better than I ever had with Rose. Some women just get more into it. Jerry's work took them to live in Washougal, Washington. I continued to stop in to play with Janet while Jerry worked, as long as their two children weren't home. Then, in 1993, Jerry divorced Janet, claiming she was having an affair with me. No, she wasn't! We were just fucking!

As I drove for Midvalley Equipment, I began seeing hot spots for us truckers to stay away from, like the same rest areas. Why? Hookers! Girls that sell themselves for money. In Canada, I had gotten into a health nut kind of plan to lose weight to look better. I joined the Lethbridge Boxing Club and won a few fights. Mostly to get into shape, I lost 80 pounds, and this pissed off Rose because women paid more attention to me. I continued my running and exercise program back in the States. Janet loved me for how I had slimmed down. That is probably why she wanted to fuck me.

Trucking is not a holiday. We drive for long periods of time to make deliveries and to pick up loads. Rose believed it to be a holiday because I seemed glad to be going on my next run. Not so happy to be at home. Life had become a normal response. My kids would say, 'Daddy's home!' and run to me, expecting me to lift them up. I'd kiss Rose hello, and we would talk about what was wrong. At night, I could get sex if I pushed for it. Sometimes, Rose pushed for it. Mostly home life was to catch up on my sleep. I'd wake up with my kids sleeping all over me. It's not really a regular home life. Maybe I will be home for a day before I go again. That makes it easy to fall for women in truckstops and rest areas. Flirting makes life better as we talk to the waitresses. Mostly, they are used to us truckers. Leading us not to follow through with our desires. However, there are a few who will act on our flirts.

At the Denver West Unical 76 truck stop, my boss paid for a motel room for me. At the restaurant, I flirted with a woman named Dee Dee, and later, at a bar, I ran into her. After a few drinks, we fell into bed, and clothes came off, and we played all night. Did I feel guilty? Not since Janet had invited me into her bed. She had made me believe it to be okay now to have sex with different women. God didn't strike me down for having sex with Janet. I was pussy whipped, for sure. Just be careful not to bring anything home to Rose—no sexual transmitting problems. Use protection to be sure! But not all the time. Thank god I never brought anything home. I was lucky- I guess.

The best prostitute I had sex with has to be Linda, down by the Ocean Side, California. That was a night to remember! I arrived at the rest area and parked in the last truck parking lot so I could be the first one to leave come 6:00 AM. I had a hot load of apple juice on from Selah's Treetop Warehouse heading for Miramar- *Top Gun*'s airfield.

I walked around the rest area for a while before deciding to retire for the evening. Back at my tuck, I saw a woman walking around. Call me naive because I thought she was another driver. Talking to her, I soon realized she was selling her body, and of course, I was very interested in a close friendship with her. She wore a long plaid dress and a dark top. Large-rimmed glasses. Her body was perfect: about 5'7 tall and 120 lbs. Slender built with not-so-big breasts. We climbed into the cab of the freightliner to conduct business. She asked for just twenty dollars. I think she liked what she saw, too. We began to kiss and slowly took off our clothes as we entered the sleeper. Kissing her, I went down on her to get her wet and horny. After a time, she guided me into her, and we made love, not just fuck. The love session took hours to complete. When we were done, we fell asleep together. My alarm went off at 6:00 AM, and we just didn't want to move, but I had to get going to make my delivery on time.

A lot had changed in the rest area since I went to sleep with Linda. Cars were parked everywhere. A VW Beetle was parked to my left, and the way he was parked, I couldn't leave without running over the front of his car. So I knocked on his window and asked him to back up ten feet. He told me to fuck off. He wasn't going to move. I was being nice to him, so I tried to move my trailer over more so I would miss his car, but to no avail. Again, I knocked on his window and asked him to move. And again, he told me to fuck off, and this time, he gave me the finger. Okay then! I climbed into the truck, put it in gear, and drove over the front of his car. I kept going all the way to Top Gun's Miramar to deliver my apple juice load. About a month later, there I was parking at the ocean sid rest area at around 7:00 pm and noticed Linda sitting at a picnic table. I went over to her and she knew it was me and began to laugh. After I had left the car squashed on the pavement, the prick called the cops. When the police asked him about what happened, he admitted the driver of the semi asked him to move. Witnesses told the police the guy in the car told the semi-driver to fuck off. Well, maybe next time he's blocking in another vehicle, he'll think twice about it.

At 9:00, Linda joined me for another full night of being together. I didn't set my alarm at all. We woke up together later the next morning. My boss Jeff Harris was nicknamed Hooker Harris because he had been caught in a sting and arrested for soliciting the services of a hooker. His pretty wife had to bail him out of jail. Deep down, I feared the very thing when talking to hookers. All truckers who seek warmth from prostitutes fear one day they, too, will be caught.

Back at home, I told Rose of my adventures out on the road, not telling her I had had sex with girls. I was justifying my actions because Rose and I were not having sex very much. I know, a lame excuse! She heard me talk about places I've been and people I've met, and she wanted to see for herself what trucking was all about. So, my boss allowed me to take my wife out for a week. We had a load of apples going to Phoenix, Arizona's Fleming Foods. I had to keep telling her this was not a vacation. This was work! She had called ahead to her cousin in Phoenix to say we would be in town. We pulled into Phoenix at 2:00 AM, and she slept as I unloaded the apples and headed out to Interstate 10 to Tuscon and Nogales for our pickup of produce. She woke up at 9:00 pm, asking when we would be arriving in Phoenix. Pissed off over missing it. Later that afternoon, we were heading back north with a load of tomatoes. We stopped at the truck stop on Buckeye Street in Phoenix called the Circle K.

we sat there parked, and I pointed out several hookers working the lot. She argued with me at seeing the pretty young girls that looked like girls living next to us in Toppenish—maybe sixteen or early twenty-something. To prove my point, I called the youngest looking one over to talk to me while Rose hid in the sleeper. She heard the costs rundown on what this pretty woman would like to get paid for. When I mentioned my wife was in the truck, the hooker told us we could have a threesome. Rose blushed.

When we drove over the Hoover Dam, looking down, Rose threw herself into the sleeper and would not come out until we were on open ground headed for Vegas. After just a week of Rose in my truck, she got out and promised she would never get into a semi again. Not fun for her. All the driving made her sleepy, and she slept most of the time.

My son Jason came with me for a week. He had fun spending time with me. I had to be careful of truck stops, though. He stayed close to me when we went into large truck stops. At the end of our week together, Jason was all smiles when Rose came to pick him up.

True to form, my father decided to inject himself into the trucking company I drove for. I called my boss, and I was told to drive to Toppenish to Trade Trailers. He had a load that needed to be delivered overnight to Lucky Stores in San Leandro, California. I couldn't understand his thinking. I had been awake for two days straight! I was in no condition to make it three days.

In Toppenish, my father was there waiting for me. He had convinced my boss that he could drive a semi and do what I could do. We were to be a team and drive a load of apples to San Leandro by morning. And what is really bad, Les Jesperson didn't know how to drive a tractor-trailer unti at all. I would have to teach him how even to start. There is a picture floating around the internet of me standing in front of a brown Freightliner with a splint on one of my ringers. Les Jesperson took that photo in the summer of 1987.

Slowly, my father began to learn to drive. Maybe drove fifty miles in central Oregon on Hwy 97. Once in California, Les Jesperson went to sleep. At 6:00 AM the following morning, we were backed into a door at Lucky Stores. Dad helped me unload two pallets of apples and then returned to the sleeper to rest as I unloaded the trailer. He was still asleep when I pulled into Salinas to get our load back to Seattle. Worthless! My boss pushed us like we were a team of drivers. Only he rode the passenger seat or bed in the back while I had to cover for him. One trip was plenty. He didn't want to drive again.

Driving for Mid Valley Equipment came to a close when I wrecked my truck. In 1987, police were implementing a mandatory seat belt rule. Driving south out of Toppenish on Hwy 97, I looked up to see the scale house was open. Remembering I needed to have my seat belt on, I reached down and flipped the lap belt over my lap. I had a problem. The end of the seat belt landed on the steering wheel and didn't allow me to steer. As I slowed down to go to the weigh station, the truck pulled to the right on the two-lane roadway. I turned right with a quick push and pulled out the seat belt. But it was too late; my tractor-trailer had drifted onto the loose gravel side and was being pulled into the ditch. The load of potatoes destroyed the trailer. Not much damage was done to the truck. I walked into the weigh station to see my friend George Hefner being inspected. He asked me where my truck was. I pointed over my shoulder and told everyone who was listening, 'It's on its side in the ditch!' They called my boss.

I lied to the police to say a brake locked up. My boss told me what had happened. Apparently, he had heard of it happening to other drivers.

My boss wanted me to pay his $2,500.00 deductible out of my wages. I was good with that. My mistake, my fault. I was told to look for another job.

Late in September 1987, I found work driving for Rahier Trucking of Yakima. Also known as Mequine Lumber. I'd be driving Cabover Peterbilt pulling Refer trailers as I had for Hooker Harris. Sometimes, we pulled flatbed trailers, hauling lumber and containers.

My first morning at work, I was told to go to the yard and pick out a tractor and, hook up to a set of Rocky Mountain doubles (40' x 20') trailers and drive to Latman's Lumber in Naches, Washington. I picked out an old 1958 Peterbilt conventional and, fired it up and hooked it to a set of trailers and drove out of Rahier's yard. As I was leaving, I saw some of them waving at me, and I waved back and kept on going. Twenty miles away in the Layman's yard, several other Rahier drivers came over to me to tell me I just lost my job. No one was allowed to drive the boss's baby—his original tractor with a 5 and 4 transmission. What Rahier didn't know was I cut my teeth driving twin sticks. I loved them the most! Even better than the new 13, 15, and 18-speed gearboxes. Before long, my 101,000-pound load was severed, and I was on my way back to the Yakima yard. As it turned out, they had called up the boss to tell him a new driver had taken out his baby. He waited out in the yard for my return.

As I drove, I shifted the old Peterbilt perfectly. Hit every gear correctly. The boss heard the straight pipe sing as I drove back into town. I came down the road and pulled into the yard in front of a crowd of bosses. I parked the trailers and returned the 1958 Pete to where I found it. I walked over to hand my paperwork to them. The big boss, the old man who loved his 1958 Peterbilt, shook my hand and said, 'Anytime you want to take her out, go ahead. You certainly do know how it is supposed to be driven.' His sons were shocked. I would use 'his baby' many times over my employment there. The only driver allowed to take it out.

I was issued number 45, a 1984 Cabover Peterbilt, to pull a Refer trailer. Most of our customers were the same people I met working for Hooker Harris. In fact, most trucking companies in the area pulled Refers and competed with each other overloads of produce.

For a time, our boss ran out of loads and decided to pair us up into teams. Dwight and I drove a few loads together on one trip, our boss put us up into a motel in Fresno, California. We went to the local bar and had a few drinks. There were several women there paying attention to us. A cute blonde-eyed Dwight, but Dwight didn't see it, and he retired to our motel room too early. I got to talking to a larger woman. She told me she had a Cobra 29 LTD radio she'd sell me for $20.00. She pulled it out of the trunk of her car, and we went to our truck to put it in. We also got into a love bite and ended up fucking. When she left me, she told me, 'I fucked you for free. You paid me the $20.00 for the radio.' I never used the motel room.

Dwight and I made our run back north to deliver to Seattle and pick up another load going south. All the while I kept teasing him how he missed out in Fresno with the good looking blonde. As it turned out, Dwight pulled into Fresno while I was asleep and parked again in the same spot. He went into the same bar and saw the same woman. She was excited to see Dwight for all of the wrong reasons. Finding out I was in the truck asleep, she called the woman I had been with and fucked, to tell her I was back in Fresno. She woke me up in the truck and talked about me meeting her father.

Bad idea! Her father was the Fresno Chief of the County Sheriff's Office. Daddy the cop! She had told Daddy she met the man of her dreams. We walked to the bar after the shorter version of the previous time we were together, and I told Dwight to pretend to make a phone call and come back and tell me we had to leave.

He didn't want to until I told him about my girl's father. He will no doubt look me up to find out I was married and probably make my life a living hell. The plan worked, and we drove off. Never to go to that place again. But Dwight did when he drove alone on a run. Reporting back that 'I am an asshole!" Okay, I'm an asshole! I'm still an asshole!

I was alone in number 45 when I parked at the Texaco truck stop at Exit 161 on I-5 in Rice Hill, Oregon. I walked into the crowded restaurant and noticed a beautiful woman eating alone. I walked over to her and asked if I could join her. We sat together, enjoying conversation, and I ended up paying for her meal. Out in my sleeper, we made out. Clothes came off, but we never got to doing regular sex. I went down on her only, and then we were done. She gave me her phone number and got dressed. What a tease!

Several weeks had passed until I was coming north and called her. She gave me directions to a place where she would meet me by Rogue River. She lived in an octagon kit home west of I-5 and past a small store along the River Road. We had a good time even though we didn't have sex. Not all relationships are about sex. She made her money selling nude pictures of herself in Swinger magazine. I'm sure Jerry and Janet probably saw her advertisements. Beautiful! And I kept stopping in to visit her. Nancy Flowers.

On a trip on Hwy 97 near Goldendale, Washington, I got to talking to a man named Bruce, driving a Ford van. He had a couple of girls with him and talked me into stopping at a restaurant on the road up ahead. Bruce, around 70 years old, had opened up his home in Zillah, Washington, to these two beautiful young girls who just could not get along with their parents. The younger girl, Roxy, had a baby. Mary, 18 years old, wanted to see my sleeper. She climbed up into it with Roxy while we looked after the baby and talked. Mary came back and asked if I'd take her out trucking sometime. I told her I was married with three children, living on Germantown Road near Toppenish. I explained to her that if she came along, we would have fun but not fall in love with me. I got Bruce's number to call when I decided to have an illegal stowaway named Mary.

A week later, I picked up pretty Mary, and we headed to Los Angeles to deliver some tree-top apple products. At the very first rest area, we got it on. Several times that trip, we fucked like rabbits. We were having a meal at Jake's Truck Stop in Bend, Oregon, when a friend of mine saw me and leaned over to ask me if Mary was my daughter. I guess Mary did look that young. I felt uneasy having friends thinking like that.

We made two more runs together, and each trip was like the one before. Stopping in to see Bruce, we talked about the girls. He tells me Mary is in love with me. And that is a problem. A week or so later I parked Rahier's truck at the yard in Yakima and rode my bicycle home to find Rose missing. My three children yelled, "Daddy's home!' and came running to me as I put my bicycle in our home. Mary was standing in the kitchen when I walked in. Our eyes met, and I told her I needed to talk to her in another room. Behind closed doors, we kissed. I was angry, not really at Mary but at myself for this.

There is a movie called *Fatal Attraction,* and this whole episode comes too close to home. Mary wanted to take over my family. She walked in and offered to babysit for Rose, and Rose allowed it to happen. Just saw free time to herself and hopped into the 1984 Mercury Topaz and left them in the care of my Friday night girl that she didn't know about. Rose soon came home and told me to drive Mary home. My three kids hopped in the back seat, and I drove Mary home. No one wondered how I knew where Mary lived. Leaving my children in the car, I followed Mary to her bedroom, and we got undressed and fucked like rabbits.

'What took so long, Dad?' asked my oldest, Melissa.

'We needed to settle her bill for sitting.'

I have to be completely honest. Having Mary meet me at home was a real turn-on. What if I really got rid of Rose? Our marriage was not going anywhere. Sex was non-existant. But maybe all of my extra sex life had something to do with it. I needed to try to love Rose more. This thing with Mary scared me. Rose was unhappy living there in the old home. My father had talked to Rose about moving to his mobile home out of Wiley City. He had moved his home there to be next to his new wife's home. He needed a reliable renter to help look after their home when they were traveling.

After fucking Mary, I spent time with Rose after putting my children to bed, trying to cover up my lack of sexual attention to her. I told her to go ahead and move into Dad's home if she really wanted to. The idea of moving into a better homemade her excited. She couldn't wait to call Dad to make the arrangements to move. Early the next morning, I rode my bicycle to Yakima to go on another run. Several days later, back in Yakima, I hopped on my bicycle and rode to Toppenish. I walked into the kitchen to see a note on the counter telling me we already moved. She could have told me on the phone we were going to be out of the home by the time I got back. I rode 15 miles home to find the note and had to ride 30 miles back to our new home in Wiley City. And I was tired when I started in Yakima at Rahier's yard. Reading the note, I kind of wished Mary was there to play house with all alone. She wasn't, and I made a point never to see her again. I really didn't want to move. But coming home to find her waiting for me and looking after my children scared me.

We had moved down to the States to be near my mother so she could spend time with her grandchildren before she died. About three months before their medical insurance runs out, Mom and Dad file for divorce so their retirement money wouldn't be attacked by the hospital and lost. My mother would become indigent, and her medical bills would be picked up by the taxpayers.

Having my mother and father divorced because of the financial issue was not the problem. My father was the problem! Because he was legally divorced from Mom, he went out to find a replacement for her.

One day I get a phone call from dad asking me to fly down to Powell Lake to drive him and his large camper home. He had had a spell with his hyperglycemia and needed help. In the background, I could hear a woman tell him they could make it on their own. My mother was at home having a rough time of it, suffering from cancer. As it turned out, he was able to return home to Yakima, and I saw him pull into town and follow them to his new girlfriend's home near Wiley City.

My mother passed away in April 1985 at 56 years old. Six months later, our father walked into a church by Wiley City and married Betty, the woman he dated while mom was still alive.

A little over a year later, he had his large mobile home moved to a space not far from Betty's home. At the time, I worked for Muffett and Sons again, and he had me borrow my boss's backhoe to install the septic tank and sewer system.

Now, in early May 1988, Rose moved us into the double-wide three-bedroom home. I just didn't get it. She hated Dad for messing around while Mom was still alive. And here we were, just 50 yards away. Don't get me wrong, Betty is a very nice woman.

My mother's mother in Chilliwack hated her son-in-law for getting married so soon after her daughter passed. Normally, when we went to Canada to visit the Chilliwack area, we stayed at her home. Les Jesperson was no longer welcome. And then there was Roberta. I met Roberta at the Truck Village truck stop south of Weed, California. She was a waitress there when I asked her for her phone number. 5'6 tall and 101 lbs soaking wet. One night, with eight hours to sleep in Weed, I called her up at her brother's home in Dunsmuir and asked if she would like to shoot pool.

I had a wedding ring at home. I refused to wear it. I told Roberta Ellis I wasn't married like I told all of the women I tried to have sex with. Selling a bill of goods that just wasn't true. Roberta did the same! Both liars trying to have a good time. She was really still married to Robert Donnelly, and her husband had their children. This was not my concern at the moment. I dropped my loaded trailer at the truck stop and bobtailed back south past Shasta and the weigh station, following her directions to the Dunsmuir exit and to where I'd pick her up. We drove back to Weed and parked next to a park. There were several taverns and bars we went into until we found one with open pool tables we could get on to play. We ordered a couple of beers and spent a couple of hours flirting with each other before returning to the truck to make out. We engaged in raw sex over and over. I went to sleep at the truck stop and woke up early to have sex again at the end of the road, where I picked her up.

'We are compatible,' Roberta said, 'When will I see you again?'

'I'll be back in a couple of days.'

Because Weed was about halfway to southern California for my trips, I would be able to see her about every two to three days.

Man, what a setup for both of us. Especially me! Roberta had a lot to give and a lot of her I didn't like. She is a brat and a flirt and very spontaneous when it comes to sex like she just could not get enough sex. That part I loved! What I hated was her smoking and mouth talk that she expressed. She could be a real bitch at times. But for now, all I saw of her was 2 to 4 hours every 2 to 4 days to get a booty call.

Two months of great sex had Roberta asking for more of me. She talked of moving north so she could be at my home when I came north. Just like Mary had wanted. All good things come to an end, and on my trip south in mid-July 1988, Roberta met me with a problem. She had called on her phone information for a Keith Jesperson of Yakima and talked to my brother. The gig was up. She now knew I was married. What was I to do? Sure, I wanted to have sex with her at least one more time. Plan B I told her I was planning on leaving Rose to be with Roberta.

And right then, Roberta picked up her suitcase and tossed it into my cab. 'I'm going with you!'

As we drove south, she opened up to come clean with me, too, about having children and a husband. Telling me that as soon as our divorces were final, we would be getting married, and she would have her two children again. Have I mentioned how great the sex was?

Back in Yakima, I dropped her off at the Thunderbird Motor Inn. She told me she would get herself set up somewhere and get a message to me where I could find her. I had no intention of leaving Rose and my kids. A week went by before I got a message at work from Roberta. She had landed a job and room at the White Pass Lodge and Restaurant on White Pass—a great hide-a-way place for formal dining.

There was something I missed at home, and I just couldn't put my finger on it. I checked the bank account and saw some weird transactions happening. Just like it was when I noticed money had gone to her mother. Melissa's birthday was fast approaching and our oldest would be turning nine soon. I asked her what she wanted: a boombox tape player radio. I just couldn't leave it up to Rose to get it for her. Why? Ever since we were married, Rose always gave the cheapest presents to me. In 1976 I asked for a Cobra 129 CB radio and Rose got me a Cobra 19, the cheapest one she could find.

For some reason, money was tighter than normal, and on that trip south, I really scraped by to save enough to buy Melissa her boombox. Back in Yakima, I went to Shopco and bought her her wanted radio. I strapped it on a luggage rack on my bicycle and rode home. No one was home when I showed up so I took her radio out of the box and plugged it in in her room, tuning it to her favorite station and shut it off. Boy, won't she be surprised when I walk into her room and turn it on!

A couple of hours went by, and finally, our car pulled in, and everyone got out to find I was home. Rose pulled out a bag of wrapped presents and, one by one handed Melissa her presents to open. The very last one is from Mom and Dad. The box was the size of a deck of cards.

'This is from us, Melissa,' Rose said with a smile.

I just lost it! Seeing my little girl's hopes crushed by the cheapest radio her mother could find. Tears fell from Melissa's face as I grabbed the radio and threw it hard on the floor, stomping it with my foot and yelling, 'That isn't what she wanted, Rose! That isn't a radio! I'll show you a radio!'

I got up, went into Melissa's room, and hit the power button. Music filled the house.

The tears on Melissa could have been because I broke the radio she had gotten. After all, it was still her radio. The look on Rose's face was priceless. The music caused Melissa to go into her room to find her new boombox.

What did I hear from Rose?

'We could've taken back the radio for our money back!'

She never took money from her purse to put gas in the car. She just drove it. I did her a favor, destroying the cheap radio that could have cost me more for gas than the radio was worth.

'Where did you get the money to buy her boombox?' came her next question.

And that was the question I needed answers to.

I had earlier talked to my father and Betty. We hadn't paid rent ever since we moved into their home.

'Where is all the money going?' I asked her. 'You haven't paid our rent, Rose! What is going on?'

Another red flag was that Rose had gotten a full-time job at a packing house a mile away, and the money she made didn't go into our bank account. She seemed to be hoarding it.

Later that night, as we lay in the king-size bed, I leaned over to her as she stared at the ceiling.

'This is the third time you've done this. I'm tired of it. Tomorrow, you are going to pay what we owe Dad for rent. This has to change, Rose. Do you want a divorce? Is that it?'

Rose layed there not saying a word. Just stared up at the ceiling. No argument at all. Silence.

It was almost 6:00 AM when I got dressed and looked in to see my children. Melissa's boombox was on, and music played softly as they slept. I got on my bicycle and rode the 15 miles to work. I was feeling pretty good about Melissa's gift. Feeling good at at least telling Rose she needed to take care of business. There are no free rides. Rent has to be paid.

I was back home after depositing my trip money into our bank account. No one was home. No one came home that night.

There was a letter for me in the mailbox addressed to me from Rose with a return address from her mother's home.

Basically, she was telling me we were done. All she wanted was everything! Everything except my bicycle, my bowling ball, and my golf clubs. I made a phone call to Spokane, telling her to get her ass and the kids back home. If not, come and get your stuff yourself! If you don't, I'll start burning it. I asked Betty if I could use her car, and I drove to the White Pass Lodge to see Roberta. Later that day, I returned home to start going through what to keep and what to burn. I was tired of moving her shit!

I made another trip south and returned to our bank, and put my check in. I had expected Rose and the kids to be back home. Just another note in my mailbox telling me my children were missing their bicycles and toys. I called up my friend Royce Kenoyer and asked him for help to take to Spokane all that my family wanted. He agreed to help when I could take time off of work. That night, I had a small fire to tend. Rose didn't need the king-size bed and dressers. She certainly didn't need the china Hutch or rocking chair.

I let Dad have our washer and dryer to cover the rent not paid. I should have taken her brand new mountain bike back to Yakima Schwinn and sold it on consignment to get my $600.00 back. Not giving her back everything on her list sent a message. We were both starting over.

Royce came with his pickup, and we loaded it up, as well as a trailer, and went to hand it off to Rose and the kids. I'd take my children to a restaurant and cry as we talked about what was going on. Back in Yakima, I closed our bank account and opened up one for just me. There was nothing in it anyway. Rose had parked at the bank, waiting for my trip money to hit, and took it before I could spend it.

What little I had kept was now up at Roberta's motel room at the White Pass Lodge and Restaurant. My bicycle ride home had gotten a lot longer. From Rahier's yard to the White

Pass Lodge is about forty miles. I could cover it in less than 2 hours each way. It kept me in shape. Visiting my kids would be a lot harder. They were 200 miles away. All I could hope for was that my loads would have to go through Spokane when my children were not in school.

Our whole family was upset at the possible divorce. They all hated Roberta. Especially my father. Why? Roberta was not a pushover, and she stood her ground.

My father loves his women to be easy to control. Roberta told him off the first time he tried to split us up. He was constantly in my ear telling me to go to Rose and fuck her and get back together.

'Rose is the one that left me, Dad!'

What I should have done is to make Rose file for our divorce, not me. She had basically robbed me of all our money and ran. She told the kids that, 'Daddy doesn't want us anymore.'

I didn't want her back as my wife. I didn't want Roberta as my wife either. I should have gone fishing back in 1975, but it is what it is.

At the same time I filed for divorce, I filed for bankruptcy.

To teach Rose a lesson on money I did keep making payments to our car. No more credit cards. No more credit to get cards. Rose had to get a job. I wonder how many times she told herself she needed to get a better-paying job.

Roberta changed jobs to work at Yakima's Gear Jammer truck stop as a waitress. Rented a small one-bedroom mobile home behind the Twin Bridges Tavern in north Yakima. I had provided her with a used car to drive. One I could also use to visit my family in Spokane.

One night, I was in town and would drive the car to the Gear Jammer truck stop to pick up Roberta when she got off her shift at 10:00 p.m. I was sitting in a booth drinking coffee and listening to two drivers from Alabama talking about waiting to capture the skinny waitress and take her to their truck to rape her. Take her on a long ride to satisfy their sexual urges. I leaned over to them and asked, 'What about her boyfriend?'

'As skinny as she is,' one said, 'She has no boyfriend.'

Just about that time, Roberta, the skinny waitress, walked over to me, kissed me, and told all of us, 'I'll be getting off work in about ten minutes.'

Both men just sat there afraid to move, ten minutes came and I got up, towering over them, 'Don't worry boys. I'm not going to get to you now. Just remember this- I'm a truck driver too, and you just never know when I'll show up.'

As we drove back home, Roberta wanted to know what that was all about. I told her, and she wanted me to turn around and go back to hurt them.

'They will get theirs.' I told her, and we went home to bed.

The following morning, my boss told me to hook up a container trailer and drive over to Othello to pick up a load of onions for Japan. I drove the hundred or so miles to the onion shed, parked my trailer up against the loading dock, got out, and went into the small shipping and receiving office.

As I entered the office, I spotted those same two men from Alabama from the night before and said, 'And you thought you got away from me!'

They couldn't get out of that room fast enough. They jumped into their semi and pulled out from the loading dock. A forklift was still in their trailer. The onion business boss asked me what was going on, and I told him. They called up those two men's bosses and explained things. They were given bus tickets home.

October 11th, 1988, would be the last day I worked for Rahier Trucking of Yakima. I'd retire #45 Peterbilt. My siblings had made it clear they did not like Roberta or that I was divorcing Rose. They all told me to make time to talk to them. By chance, my boss had me sitting in Seattle for the night, waiting to get a container picked up the next morning. As I sat there, I thought of bobtailing to Bothell to visit my sister Jill— not something my boss would want me to do, especially in the wet conditions. Against my better judgment, I drove over to I-405, heading north, and headed for Bothell.

At Kirkland, traffic all of a sudden came to a stop, and with no weight on my tires, my Peterbilt couldn't stop. I saw small faces staring back at me as I quickly was about to run into their car. I swerved over to the medium and crashed, rolling end over end down the hill. The Peterbilt came to rest on its side. I got up on my feet after crawling through where the windshield had been. Police showed up, and an ambulance put me on a backboard and ran me to the Kirkland Hospital to be examined. At 9:00 p.m., I called Rahier to tell them I crashed. They were more concerned about #45. I called my sister Sharon, and she came to pick me up.

I spent the night at Sharon's home, and our brother Bruce just happened to be in Seattle, and he gave me a ride home to Yakima. Everyone gave me an ear full. Rahier fired me.

On October 14th, I was back to work driving for Rahir's rivals, A & G Trucking of Wiley City. I had the same customers, the same everything, except my Peterbilt was a conventional cab. A month went by, and I had been teaching Roberta how to drive a semi. I thought it would be nice to have her as my co-driver and my lover at the same time. My boss was okay with her as my co-driver. More miles driven means more money made for everyone.

More to the point, Roberta was good for my log book *and* my pleasure. She was not a very good truck driver, and her mouth would get us fired. Her biggest problem was she would forget she was pulling a trailer. Often, she cut corners too short and had to back up and do it again. Once, at turning into a truck stop at Klamath Falls, Oregon, she cut it short and dropped the trailer tires into a ditch. It cost me $500.00 to get pulled ten feet by a wrecker. Of course, it was my fault. I yelled at her to stop and she yelled back, 'Don't yell at me!' and she kept driving.

My divorce became final in April 1989. Rose was impatient. She and her new man, Tom Hicke, were planning to be married. A.S.A.P. Rose had claimed to the court that the reason we were splitting up was because of our lack of communication. I just didn't know what to say to her in our foreplay during sex. Who was her new man, Tom Hicke? A deaf-mute. You can imagine the sign for wanting to fuck.

On a trip north, Roberta lied to our boss and later got into an argument over the phone with him. At the end of that trip, our jobs were terminated. Anthony Silva told me I could get my job back as soon as I got rid of Roberta. Now, that is a thought. Once, when I went to sleep, and Roberta was driving, I woke up 200 miles in the wrong direction. Why? She had been talking to another driver over the CB radio and missed our exit to Hwy 58 going west. I woke up to see a sign saying, 'Welcome to Needles.' I should have woken up in Bakersfield.

We loaded up our Ford Pinto and headed for her mother's home in Portland, Oregon. 18434 NE Everett Street. Her mom gave us the master bedroom. Roberta got a job as a waitress, and I got a job running a backhoe.

Taunja Bennett

We drove out of Yakima to the Columbia River gorge and west along Hwy 14 to Washington to see Jerry and Janet. Roberta left me at their home so she could talk to her mother to see if I could live with them. One look from Jerry told me he wanted to have Roberta in bed and trade me to his wife. I just don't work that way. I hate to share. I never asked Rose to even consider the swinger culture. Certainly, I would not entertain telling Roberta to fuck Jerry. She probably would have if doing so benefited her.

Janet is beautiful, and Jerry is, well, not the man most women would choose to take them home. Janet told me she was the first woman picked at parties, and Jerry was usually the last man selected. Oh, the girls all get prettier at closing time!

In high school, I got a card from his parents thanking me for being his friend. Because now I didn't have a car to drive, Jerry handed me the keys to his 1974 Chevrolet Nova to use until I could afford to buy something. He had a couple more cars he could drive to work. Before leaving their home, I properly thanked Janet for fulfilling her wants and needs. Women are crazy! Okay, some of them are crazy. And just maybe men make them that way. There is the sex before marriage called dating sex, and there is married sex. With Rose, the dating sex was constant; maybe every other day, we got it on, but after marriage, I was lucky to get it once a week. The very first time she asked me to go down on her, I got close to her pussy, and the smell made me gag. I told her to get off the bed and wash herself. Put some soap on it. Horrible! Maybe she thought guys liked to do it no matter what. She would never go down on me! Roberta would do everything, and because we were dating, I didn't want the dating sex to stop.

Six months after Rose and Tom were married, I was visiting my kids in Spokane and had this conversation with Rose:

'How's your sex life, Rose?'

"Remember all of the times you asked me to give you a blow job, and I said no?'

Of course, I remembered asking until there was no point in asking. She would not do it at all. Felt it was too dirty. 'Yes, Rose, I remember.'

'Well, Tom won't take no for an answer!'

'So, you're a cocksucker now, huh?'

Rose turned red and looked the other way.

'Maybe Rose,' I said, 'Maybe if I didn't take 'no' for an answer, we would still be married.'

At 18434 NE Everett Street, Roberta's mother was okay with a new man in Roberta's life. Her plan was simple: Help Roberta to take custody of her two children from the children's father. There was something a miss over the whole show. I was a welcome sight. A worker that Roberta wanted. Not the deadbeat type that Robert Donnelly's reputation projected. Of course I was only hearing one side of the story from the women.

Burrel and Roberta began planning to enter truck driving school in north Portland. They hoped to be a mother/daughter team of truck drivers! They secured student loans and entered the school. The six-week course took its toll on them. Roberta passed. Her mother just could not shift a stick shift. Like my own father, Burrel couldn't drive a truck to save her soul. Not passing truck driving school, she decided to go back to driving a cab in Reno, Nevada. Called a former boss and was able to secure an apartment and her job there. They would move down to Reno. Her mother and grandmother, leaving us the home to ourselves. We loaded Roberta's Pinto into the truck full of house furnishings so that when we dropped off her things, we could return the U-Haul truck to a dealer and drive home to Portland.

Passing truck driving school opened up jobs for Roberta to hire on to a major trucking company called P.S.T's Portland office sits over in the Vancouver, Washington's industrial park. She went out with a trainer as a co-driver and soon graduated to drive all by herself. For a while, she drove a set of doubles. Doubles pull differently than say a 48 foot trailer. They turn corners tighter. Roberta got used to driving a set of doubles. Then, on another trip, she was supposed to drive a long trailer to P.S.T's main office in Salt Lake City, Utah. As I have said before, she sometimes gets lazy and forgets she has a trailer behind her. When she enters the Salt Lake City yard, she cuts the corner too tightly, and her trailer hits the guard shack, pulling the building off its foundation with P.S.T's safety director inside. Roberta was given a bus ticket home.

She was then hired on by a small company out of Tacoma, Washington. Several trips later, she complained to me about not making much money on the road. Begged me to hire on as her co-driver. I had told her I didn't want to drive semis. I was working on running equipment I loved to operate. Driving with her had its difficulties. She needed to be pampered. Her lack of ability is made up in providing her body of love to me. Her other co-drivers were not helping her. And I was not willing to help her claim good money by making up the miles she was supposed to drive. Eventually, she quit the company and asked to be paid for her worth. We drove to Tacoma and her boss showed us her many cash draws out on the road. She had done what I suspected: spent more money than she had earned.

Back in Portland, she returned to what she was good at, waitressing. She hired on to Troutdale's Burns Brothers truck stop. A place like where I had met her. She loved being able to talk shop to truckers about trucking. Even brag about having been a driver.

My first job was working for Hughes Plumping and Excavation. I'd run a case 580 backhoe for $10.00 an hour. I could do the job, but my boss wanted his company to operate off of its employee's money. Not my way to make a living so I sought another job.

Heinz and Sons hired me to run an excavator for one day. They hired me and then filed for bankruptcy the next day. I made $16.00 an hour.

A few days later, I got a phone call from Byad Construction asking me to be part of the crew to finish Heinz and Son's contracts. To finish the job at $16.00 an hour. So for the next month, I had a good job until the job was finished. Dyad made sure to call around with good word to other contractors that we needed work. Copenhagen Construction hired me at $16.50 an hour to run their equipment in the general Portland area. Based out of Clackamas, Oregon, they also have a southern office in Sacramento, California.

I first ran a case 580 backhoe on a telephone job in Sherwood. They also tried me out on excavations. Then we had about a mile of U.S. Water pipe to put in close by. I'd also be running a Kamatso 220 excavator. My skills on the machine made quick work of the six-week-long job in under two weeks.

We also had a pressurized sewer job seven miles long between Gaston and Forest Grove. I'd run a TD8 dozer, a 580 case backhoe, and a Barber Green wheel trencher. My last job for 189 came in November, digging with a case 580 in Eugene, Oregon, on a telephone job.

Students from the University of Oregon in Eugene kept walking by our job site. The workers in the trench told me I was missing out on the view. Girls would stand above them, looking down. Our workers looked right up the girls' skirts. It is a wonder any work got done.

It became bitter cold in November 1989, and we soon had to stop work for the season. I would have to draw unemployment insurance until work would resume in the spring.

I could have gone back to trucking, but by this time, Roberta was a waitress, and I loved having her home with me.

That Christmas, money was tight. I sold off my precious Schwinn 15-speed touring bicycle and all of my fishing equipment. All of this so that I could provide a Christmas for my children in Spokane. I bought Roberta a nice snakeskin pair of cowgirl boots.

She came home from work usually at 10:30 pm from Burns Brothers truck stop. Her pockets were full of tips. I'd hear her tell me of available trucking jobs. Other drivers were pushing her to get me to get back into it. I knew what she was up to. I just wasn't going for it. Looking back, I probably should have gone back over the road to keep Roberta from doing something stupid- me too!

Have no idea what exact day/night it was when Roberta grew tired of me and decided to take a driver up on his offer to drive for the company he drove for. Maybe January 14th, 1990. the clock said midnight and still no Roberta. So I thought her car could have broken down and retraced her travel patterns to Troutdale's Burns Brothers truck stop. Her Ford Pinto was parked over by the McDonald's restaurant. I went inside, hoping to see her. She wasn't there. Another waitress told me she left with a truck driver.

My first thought was they were fucking out in his truck in the large parking lot in the back. I waited by her car to show up and decided to return home.

For two days, I waited for a phone call or her return before I had a neighbor drive me to Troutdale to drive Roberta's car back home. She had done this before. Back in late 1988, we had a break up, and she drove to Bigg's Junction and caught a ride with a driver. Weeks later, she called me through my boss, and I'd meet her in Castaic, California. Had to get her car and drive it back to Yakima.

With Roberta gone, the home seemed too large for me. I moved the mattress from our bedroom into the living room, making the home smaller. No need to go into the back two bedrooms. I spent my days doing a lot of walking around the area. Got into a routine—morning TV to watch Perry Mason until the sun burned off the morning fog. Then, take off walking south to a Fred Meyer shopping mall. First, the grocery store to see if any women needed help with their grocery load. Then over to Radio Shack to check out everything. I'd cross the street to Fred Meyers industrial store to window shop. After moving into the home, I bought several ceiling fan/light combos for our cedar living. All were bought there at Fred Meyers. Eventually I'd walk into the B & I Tavern on Stark Avenue at around 1:00 pm to play a few games of pool before returning home—a pretty dull life living off of unemployment insurance. Late in the evening, I often drove to Burns Brothers truck stop to watch a movie in the driver's lounge or just sit there drinking coffee and listening to truckers complain. With no one at home to come home to, there is no real point in being there.

Reflection on my life had me feeling sorry for myself. My kids were in Spokane, three hundred miles away, and my girlfriend had again run off and was probably fucking the man she met. Surely have made a mess of my life after my mother died in 1985. It seems like the right time to move on and find someone new. Roberta certainly had.

However, I was torn, not knowing for sure what was going on with her. I was still living in her mother's home rent free in winter. It was really hard to just pick up and leave the sweet situation I was in. I hoped for the best and expected the worst.

About a full week had passed when I woke up Saturday, January 21st, 1990, to a cold, foggy morning. Gloomy! Just another day in Portland, Oregon in the winter. It is really hard to get motivated when there is no work to get done and no one to share my time with. The smell of perked coffee and fried eggs and bacon had, me dreaming of meals at truck stops. The constant chatter of drivers telling their stories, their lies. What to do today? People watching? I looked outside at the heavy fog and decided not to drive in it. I'd wait in front of the TV for the morning sun to lift off the fog.

At around ten, I got tired or even restless to get moving; I walked out of the warm home into the harsh cold air and started walking toward the Fred Meyer stores past Burnside and Stark Avenues. Routine? It is hard to not go through my normal routine of day-to-day fumbling without a purpose in life. I'm sure some, if not all, of the shoppers at the grocery store thought I was a stalker. I'd see one roaming about looking for items and eventually walk up to them to see if they needed help. You can tell a lot about people by what they buy at the grocery store. I would never push myself on them. Take it or leave it. I had to have the attitude of 'it matters little to me what their decision is.' The moment they feel forced, they run. Let them make up their own minds. But once they invite me into their world, I'm then going to push them to get to my goal. Some things I will not do. Like, get into a car with a person who has too much to drink. Not a nice ride, being scared of wrenching, having placed my life in a drunk's hands.

Nothing was happening at the grocery store, so I moved on to Radio Shack and then the Jeep dealership on Stark Avenue. I crossed the street to Fred Meyer's lumber store. Making my daily rounds, I eventually walked into the B & I Tavern at 1:00 pm.

Mostly low-lighted, only lights over the pool tables filled the room. Two men and a woman were at a table playing pool and drinking beer from a pitcher on a table with chairs. The female bartender looked at me as I walked toward her. To my right, I saw movement toward me. The woman with the two men ran up to me and wrapped her arms around me. As she held me, I looked up at the bartender, and she was twirling her index finger around her left ear. *Crazy* was her message. I have to admit that I had an instant hard-on in my pants at the smell of perfume, and her arms held me close. Crazy? Yes! But I've seen a lot of crazy stuff in bars. People do not go to bars thinking drinking alcohol makes them smarter. IQ levels drop way down with every drink!

Sure, running over to hug a complete stranger is nuts. Then again, I'm in a bar and stranger things have happened.

She tells me, 'Join our party. Come on, play with us!'

I looked over at her two male friends, and the look on their faces told me not to join their party.

'No, thank you, lady.'

She looked unhappy hearing my answer and let go of me and returned to their little party of drinking. I walked over and sat at the bar, and ordered a bottle of beer. The bartender is pretty. I also know she has heard all of the come-ons before.

'That girl is nuts!' she volunteered to me, 'Real coo-coo!'

I turned around and looked over at the nut playing pool and flirting with the men. Too much competition! A lot of fights in a bar have been over a woman. Best leave that fight alone. I walked over to another pool table and played a couple of games, leaving the B & I Tavern after returning my empty bottle to the bar.

I left the empty parking lot and made my way back to 18434 NE Everett Street. The sun had destroyed the morning fog, and it became a really nice sunny day's walk after all. I sat around the house for a couple of hours, trying to make up my mind on what to do. Either drive to the truck stop or over to the B & I Tavern to hopefully find a good game of pool to play. I decided to do maybe both.

First to the B & I.

It was around 5:00 p.m. when I parked by the sidewalk on Stark Avenue next to the now-crowded B & I Tavern. I walked in to find every pool table occupied with people. Several quarters on each table.

I had waited too long. I walked over to the counter and turned to study the people for a possible 'in' on a table. At that very instant, the woman who hugged me earlier walked past me and out of the building. Where were the two men she was with earlier? Who cares! I followed her out into the parking lot. I stood by my car and watched to see her walk up to the building east of the B & I to find the restaurant closed. She slowly walked back over to where I stood. Her actions fueled my story to hopefully get her to come with me. Crazy or not, she certainly is a pretty girl, and all I could think about was getting her home.

'Remember me? I'm the one you hugged earlier.'

Something clicked on in her stare at me. 'Yeah, I remember.'

I made my pitch: 'Do you want to come with me to a restaurant and find another bar to hang out at later?'

'Okay.'

I opened the car for her, and she slid into the 1974 Chevy Nova. 'Nice car!'

I got in and started it up, and pulled out onto Stark Avenue. 'I have to stop by my house first to get more money. I never thought I'd be with you and we need more to have a good time.'

'Okay.'

I drove into my driveway at 18434 NE Everett Street and turned off the car.

'Why don't you come on in? It will take just a few minutes. Better than sitting out here all alone.'

'I'll leave everything out here.' She set down her small black purse, her tape player, and headphones. We exited the car and walked to the front door.

Good, the door was locked. Roberta had not come home. Here I was about to enter her home with a strange woman that I didn't even know her name yet. Certainly would be a sight if Roberta had been home. What was I doing with a beautiful young woman in her mother's home? I'm sure she would have figured it out. The thought? What was I going to do with her?

'I'm Taunja.' she told me, but what I thought she said was 'Sonja.' Close enough.

She walked into the dining area while I pretended to go to another room to get more money to party with. Staring at her as she looked at a painting over the dining room table of Jesus Christ, I made up my mind to go up and return the hug and propose we play on the mattress there on the living room floor. Spontaneous! Not well thought out. Certainly, she will accept my advances! She started it!

She had been drinking alcohol all day. This would be no different than driving the drunk girls home from our teenage kegger parties in Selah. Hug her, kiss her, and then fuck her and fuck her some more. That was the plan.

Plans don't always work out, though.

Roberta always told me, 'You can't rape the willing.' and Roberta was always willing at every moment I tugged at her.

I slid in behind Taunja and wrapped my arms around her. My right hand found her crotch and fingered her. She pulled from me and headed to the door.

'I guess sex is out of the question?' I asked her after capturing her and pinning her against the wall. She said nothing as I pulled her over to my bed and lay her down on her back. I kissed her over and over again while she refused to kiss me at all.

Staring up at me, she said, 'Hurry up and get this shit over with!'

I've heard that before from Rose. Hurry up and take care of it. Mostly, she told me to get rid of it. Go stick it in a keyhole or hole in the fence. So I went into our bathroom, opened a JCPenney catalog to the women's section, and masturbated, staring at a beautiful picture of.... Rose had opened the door to see me with JCPenney. She was angry. Not at me masturbating, but because the photo I held was not of her. And I never masturbated looking at Rose's picture or even of her memory. There is nothing there.

I kissed Taunja, and nothing. I felt her through her clothes, and still, she just lay there telling me to hurry up and finish it. I sat up on my knees, straddling her and looking down. This wasn't turning out the way I hoped it would. I wanted her to like it. I wanted her to be in for a great sexual love-making session. Taunja just wasn't cooperating. Call it anger at Rose. Call it frustration. Call it me being pissed off at Roberta for leaving me. Whatever it was racing through my head, I just started to punch Taunja in the head. Rights and lefts as hard as I could, I plummetted her once beautiful face into something that looked like a meat grinder. And then I heard her beg for her mother: 'Mommy, make him stop! Make him stop! Please, Mommy, make him stop!'

I froze.

I stared down at what I had done to her. Teeth were protruding from her lips, broken jaw, broken nose, broken eye socket, blood was everywhere. On the ceiling. All over the walls and me.

'What the fuck have I done?' I said to myself.

'Panic' is a good word here. What to do next? Take her to a hospital; I'm going to prison. Call 911 I am going to prison. Drop her off and run, and I am going to prison. What would my father do? He ran over a man with his car, went someplace to sober up, and got away with it. If I am to believe his story to me while he was drunk. I realized I needed to kill her, drop off her body someplace, and hope no one saw me.

'I'm sorry.' I told her when I wrapped my hands around her throat and squeezed until my hands turned white and ached. After just a couple of minutes, I had to let go, and she was still alive. Breathing, but not conscious.

I found out that killing by strangulation is way harder than it is on the TV. I had to figure it out. I realized I could use my fist and push down really hard onto her throat for several minutes until I smelled urine from her. A smell I had smelled before when I was with my father's friend Smitty at the retirement home. Smitty was dying of cancer or old age. Dad had me there talking to him and holding his hand until he passed. I was just eighteen years old, and my father introduced me to death. Dad was in the cafeteria when Smitty died. The following day, both my father and I went to Smitty's home and robbed it of all valuables.

My father explained, 'If we don't get it, someone else will.'

I learned four minutes is all it takes to kill someone with my fist on her neck. I timed it as I waited for her body to relax, to smell her relieve herself.

I had never killed anyone before. This was all new to me. She had been drinking all day. What if when I moved her, her stomach contents poured all over me?

I went into the garage, got a length of ½ inch nylon rope, and tied it tightly around Taunja's neck. Using a kitchen knife, I cut the rope short. Originally one end of the rope was burned to keep it from unravelling. It is all in the details. Things were happening too fast, and I would believe years later that one end was left burned, not cut. But in reality, I had cut both ends short.

Because I had fondled Taunja's pants buttons in her fly area, I feared I'd leave fingerprints on the metal, and I used the same knife to cut out the fly area of her jeans. Not really smart. No buttons. Nothing to hold her pants on her hips. The moment I moved her, her pants slid down to her ankles.

Remember I said 'panic'? I was paranoid, to say the least, when all of a sudden, the phone rang.

'Do you accept a collect phone call from 'Roberta'?'

'Where are you at, Roberta?' I didn't want her close by at that very time.

A body lay there in my living room with a rope tied around her neck, all bloodied. For the next hour, she told me her story about climbing into a truck and promised a job working for Country Wide Trucking of Knoxville, Tennessee. As we talked, I noticed blood all over me and took off my clothes and put them into our washing machine, then dryer.

She had called several times while I wasn't home, hoping I'd send her some money to live on while she went through Country Wide's training course. I explained to her that Country Wide rarely came to the West Coast, let alone here in Portland. I told her I had not gotten my unemployment checks yet. A lie. She would be given a bonus to hire on to the company. More likely, she had already spent it on games and food. Talking to her slowed down time. It allowed me to think out how I was going to take care of dead Taunja. We said our 'I love you's and said good-bye.

I got dressed into the same clothes, now cleaned, that I had worn to the B & I Tavern earlier. I locked the door behind me and drove back to the B & I Tavern to establish my alibi. I made sure the bartender saw me leave the building alone. Drove to Troutdale past the police station and across the bridge over the Sandy River to the Columbia Gorge scenic roadway and headed to the Crown Point's Vista house monument. Saturday night, the place was packed with lovers and tourists watching the traffic go by on Interstate 84 below. It is a regular make-out point for the locals, too.

I kept driving down past the point to hopefully find a ravine to place her body into. The road hugged the steep cliff side until it turned sharply to my left, going northwest. On my immediate right were large trees guarding a deep ravine. I stopped and got out to look. At the top of the ravine, there is a bush I'd later call 'the finger tree'.

'This will do nicely.' I said to myself.

I got back in the car and drove back the way I had come, making sure to be aware of everything along the way.

At the AM/PM 24-hour market on 181st Street, I stopped to put gas in the car and to make sure every light worked- except my dome light. I removed the bulb. Drove home and backed into the driveway. I opened the passenger door, leaving it open. The smell of death hit me when I walked into the living room. Her body stiffened on my floor.

'What a waste? I didn't even fuck her.'

I spent time with her, lifting her clothes to check out her body. I have heard of people having sex with dead bodies before. That wasn't me.

The curtains pulled tight, I peeked out them studying everything. There had to be a moment when I could lift her body and carry her to the front seat of my car, Jerry's 1974 Chevy Nova.

Kept the house dark and kept looking out at the road. I stepped from the house to walk around the neighborhood, checking to see if anyone was out walking late at night. It was near midnight when I felt it was safe to carry her to my car. I picked her up, and her pants fell to her ankles. Dropped her back down and pulled her pants back up. Then reached for a belt loop and held it tight as I carried her out the door and sat her up in the passenger seat. She shut the door, and she fell against the passenger door window.

A lot went into preparing for this journey. Since I no longer had my bicycle, I no longer needed my bicycle shoes. I wore them to where I would drop her body—planned on tossing them away and putting on my 'New Balance' running shoes. Jerry's car had Washington state license plates on it. Being up on the scenic roadway would be a good fit. Just another tourist.

And then there is luck. There is so much that can still go wrong with me driving a bloodied dead body into an area I'm not familiar with at a time of night I'm not familiar with. A traffic stop could catch me. There has to be some luck going my way to help me get away with it. Often, success comes down to timing.

I got into the Nova and pulled out into my pre-planned route, making sure to follow it all of the way. It's midnight to 1:00 AM when I'm doing this. The roads are mostly empty. I worried that if a cop saw me, he would follow me just because chances are I came from a bar, expecting to catch a drunk.

However, I also knew that as soon as I could get to the scenic Highway, I'd be a tourist out to see the falls and lights at night in the Columbia River Gorge.

I drove along Gleason Avenue to the road dropping down to Troutdale and turned right, driving past the Troutdale Police Department.

Crossed the Sandy River and turned south on the Sandy River Road, A.K.A. The Columbia River Gorge Scenic Highway. So far, so good. Past a small community and follow the signs to Crown Point. The road drops off of the upper ledge of the canyon and winds down to the Vista House parking lot. At every wide spot is at least one car with people enjoying what they must have been enjoying. Certainly, the women in their cars were not dead. Maybe a dead fuck here and there, but not really dead like the one in my car.

I never lost sight of what I had with me. Kept looking over at her fucked up face. I was ashamed of what I had done and what I was about to do.

The Vista House parking lot was just as packed with cars as it had been the last time I drove by. What little light shined into my car as I drove past made me speed up a little to not have anyone notice her. It is funny, and maybe not the right word for this. But in my car, I know what I did. My mind played tricks on me, thinking of all of God's teachings- the whole book of life- all-knowing God stuff. It is as if I wasn't fooling anyone. That they all saw what I was doing and didn't care. Went about their business as if I wasn't there. God will sort it all out. And maybe I was doing what God had planned for me? If you believe the Book of Life that everything we do is already written in the book, kind of crap. Right? Just in case it wasn't written in the book, I had to do this on my own. No one pulled in behind me at Crown Point. Drove to the ravine I had picked out. I parked, got out, and started back behind me to make sure no headlights were following me down. I looked ahead of me to see all was dark. Time to move!

I ran around to the passenger door and opened it. Taunja seemed to want to move, too. She fell down with one arm out, reaching to me to grab. I pulled her by her arm. Immediately, her jeans slid down to her ankles as I dragged her down into the ravine past the finger tree on the left side, sliding on the cold, wet, slimy old leaves that the finger tree shedded in fall. At about 90 feet from the road above, I froze. Headlights came at me from below! Man, I was fucked! The ravine was in the middle of the same road. It crossed the bottom coming up and crossed the top going down.

A switch back in the middle. I dropped her arm. She layed there face up, her head on the downhill side, one arm out reached over her head, her jeans by her ankles. Her white skin is in complete contrast to the gloomy backdrop of winter in the woods. I ran to the car, slipping and falling twice because of the hard-soled bicycle shoes I had on. It was like skis they were. I closed the passenger car door and got into my seat, put the car in drive, and tried to act calm as I drove to the switch back. I knew that the further I made it away from her, the more safe I'd be.

That was close!

How close was it?

Like I said, it is all about timing and luck. Imagine if I had waited 20 seconds longer before dragging her body into the ravine. I would not have seen the car at the bottom coming up the hill. I would have thought I was safe and covered her up with leaves. Maybe the passing car would have stopped to see why no one was in the car and investigated to find me covering up a very dead, badly beaten girl. At the switch back, I slowly entered my turn to the right as the car coming at me entered the turn turning to his left.

My headlights lit up the side of a Multnomah County Sheriff's car.

We passed each other. I was careful not to do something stupid to make him stop me and have it in his log book that I was in the area where her body would be discovered. All in the details.

I continued to drive past the next waterfalls and to a 'Y' in the road and stopped. I pulled off my shoes and put on my running shoes. Set the shoes beside me and took a left turn to enter Interstate 54 West. If I had gone to the right, eventually, it would go to Multnomah Falls Lodge and beyond.

As I drove along westbound I-54, I opened the passenger door window and tossed one bike shoe out toward the river. About a mile later, I tossed the other.

(Okay, collectors of murderabilia momentos, those shoes are probably still there next to the river off Westbound Interstate 84. I doubt that anyone in the last 34 years as of this writing has ever picked them up. If someone were to actually find them size 13 Cannondale Bicycle shoes, that could be one hell of a collector's piece. If by chance you find a used shower curtain, I'm sure it isn't Laverne's.)

Driving back toward Troutdale, I looked down to discover Taunja's small tape player and headphones. I opened my window and tossed them out onto the bridge passing over the Sandy River. Certainly, they would be destroyed by traffic. Having kept it, had cops come to a calling, they would be looking for her tape player. I had to get rid of everything Taunja to to be clean of her. I pulled into Troutdale and parked outside of the Burns Brothers B-Bar

B Restaurant. My car in view of the tables inside. I went in and spotted a table in full view of my car and just about everyone in the restaurant, including the cash register.

'Coffee, please.'

Just minutes later, three Oregon State Police cars rolled into the parking lot and parked around my car.

That was fast!

They got out and mingled around my car before coming into the restaurant. Stood by the entrance next to the cash register and pointed over at me. Were they super cops? They came over and sat in the booth next to me. No, they were not super cops! They had pointed at the empty table next to mine. We even talked. And they had no idea I was a murderer.

After several cups of coffee, I left to watch a movie in the driver's lounge. As the sun came up, I decided to go home and sat in my car to notice I had fucked up again. Taunja's little black purse lay on the floor.

The state police cars were gone. What to do with her purse? I opened it to find two dollars and seventeen cents and her Oregon ID, plus assortments of makeup. Saw a dumpster and decided against it. Some force told me to put the purse and ID where it could be found later. I can't even explain it now as I write this out in May 2024, but there was a feeling deep in me to hide it. Not back home. Somewhere, no one would find it. I drove past the Troutdale police department and south on the Sandy River Road. The road starts to climb up from the river below. I passed a Y in the road. The road on my left had come down a steep hill to a stop sign. Across from that road was a deep ravine full of blackberry vines. I continued up the road a hundred yards or so and spotted a small turnout under a small tree. I continued up the road to where Sandy River Road swung sharply to the left and decided I'd drive back to the small turnout under the small tree. Parked, I got out, holding her purse, and looked down toward the Sandy River. A small pathway wound down to the river that fishermen used to access the river for fishing. To my right and on the right side of the path was a large old dead cedar tree stump under the telephone lines. To the left of the path, about fifty feet was some small brush and poison oak. There, I tossed her purse and contents. Forty feet from the roadway and forty feet from the large cedar stump. I got back in my car and drove home to 18434 NE Everett Street.

The smell almost floored me when I walked into the warm house.

Murder is messy!

I opened all of the windows and drove to the Albertsons Grocery store on the corner of 181st Street and Gleason Ave, a block away, to rent a steam vacuum and floor deodorant to clean up blood and urine. I got a bucket of warm water and tried to wash off the blood on the ceiling and walls. Because Roberta smoked and everyone else smoked, the walls were coated with nicotine so badly that all I managed to do was to cause streaks of yellow and red to drip down. The whole room needed to be cleaned. Before I handled the task, I lay on clean sheets and fell asleep.

Murder is a lot of work!

The popcorn ceiling was the hardest to clean. Pieces kept falling onto the carpet. So, to speed it up, I used a large push broom to go over it before I washed it down, loosening up the bits. Took two full days of cleaning to feel safe I had washed all of her blood and urine out of my home. Returned the machine to Albertsons on Monday morning, January 23rd, 1990, and picked up an Oregonian Newspaper.

And there it was in the metro section, a small report of a murdered woman found in the Columbia River Gorge with a rope tied around her neck. A couple of bicycle riders had found her on Sunday morning, January 22nd, 1990. They would be the first suspects in the case. Especially with footprints of bicycle shoes left behind. The irony!

(I need also to explain something at this point. I only washed the room. I didn't paint the room. In 1995, I told the police I had painted the room. Why? Because I knew only Roberta would know if I had painted the room or not. See, I was fishing to find out if they had talked to her.)

Later in the week, I saw news reports that the police were trying to identify the body found with a rope around her neck. A composite sketch was being shown to the public. And it must have been January 31st 1990, when a positive identification was made by Taunja Bennett's mother. Two weeks later, in the Oregonian Newspaper was a request for information the police placed, hoping the public could help them solve her murder. They were looking for the two men she had been playing pool with at the B & I Tavern.

I don't know when exactly I saw news reports of two people captured in Taunja Bennett's murder. One had confessed. Was this a joke? A play to get the real killer to come forward? Only in America can I kill someone, and two people will confess to doing it. This really messed with my head.

Just like a Perry Mason moment. The police arrest the wrong people, and Perry Mason proves them wrong. Every time!

However, where is Perry Mason on the case? Seriously, I was really troubled by their arresting people I know didn't do her murder.

I had acted alone. Who were John Sosnovske and Laverne Pavlinac? I certainly have never met them, or have I? I had no idea how the police went to them. What evidence did they have? Regardless of how I felt about their arrests, one thing was certain: they were not looking for me!

I'm guessing it was around late February or early March when I'd get a phone call from Roberta's brother Rick Ellis in Dunsmuir, California. He told me that Roberta's two children were dropped off at his home by their father, Robert Donnelly. He had told Rick that is was Roberta's turn to look after the kids. I told him that when Roberta checked in with me, I'd let her know. Part of me didn't want kids around. But having Roberta home every night would be a welcome distraction. The first time she called, I didn't mention the message. A couple of days later, I told her about her kids.

As it happened, Country Wide Trucking had sent her with a man co-driver to Seattle. They were held up in Ellensburg due to avalanches on Snoqualmie Pass I-90. That would never stop me. I would have rerouted my route North to Steven's Pass or South to White Pass. And if all of them were closed, drop down to Interstate 84 West to Interstate 5 North to Seattle. Country Wide Trucking kept them in Ellensburg. So I drove east to Bigg's Junction and North on Hwy 97 to Toppenish, Yakima, and Ellensburg. Found Roberta in my friend Dave's restaurant next to Ellensburg's Fly 'N' J truck stop.

I loaded up my Nova with her stuff, and I talked to her co-driver before leaving to come home. They both had stories to tell about each other. I believed his more than I believed hers. Again, Roberta claimed she had a check coming, and he told me she owed money back to the company due to her maxing out her money draws out on the road.

It was a long day of driving for me. We got home, and I mustered up enough energy to screw her a couple of times before sleep overtook us.

Where is the money? I was broke! My unemployment checks had not come in yet. Could be a week before she could go south to get her children. She pulled out of the closet those snake skin boots I bought her at Christmas. Went to Western Outfitters to turn them in for a refund. Just about three months too late. When she explained her problem and the fact she hadn't worn them, they gave the money back to me, almost $600.00. we filled the Nova with gas and headed south to Dunsmuir to pick up her kids. We were supposed to be one big happy family now.

Right East

Switch back on Scenic Hwy

Vista House

Resting

Daun Slagle

Alisha and Roberta had been in the care of their father, Robert Donnelly, a child molester. That is how Roberta described him. If he really was a child molester, why did Roberta leave them with him? At hearing her claims, I asked her to file on him. Her real solution had always been to kill him.

"Invite him over, Keith, and kill him!"

After hearing her rants about murdering her former man, the man actually legally married to her, I wondered who she had in mind to kill me after the deed was done. And I believed she was dead serious.

Her co-driver's story was right. Roberta had no money coming from her boss, Country Wide Trucking of Knoxville, Tennessee. Another wasted time trucking. Back home, she had burned her hopes of a job at Burns Brothers in Troutdale and ended up working as a waitress at Elmer's a mile away. The money she made as tips kept us afloat. My checks went to most bills. Her children needed everything. And two more mouths to feed. I became Mr. Mom. I was torn by this new development. I wanted to look after my own children and not someone else's

It didn't take long before I saw the real parent Roberta Ellis was. She yelled at the kids and spanked them every day. They seemed to push her button to react. Me, they didn't know how to get to me. One day at Toys 'R' Us, I caught her son stealing a toy and took him to the manager. He didn't think he had done wrong because his real dad had taught him to steal.

Stealing is bad... so is killing. Hoped to stop the kid from becoming like me. Unlike my own father rubbing my nose in it for getting caught, I let go of it soon enough and moved on—no point in dwelling on it.

Once, I was called by my ex to go to the school to talk to my son. He was accused of a phone call to 911 with another boy. I entered a teacher's room to see my son and the other boy and mother already there. The woman teacher had a stern look on her face. I felt I had to defuse the situation and walked over to the teacher and leaned into her and kissed her. Startled, she smiled and in her voice told us what had happened. The both of them had dialed 911 and hung up the phone once the operator came on the line.

"Did you dial the phone son?"

"No, Dad."

I looked at the other boy. "Did you pick up the phone and later hang it up?"

"No sir."

They hadn't really lied to me. So I told them. "This is what I think happened. Jason, you had a hold of the phone while you dialed it."

"We have to punish them. You need to teach your son not to— " said the mother of the other boy.

"Where are your sisters at?" I asked Jason.

He told me they were in class.

"Let's go get them, and we'll go to Dairy Queen and put this behind us."

"Dairy Queen? Aren't you going to punish him?"

"You have embarrassed them both by marching them in here. Several of their own friends told on them. They know by all of the fuss that they did wrong. Put it behind us and move forward. Spanking our children only makes them hate us more. I don't spank my kids. I'm not my father."

I gathered up all three and we had what they wanted to have at Dairy Queen. Many years later after I came to prison, I asked Jason if I got it right on that incident. 'Spot on!' He turned out okay—25 plus years in the United States Military.

Being Mr. Mom was wearing on me. Every week I called up Steve Burton at Copenhagen asking when work would resume. I needed to get out of being Mr. Mom. Steve told me to keep calling back. At any time, work could pick up. Then one call, he mentioned they had an office down in Sacramento, California. Would I like to travel there for work until I'm needed up north? "Hell yes!'

One night I was in bed and little Alesha climbed into the bed and tired to touch things she shouldn't know about and saying 'I'm pleasing daddy.'

"Roberta! Get your ass in here!"

"What's the problem?" she asked.

I told her what her three-year-old had said while she was trying to touch where she shouldn't.

'That son of a bitch!' she started.

'You have to file on him!' I told her.

Her ex-husband was/is a child molester, and she let him keep their children. I just didn't understand her. Even after this revelation, she refused to file charges on him. She kept in my ear about killing him. Okay, I'm a murderer. She didn't know that. Murder is messy. Murder is work. Killing Robert Donelly for Roberta was something I just didn't want to be involved in. Let the legal system have him.

"If you're not going to take care of this problem, Roberta, I cannot be a part of all of this bullshit."

And there it was.

Steve Burton had secured me a spot at their southern office. All I had to do was show up. I hate goodbyes. Okay, call me a coward, but sometimes walking away is the best policy. While she was at work, I loaded all of my property into the Chevy Nova and waited for her to come home for one more love session. After she fell asleep, I got dressed and got into my car and drove south out of Portland and on my way to work in our southern office. At the very first rest area, I pulled in and slept.

At Exit 86 on I-5 the next morning, I pulled into the 'Heaven on Earth' Bakery and Restaurant to get a large cinnamon roll they are famous for. These two beautiful women run this great bakery. Had known them for years. (Every time I'm taken by police to settle cases, I talk the cops into stopping there at 'Heaven on Earth.')

I was taking my time driving south. Stopping here and there to visit people I had come to know while trucking. I wanted to catch up with Nancy Flowers, but found out her ex-husband had killed her. What a buzz kill!

I stopped at the Pear Tree Restaurant in Phoenix, Oregon, for coffee, careful not to spend too much because my recent unemployment checks would have to last until my next paycheck. Late that afternoon I pulled into 'Porky Bob's' a small restaurant next to the rest area just north of Weed, California. At 9:00 pm on April 13th, 1990, I found myself parked next to the US Bank at the Shasta City Mall. I had gone into the grocery store and bought my evening meal of a jar of peanut butter and a stack of celery.

It was a little cool outside as I leaned on the back of the Nova, eating my meal. I soon saw her walking toward me. A woman carrying a newborn as the baby sucked a nipple. She was drinking from a pint of Jack Daniel's Whiskey. She sat down in front of me about 20 feet away on one of the railroad ties to keep cars away from the light poles.

"Dinner and a movie!"

The baby had finished a nipple. The woman sat her whiskey bottle down, opened up her other nipple, and moved her baby over to it.

She seemed to be advertising to me. Slowly, she covered herself back up and picked up her whiskey to drink. Been a very long time since I had milk from a woman's breast. When Melissa was born, I asked Rose to allow me a drink. Her milk soured my stomach. Staring over at this stranger, I stated a fact: "I wish I could do that."

"Do what?"

"Suck on your nipple."

And all she did was smile. "No, 'go fuck yourself'." Her whiskey empty; she set it down and got up and walked over to me.

"Do you want to party?" she asked.

"No, I can't afford to. I'm on a strict budget."

"I'll buy." She said and pointed over her shoulder to an all-night mini market.

"Get in the car. I'll drive over to it."

"No, let's walk."

We walked over to the store and went inside. She passed me her baby and went to the cooler and pulled out a 12 pack of beer. Like she said she would do, she paid for it and we walked back to the Nova and sat inside. We opened a couple and drank. During our conversation while drinking we both learned about each other.

The thing is people, I was not being deceptive with Daun Slagle. I told her where I was going and why. She wants to have a drink and maybe play with me- great! She was paying for it all. I was just on it for the ride.

Daun fought with her husband and stormed out of their home to cool off. Walking down to me was just curiosity at best. Too occupied with drinking and caring for her child to be making plans on what to do next. Just maybe being with anohter man would teach her husband a lesson. Whatever she was planning wasn't a plan. She was shooting from her hip. I just happened to be where her bullets hit.

We had put away two beers each when she spoke out loud. 'I have to pee!'

We were parked about 25 yards from Jerry's Restaurant and I pointed to it saying, "Let's go up there to Jerry's."

"No, I have a better idea! Drive and I'll tell you where to take us."

I get it.

Daun, a local girl, didn't want to be seen with another man.

I drove past Jerry's Restaurant and across Interstate 5. Up ahead is the California Highway Patrol Office in the Shasta City area. We turned left on the next read before the police parking lot. We drove about a mile to a large turnout area to our left. Deep into the area off of the road we parked in the shadows of large trees. She got out and walked about twenty feet, pulled down her pants and squatted right there in my headlights, showing me everything.

She left a large wet spot on the ground and pulled her pants up. A smile came over her. She had been holding it for a while.

When I loaded my car with my luggage, I folded down the back seat. Daun moved her baby onto my bedding just behind her seat. Freeing both of us up to do whatever we wanted.

We were two adults in a car at the local make-out spot. What do you think we were there for? Talk went to sex.

(Now, there is a problem here: several years ago, crime writer Matthew William Phelps interviewed Daun Slagle, asking her what she had told me about her ability to give a man a blow job. She told him she told me that her husband told her that she gives the best blow jobs in Shasta. Suggesting her husband has had blow jobs from every woman in Shasta City, and hers were the best. But that isn't what she told me while we were all alone in my car in Shasta's make-out spot.)

Daun rubbed me on my crotch and said, "I give the best blow jobs in Shasta."

Well, 'okay then,' I thought.

I had wondered where this was going. Dinner, sex, and a movie. I unzipped my pants and pulled Keith Junior out for the best blow job of Shasta. I'm a big guy, and Daun wasn't so small, either. Not much room in the car for such a maneuver. My right hand was on the back of her neck as she leaned down.

And she then stopped and said, 'What am I doing here? No, I'm not going to do this.'

Seriously!

Maybe she needed a little nudge and I pulled on her neck a little. The more I pulled, the more she resisted. I got angry and twisted her neck. I even violently tried to break her neck with tugs with my right arm. I was about to position myself to really hurt her when out of the back seat came a cry. Her newborn was awake and voicing her opinion of the activity going on up front. Like when Taunja cried out for her mother, I stopped what I was doing and relaxed, letting go of Daun.

She reached for her baby, yelling, "My baby! My baby!"

Her door opened, and off she ran.

For a moment, I sat there thinking of what had just happened. I didn't want it to end like this. I had to stop her somehow. Defuse the whole situation or end it. I drove after her and her child. Pulled alongside her as she walked back toward town.

"You asshole!" she spat at me.

"I'm sorry, I don't know what came over me. Get in the car and let me take you back to town. Think of your baby out here in the cold. Come on, get in."

She reached for the door and got back in. Kept her right hand on the door handle just in case what I told her was a trick. As I drove, over and over I told her, "I don't know why I did that. I am sorry."

Just as we crossed Interstate 5 and stopped, she flew open the door and jumped out, yelling at me, "You asshole! I fucking hate you! You mother fucker!"

Flipped me her middle finger and ran off toward Jerry's Restaurant. I drove north to an exit and sat there wondering what to do next. Work awaited me in Sacramento. I decided to drive south to go to work. About ten miles south of Dunsmuir, I realized I had open containers in the car and pulled over and made sure no beer, empty or full, remained with me.

Two hours later, I pulled into the Burns Brothers truck stop in Corning, California, toured the parking lot, and saw a local cop eyeing me as I drove past him. I made my way to the parking area close to the diesel fuel desk, got out, and asked a cashier I knew if I could use a shower. I returned to the parking lot to get my shampoo and change of clothes. I made it maybe 20 yards when I heard, 'Hold it asshole!'

I saw maybe six policemen with guns pointing at me.

"Get down on the ground!"

"Get on your knees!"

"Now lay down on your belly, arms to your side, reaching as far as you can."

I lay there while one of them placed me in handcuffs. The other read me my rights.

"You have the right to remain silent; anything you say will be held against you."

You know the drill. Right to an attorney and everything else...when that ended, "Are you willing to talk to us?"

Comedian Ron White had been thrown from a bar and when cops read him his rights to remain silent, he didn't have the ability to.

That is how I was at this point.

'Yes, I'll talk to you,' I said.

Daun Slagles' husband tried to convince his wife not to press charges because she had brought it on herself. That she has a history of starting a lot of trouble for men. But this time, she felt a need to complain to police. She filed a report of assault.

The Corning police listened to me tell the story how we met. How she bought the beer and asked to be driven to the locals make-out spot. Told them we were in an uncomfortable spot, that I didn't hurt her. She had filed it to make peace with her husband, that she had a fight with early on that evening. The Corning police relayed my message to the Shasta police.

"Are you willing to drive back to Shasta to talk to detectives?"

"Yes sir! I'll be back there by morning."

They put me in a car and drove me to their station to fingerprint me and take my photograph. Brought me back to my car and released me. One looked at me and said, "Be careful who you pick up at night from now on."

I spoke back, "She picked me up."

I went to my car and grabbed my shampoo and change of clothes and went inside to get a shower room. I told the girl behind the counter that I was a mistaken identity. They got me, the wrong guy, for a robbery up north. She bought into my story. I was there and not still arrested. She even felt sorry for me having to go through such an ordeal.

The shower and change of clothes felt good. I I Sat there in the car, actually deciding if I should go back to Shasta or take off. I couldn't go south. The police probably were waiting for me to try something like it. I was able to talk myself free in Corning and they were willing to let me go back to Shasta. To not do what I said I would, would prove I'm more guilty. I felt I could tell Shasta to believe my story, and it would go away.

I had a couple of hours of sleep in my car before driving back to Shasta. Found a parking spot next to the office of the county sheriff's office past the store where Daun had bought the beer. Locked the car and went inside to confront my fears. Stood there waiting for someone to ask me, 'Why are you here?'

Upon answering the question with 'I'm Keith Jesperson, you wanted to talk to me?' Both detectives pulled their guns and pushed me against the wall, handcuffed me and led me into a small room to ask me questions after my rights were read to me again.

When police come at you head-on for the first time asking what happened, any lie you tell them has to become the story.

Telling Corning police my story about what happened between me and Daun Slagle was now the story. I had to tell the Shasta police the same story.

And continue to tell the same story for the last 34 years.

Why?

Because each case I have feeds off of the other. If I told the truth about one case and lied the next time, someone would notice.

I remember my father came to me one time telling me, "You lied to me son!"

And I told him, "Don't feel bad Dad, I've lied to everyone."

Imagine telling the police a lie to secure a certain story to be sentenced a certain way. Then, tell a friend a different story. My father was a piece of shit when it came to talking to police. He told them everything! It was just like I was telling the police in person. Of course, I had to lie to my own father!

The detectives of Shasta's sherriff's office asked me my story. I told them the whole truth and nothing but the truth except the part about twisting the bitch's neck. We were in a compromising position inside the Chevy Nova. Period!

"But she told us you handled her!"

Her story lacked a lot of details. I'd hear later she couldn't remember how she got back to town. Failed to mention she bought the beer or that she had been drinking alcohol while nursing her child.

When a police report is filed, the one who makes out the complaint is always considered most credible over the person that has to react to the report. And the fact that the one complaining is female really puts the squeeze on any male suspect. Dealing with Daun Slagle was like a very hard uphill climb to clear myself. At least I had evidence to support my claims. But generally, it came down to a 'she said, he said' battle. Two hours of debating over our stories had me in a police car on a fact-finding trip around Shasta.

The clerk at the convenience store remembers Daun buying the beer. The empty whiskey bottle lay there in the grocery store parking lot where I said it would be. There was a wet spot where Daun peed at the local make-out spot. Yes, everything added up in my favor!

The Shasta police still had to take all of the evidence to the prosecutor's office in Yreka, California, the county seat where the courthouse is. They have the final word on if they planned to prosecute me. They let me out of their car, took off the handcuffs and said, 'Keep checking back with us. Might take a few months to sort this all out.'

Several hours later I pulled into the yard in Sacramento to talk to my boss. I had keys to the gates and a room above the shop to sleep in. There was a shower downstairs to clean up in. Steve Burton scholed me that their sounthern office was losing money. I was there to watch for him what exactly was going on. And the Sacramento boss felt something was up with me there, but couldn't put his finger on it until one day when Steve came to town and invited me to his motel room for a debriefing. The biggest thief in Sacramento was the boss.

Just about every weekend he'd show up to steal fuel. Taking 500 gallons at a time. After Steve left for Portland, the boss in Sacramento ran out of jobs for me to do. One job I was doing there had to do with the new Arco Arena, I dug the trenches for telephones. Mostly I ran a Barber Green Wheel trencher and a Linkbelt 3400 Excavator.

When I wasn't at work, I went to the Cinch Tavern. Even attended the owner's wedding. Also helped a feed store in my spare time, filling orders. Some of the customers thought I was too friendly. One woman wanted to take me home.

I'm guessing it was mid June in 1990 when Copenhagen called for me to return to Clackamas's employee list. I drove the Chevy Nova back to Jerry Day in Washougal. Bought a 1969 Chevy long box pickup truck and headed over to Yakima to see my friend Royce Kenoyer to buy an eight foot camper. Married the two togeteher to be my mobile home.

Copenhagen sent me to Astoria to operate the backhoe doing a telephone job. About that same time, protesters hung from the bridge over the Columbia River stopping a large battleship from going to Portland. Jokenly, I offered to run across the bridge with my ax to cut them down. The 200 ffot would have killed them. And besides, cameras were on them 24 hours a day. I might have done it, had it not been for the press. Not thinking how high it really was.

While in Astoria in 1990, the movie 'Kindergarten Cop' was being filmed. Arnold Schwarzenegger was in town. I stood by one of his shoots until a producer came to the crowd and sent all of us larger than Arnold away. Afraid a sweep of the locals would show me being larger than Arnold. And I am bigger.

On weekends I made trips over to Jerry and Janet's to visit and sometimes play. Jerry liked it when I joined in on a threesome. Both of us tag teaming Janet. She would be sucking me off while Jerry rammed her from behind. And vice versa. As I said beore, I hate to share and my best time with his wife was when we were alone while Jerry was at work.

I became a stalker with Roberta still living at her mother's home. Parked my camper at the mall and walked over to her neighborhood to spy on her. I missed the sex we had. Then one day I drove up to in front of her home while Roberta and her children played on the lawn. The meeting went better than I thought it would. They packed up clothes and joined me in my camper to Astoria. We put the kids to bed early so we could fuck each other most of the night. We were back to normal. Daytime at work and nightime between her legs!

When the Astoria job ended, we settled in to her home. Jobs around Portland would keep me busy. My father and step mother were hosts of Oregon's Sand Lake State Park south of Tillamook for about seven years. Drove to Spokane and picked up my three kids and deposited them their with their grandparents. Had to explain to dad to not spank my children. Told them that if I hear they used a belt or spoon or even their hands to punish them, they will never be trusted to look after them. On weekends we drove up to see them at Sand Lake to check on how they were doing. Both were amazed how behaved all three were. Only my son Jason needed a time out once. He wanted to control the use of the ATV four-wheeler Honda. When I drove the ATV with Roberta on behind, we looked for secluded places we could toss a blanket down and fuck like rabbits. When Melissa rode with me, 1st gear was too fast. When Jason rode with me, 2nd gear was good and he wanted to control the throttle. When Carrie got on, we needed to find higher gears we didn't have. The faster the better! For six weeks they stayed there with Grandpa Les and Grandma Betty.

I was wrestling with my three children on the living room rug at 18434 NE Everett Street when I noticed blood droplets I had missed on some of the moldings. Using a kitchen knife, I scraped several spots away. Reluctantly, a week later, I drove them home to their mother in Spokane.

The summer was over. (Melissa was 11 years old and never saw the blood droplets. And if she had noticed specks, would not know what made them! Certainly her mind would never comprehended the specks were dried blood. But fast forward to after she was on the Dr. Phil Show in 2008, all of a sudden she is recoiling a memory of seeing blood droplets everywhere in the home,)

back in Spokane, my son Jason was running and ran into a tree head on, suffering a concussion. I got a call from Rose telling me my children needed to see me.

I believe it was the first week in October 1990. took a leave of absence to drive to Spokane. My children begged me to stay. Looking in the newspaper, I spotted a job driving for Safeco Trucking, called and went to them to apply.

Drove a frieightliner pulling a set of Rocky Mountain doubles for a test drive. Of course they hired me. My home base would be Spokane. My days off spent with my children. Roberta wasn't happy. She begged me to be my co-driver. But what about her children?

This is when things really got fucked up with Roberta and everybody. She loved trucking with me more than being with her children. She had invited an older woman to babyit as a nanny living in her home in Portland while she worked. Now she was trying to toss it all away to follow me out on the road. In reality, I could care less about her children and her nanny. Having Roberta in a truck with me helped with my log book problems and entertainment every where. Told Roberta to keep her mother's home and get out of the truck from time to time to be with her children. That home coast little to maintain. No rent, just heat and other small bills. Nannys cost money!

My boss allowed Roberta to drive on my say so alone. Climbed into the job in November after shutting down the home in Portland, moving her two children and their nanny to a motel above Spokane off Interstate 90. these are her bills.

Her mother was not happy, and then again she was able to sell the home and helped her out a lot.

We drove 48 states and Canada pulling flatbed trailers. I became known as 'the man of action' because I could get loaded when others could not. They gave us all of the difficult loads. For the next two months we drove more miles than the other drivers and teams. 26,000 miles a month! Every two weeks or so, Roberta would go to the motel to check in, buy groceries and not pay the nany. Always out of enough money to cover it all. I had my own bills and child support of $750.00 a month. Just a couple hours and we were off again.

In trucking one load leads into the other. Time runs into time. Hard to keep track of exactly when things happen. Sure, I can remember, but not exactly when on the exact day. January? 1991, Roberta and I had a load of lumber going east to Illinois. It had been snowing all day when I pulled into Rock Island weigh station on Interstate 80. my heavy load had gained 2,500 pounds of snow pushing me over the limit and the femal scale master red lighted me.

'That will be $84.00 Mr. Jesperson. You'll have to legal it before you leave.'

'That's bullshit,' I yelled.

It was just one more way for her state to get over on us truckers, charging me for her snow that will fall off on her ground. The fact that she allowed me to use her shovel to knock off the snow weight to legalize my load is proof of the corruption at play.

Of course I was pissed off! And then sh ran my name across the National Crime Index Computer and out popped a felony warrant for assaulting Daun Slagle in Shasta, California.

She called for backup to take me to the Rock Island county jail in Rock Island, Illinois. But first allowed to legal the load for Roberta to take over the load on to be delivered.

In typical fashion, Roberta would leave the weigh station without the truck's paperwork. The paperwork, and permits made it back to Safeco before she did. Also before she left me, she asked for every penny I had because she was broke again.

And this is the very important part: I told Roberta about having a problem in the home while she was in Knoxville. Didn't mention exactly a murder, but felt that maybe the police in Shasta contacted Oregon and added it up. This is paranoia speaking!

(This conversation came alive in Portland on October 16th, 1995 when police talk to Roberta about the Bennett murder.)

They book me into their jail and at 10:00 AM the next morning I'm in front of a judge telling California to come and get me as long as they drop the $84.00 over wieght ticket. Fighting extradition only makes the case against me stronger. And in the end, they will get me anyways. Just futher down the road is all. Agreeing to go back to California under felony warrant, they have just ten days to do it. Rules. Until they made up their minds, I sit in the Rock Island jail. I called home to talk to my kids and the call upsetted them. A learning curve.

Three days later after calling my boss with the news, I'm called down to the Sheriff's office. Seems, California has a change of heart and drops the felony to a misdemeanor warrant. Meaning: I was going to be set free!

The new warrant is only enforceable in California. Should I be arrested in California, then they will send me to Yreka to face the misdemenor charge.

He gave me papers that told anyone who needed to know that I no longer had a felony warrant pending. I called my boss and told him I was broke and he would set it up for me to cash a com-check for bus fare at the Iowa 80 truck stop. It wasn't far of a walk to the Iowa 80 truck stop to get bus fare back to Spokane. Roberta had made the delivery on time. Then had some trouble getting her load on for Spokane. I was ahead of her and she was driving. A driver gave me a ride to Des Moines, Iowa to catch a Greyhound bus ride to Spokane. The bus I was on made a stop in Livingston, Montana.

Sitting in the restroom, I saw all kinds of notes written on the walls.

I pulled out a pen and wrote my own message:

"I KILLED SONYA BENNETT IN PORTLAND, OREGON ON JANUARY 21, 1990. TWO PEOPLE TOOK THE BLAME SO I CAN KILL AGAIN. CUT THE FLY OFF OF HER JEANS- PROOF!"

I finished writing and got on my bus to Spokane. What was I thinking? Sort of gloating over the whole mess. I had gotten away with murder and Slagle's felony was now a misdemeanor. It was just a note written on a wall. Who was going to pay attention to it anyways?

(So what I didn't know was Laverne Pavlinac was actually in her trial in Multnomah County courthouse at the very time I wrote the note on that wall. A janitor was called to the wall and a call to the Livingston police confirmed Taunja Bennett died on January 21st, 1990 and the suspect was in trial for it. The wall was removed and sent by bus to Portland, Oregon's Multnomah County courthouse to appear as evidence in Pavlinac's trial. However not allowed because the actual writer of the note as not known. The lead prosecutor Jim McIntyre believed or at least said he believed it to be written by one of Pavlinac's family trying to convince her jurors that the real killer was still out there.)

Had I known what a fuss they made out of the note on that wall, I might have written more. Then again, I might have never written it at all had I known they would treat it as evidence.

Simply venting is all.

I made it to Safeco before Roberta came to town. Even met her as she exited Interstate 90 by the truck stop. Seeing me, we hooked up and stayed together all night. What she didn't tell me, was her load was to be at the yard as soon as possible, just another mistake of hers not to follow orders. Another nail in her trucking career with Safeco. Her 300 mile days behind the wheel didn't help either.

Because I still had a misdemeanor warrant still active in California, Safeco could not allow me to drive until it was resolved. And Roberta wasn't any good behind the wheel without me. So we both lost our trucking jobs.

At the unemployment office, I signed on to work in Alaska on the Ocean Pride Alaska processing ship in Dutch Harbor for a three month tour processing crab and cod. I'd be flying out in days. Pay was low, about $7.00 an hour and time and a half after eight hours. Days were 20 hours long of work, so it all adds up to be a good deal for work in January. Better than collecting unemployment insurance. While I was there, I set the boxing of crab hour record by filling 185 boxes of crab in one hour. A short time later, I felt a need to exit my job because of an arm injury. Flew back to Seattle and bussed back to Spokane to find Roberta had been living in my camper in front of my ex wife's home. You can't make this type of shit up!

Of course her nanny had split with no money to pay her or the rest of the motel. She had eventually moved into a room in a home using my checks sent to her from Alaska. I came home to her to find she had spent all of my money.

Ocean Pride Alaska was self insured by Crawford and Company. Instead of State Industrial insurance paying for my injury, I had to prove I had an injury to be paid compensation. It took just a week at a doctor to confirm I was under the care of a specialist to treat my tendinitis. All in all, my monthly checks came to around $2,000.00.

When I was downstaris at our new home, the homeowner made an observation on me and Roberta.

He said, 'Keith, you're pussy whipped. She just has to wiggle her ass and you follow behind her.'

This pissed me off. Yes it was true. I hate nicknames. Roberta and I had a falling out over this and how she used up all of what I made in Alaska. What her nanny told me about nights of hooking she did also pissed me off. She hadn't looked for work as long as money was there.

Roberta had a small job driving Eldon Schwilke to all points he requested to go. Suffering from MS, he was fastly falling apart. I went with Roberta and found out Eldon was a big cribbage player. Also soon learned that cribbage has a large following around this country. Clubs and even tournaments. I joined Spokane's Cribbage Club #69 and played in their weekly games. My American Cribbage Congress number is WA 507. as it just so happens, the second weekend in March every year Baker City in Oregon has their annual cribbage tournament and Eldon told me he would pay my enty fee to play if I drove him to Baker City. Eldon rented a car and I drove all of us to Baker City. Roberta helped Eldon deal while I played the main tournament. My cribbage play has always been good. Have played since I was 4 years old.

Out of over four hundred players, I placed 3rd overall and was paid over $450.00 and won a trophy cribbage board. That Sunday evening as we headed back to Spokane, we stopped at the Umatilla, Oregon truck stop to eat. Sitting in the truck stop's restroom, out came my pen and I wrote another note on a bathroom wall.

"I KILLED AND RAPED TAUNJA BENNETT ON JANUARY 21, 1990. BEAT HER UP BADLY. TWO PEOPLE TOOK THE BLAME SO I CAN KILL AGAIN."

I know I had not raped her. The public didn't know. I was just telling stries to tell stories. There is a rub here. Everything a killer says is taken seriously as if it has to be true. I wasn't caught. Didn't think I'd get caught. (AS it turns out, I had to prove I hadn't had sex with her. However, my intentions were to have sex with her. And in the news, police said Sosnovske had raped her. So maybe that is where I got rape from.)

Roberta and I split up because she was pregnant and didn't know who the daddy was for sure, could have been any one of the Johns she messes with while I was in Alaska. Where did I end up? Floyd Eldon Schwilke has a guest room downstairs and he offered it to me if I drove him everywhere. We went to every cribbage tournament we could and I was on a hot streak. Another thrid place in Nyssa, Oregon, a first place in the consolation tournament in Bend, Oregon and another thrid place finish in Portland, Oregon. Each paid me hundreds of dollars and won me trophy boards.

You can always see the results of tournaments in Cribbage World Newsletter/Magazine. Get issues for 1991, 1992 to 1995. I'm in them someplace.

Eldon and I joined a singles meeting dub in Spokane called 'New Friends'. We met at the IHOP restaurant on Drusen in Spokane. I found love in a few of those lonely women's home. The one I liked the most was Betsy. But she cheated on me later in November 1991 with a man that had herpes. I refused to get involved with her any more. Actually, I had a woman stalk me and complain to management that I jaded her. And we actually never met.

Roberta contacted me again in June 1991. we had sex a few times. She had lost the baby. Or it was taken care of. We never lasted because I just wasn't into her any more. Okay, go ahead and laugh... I was in her a few times... just not into her life any more. When she was in my life, no one could be pleased. She was hated by both sides of my family.

In the fall of 1991, my son Jason came to live with me and Eldon. All was good until Eldon wanted a female driver. A woman named Mary came into the picture. Forced me out. A very heavy and out of shape girl. One time Eldon fell out of his wheelchair and she could not put him in it. They had to wait for his neighbors to come home to help. At the next club play, Eldon yelled at me for not giving him my phone number to call. Jason and I had moved to Cheney, Washington about 20 miles from Eldon's home.

'Sorry, but Eldon you kicked us out of your house remember?'

Even Eldon's brother and parents contacted asking me to convince him to get rid of Mary. She eventually did it herself after stealing just about everything not nailed down in his home and bank. She left him almost penniless until his next VA check arrived. A sad story!

Eldon was a mechanic in the army. When he was diagnosed with MS, his wife divorced him and moved away, because he had friends in the service, powers to be pushed paper work ahead so when he retired he was a major or even higher ranked, allowing him a good pension that he could live on. After he went down hill almost to death, his ex wife remarried him so she could get the survivor's pension upon his death. At least his daughters will be well taken care of.

I kept going to therapy and taking my medication. In March 1992, Crowford and Company believed I was cured enough to again join employment. They told me I could go back as a truck driver because there was no heavy lifting in the job description. They don't know trucking! Who do they think unloads all of the stuff truck drivers haul? They were cutting me loose.

My son went back to his mother now living in Vancouver, Washington. I went to work for Jim Wiley in Moxee, Washington, the small town east of Yakima. He had a project for me to weld up a three axle tilt bed trailer to haul a paving machine behind a dump truck. It took me about a month to complete. I was also requested to work for a wood molding plant also in Moxee as a welder building haul trailers for the various chips of wood. My brother Bruce worked as a foreman for the company. He would later lose three fingers in an accident at the plant and they would be put back on in Seattle. My job ended soon after. Not because of his accident, but because I worked myself out of a job.

Where to work now? In order for me to go back trucking, I needed to take care of the misdemeanor warrant.

I left my vehicle with family and hopped on a Greyhound bus to Yreka, California. Took a cab to the courthouse, walked in to see the clerk to turn myself in for the crime. They gave me a lawyer instead of arresting me. Walked to the lawyer's office and he told me to go to lunch and come back in an hour. Apparently, Daun didn't need me to show up. She had her own problems and refused to come to court to argue nothing. It was April 1992 and the Daun Slagle case was dismissed. Given proper paper work, I hopped back on a bus home to Yakima to once again go back to work for A & G Trucking.

(After I was arrested and convicted of murder and Daun Slagle went on the Oprah/Dr. Phil shows with my daughter someone in records of Yreka courthouse rubbed out the Slagle dismissal and rewrote the decision to say Mr. Jesperson pled guilty to misdemeanor battery and got time served in 1993. Crime writer Christopher Berry-Dee wrote in a book that he has seen documents claiming Mr. Jesperson was convicted of rape in the Daun Slagle case. I read the text and wrote John Blake publishing in the UK to accuse them of fraud.)

The Learning Curve

While I am writing this material to send to my friend Nicole D. Phoenix to type up for this book, I'm watching one of America's favorite series on the Paramount network called *Yellowstone*. I've seen all of the episodes at least five times over the past few years. Kevin Costner is the leader of the Dutton Ranch in Montana. A family of monsters. They are all serial killers that empty their victims at what they call the 'train station'. A canyon in Wyoming where all of their secrets go to rot and decompose. My favorite episode has Rip walking up to a fisherman and he shakes a cooler with a rattlesnake in it- exposing it to the face of the man and the snake bites him, killing the man in just minutes. Good riddance! The show is full of murder. Each death different in some ways. The learning curve of death. I also have to learn to kill. How to get what I want out of things. A progression of how I evolve unchecked by anyone. I'll have to develop my own kind of 'train station'.

With the Daun Slagle case settled in April 1992, returning to Yakima I soon discovered my chauffeurs license wasn't any good to drive semis anymore. Between 1991 and 1992, the department of transportation decided to have truck drivers have their own license to drive, the Commerical Drivers License, or C.D.L.

First off, I had to pass a written test and get a medical card. Then locate an office to take my drivers test. Passed the written in Ellensburg and went to Yakima to get my job tractor and trailer, taking it over to be road tested. Anthony and Gina Silva hired me right there and sent me to Ellensburg to get my CDL at the DMV. Pulled up outside and parked on the shoulder and the nice officer looked over my medical card and driver's test report, looked up to see a Plum colored Peterbilt pulling a 48 foot refer.

'Is that your rig?'

'Yes it is.'

A smile came across her face as she took my photo for my new CDL.

'You drove that here?' she said as she handed me my license.

'Yes miss, I have to pick up a load of boxed meat in Ellensburg Washington beef plant.'

And off I drove to Glendale, Arizona to Glendale Meats. A & G Trucking hired me providing Roberta no longer was with me. After murdering Taunja Bennett and dealing with Daun Slagle in the 'she said he said' battle for over two years, I decided not to be with women out on the road.

When I saw hitch hikers I just never stopped. Now I'd meet women at stores and restaurants and have them waiting for me where they were. Out on the road they were trouble. I wasn't looking for any more trouble any time soon.

I'm guessing it was August 1992 when I had a load of frozen potatoes fries going to Smith Foods in west Phoenix, Arizona. My 3:00 AM off load time was seventeen hours away when I pulled into the brake check area on Interstate 15 north of San Bernardino, California at 10:00 AM. The scale house a couple miles ahead was open and I didn't take any chance and parked.

Over the years I haven't had much luck dealing with scale houses in California.

In 1990 Roberta and I drove out of Reno heading to Sacramento over Interstate 80 driving a cab over freightliner that had some recent damage repaired over the first driver's good wheel. At Truckee's weigh station the officer had me in his building doing an inspection. He claimed my driver's side front wheel was cracked and I could not move until it was fixed. We parked behind the building and waited. It wasn't 20 minutes when a repair truck showed up with an exact tire and wheel to put on my truck.

We hadn't called anyone. The name on the side of the truck was the same name on my fix-it ticket. The officer had called his relative with the news. Told him we will wait until we call our boss before authorizing a switch. He gave us his card.

Before the sun came up, I got my aluminum wheel polish out and went to town polishing both front wheels until they looked brand new. Waited for shift change in the cops office and then pulled up and showed the new on duty scale master my polished wheels. He signed the fix-it ticket as fixed.

I wasn't going to take any chance on I-15 and crawled under my trailer and tractor to adjust the brakes. My log book needed help too. I had written in the current book that I had been at the brake check area for five hours sleeping. I needed to stay there for three more to show I had my eight hours in the sleeper before being back in the driver's seat. Rules!

When I pulled in and parked in the middle of the paved lot, my truck was the only one there. Under doing my brakes, I hadn't heard anyone drive in. so when I heard a voice asking for a ride I was sure she had walked off the freeway.

'Hey mister! Can I get a ride?'

had looked around and didn't see her. Then I heard her again.

'Hey mister! Can I get a ride?'

finishing up my task, I slipped out from under my truck and looked up at a blonde shaggy haired woman dressed in light blue jeans and a white t-shirt with some kind of motorcycle picture on it. She was really nicely put together.

'Where did you come from?'

I followed her to the back of my trailer where she pointed to another semi. An Albertsons Grocery carrier. Probably out of Brea, California. Without asking a question, the message was clear. The scale house was open and the driver could not drive over the scale with an unauthorized passenger on board. He would certainly lose his job. Me, on the other hand, had a sleeper I could hide her in.

'Where are you going?' I asked her.

'Los Angeles.'

'I'm not going to Los Angeles. I'm going to Arizona.'

'Can you give me a ride to Fontana?'

'No, I can give you a ride to Cabazon in about two hours. I have to wait til my log book is legal.'

'I guess that will have to do.' she said.

I waved off the Albertsons truck driver and he took off. Got out of my cover-alls and we got into the air conditioned cab. She had nothing with her. No purse, no money, no identification, nothing. She never even told me her name. True to form. Most of these women don't want to be known. They are opportunists. Ride to where they want to go and live off of what they are able to grab along the way.

'Are you a hooker?'

'Sometimes?'

Well as we sat there, I kept remembering Daun and Taunja. The good things and bad things. What I didn't get to do to both. Wishful thinking only goes so far. And at that moment I added up what I had been given like a spider to a fly, I am in control to a point. Getting past the scale house is key. No real problems until after getting past my road block up ahead. Her saying, 'sometimes', opened a door while we were alone for the next two hours. Our sexual play time helped to spin off an hour or so. Back dressed, I drew a line to being in the driver's seat and pulled out into Interstate 15 south. Had given her specific instrucions to hide in the sleeper until we were past the scale house.

Hell, the weigh master never blinked at me. We drove on through without a hitch. I hear that now scale houses have heat sensors to be able to see if our brakes are working and how many people are in our cabs. Infrared sensors. Back then in 1992, they had to physically inspect us. We went by after I had freshly fucked her.

There is something about sex when it comes to control by a woman. They seem to think what they say makes a difference. This one was no different. The split was coming up for I-15 to to Fontana or the I-115 to out east to connect to Interstate 10 to Banning and Cabazon and beyond.

'Can't you just take me to Fontana?'

'No, a deal is a deal. I'm heading east.'

Telling her 'No' struck a cord with me. A control thing. Even a turn on really. The sex we had had been okay. I was wanting to do her again. Also knew she would be getting out of my truck up in Cabazon where Pee Wee Herman had his great adventure in Dinosaur Park next to the Chevron truck stop. I made up my mind she wasn't going to leave. I had too much time to kill to let her go just yet.

We pulled into Cabazon and I parked, two K-9 units pulled in beside me to use my shade from my trailer to shield their dogs from the sun. one cop asked how long I'd be there and I told him to take their time. I would not leave until they do. As for my passenger, I pushed her back into the sleeper and began taking her clothes off. She complained that I had hurt her. Had I asked, she would have gone back into bed with me willingly. I had sex with her for the time it took for those K-9 cars to leave. Then I tied her up using duct tape.

It was close to 4:00 pm when I pulled back out onto Interstate 10 east. As I drove I heard some noises from behind me. She had been able to untie herself and get into her clothes. Her hand on the sleeper door waiting for me to come to a stop anywhere.

'How could I be so fucking stupid,' I told myself.

Letting her be behind me and able to untie herself. Up ahead I saw a wide pull out I had once used when seeking directions to a shed. It was a gravel area at an exit and was clear of other trucks when I pulled in to secure her again. Pulling into the parking area, I slid out of the driver's seat while the truck was still doing 20 mph, pulled out the maxi brakes valve that would engage the trailer brakes and brought us to a stop. I jumped into the sleeper about the time I heard her yell.

'I'm tired of this shit!'

I pushed her down on the bed and ended her life. My fist into her throat for a good time to be able to feel her body relax.

'That was close.'

I pulled back onto the interstate and drove to Coachella's Dillon Road and the Burns Brothers truck stop, parking in the rear of the lot. Sat there for a long while to make sure she was really dead. Then went inside to sit down to some ice tea. Killing is hard work. My attempt at kidnapping was a failure. Maybe next time? I had to admit that forcing them to love me wasn't working out. A lot easier to just pay them and let them fuck me willingly. Back in my truck, I rolled her body up into a blanket and pushed her against the back of the sleeper. Just then a small blue security pick up drove by with a flashing amber light flashing on top. I needed to get moving to find a place to put her.

The hill climbs up steeply going east from Coachella on Interstate 10. On top of the hill at the next exit sits General Patton's Museum. Went on past to an exit further toward Blythe. Parked on the on ramp and got out in the afternoon heat to try to locate her resting spot, a ravine with tumbleweeds I could use to cover her with. Layed down beside her and listened to my CB radio and stereo. Rigor was setting in with help from my air conditioner keeping everything cold. As I layed there with her, I heard truckers talking about a full grown smokey bear parked net to a plum colored semi on an on ramp heading east.

'Hey wait a minute!'

Leaned over and looked out the window to see the California Highway Patrol car with all his lights on top sitting in my shadow away from the sun. I could only guess as to why he was next to me. There is no way he knows I have a dead woman in my cab. So I open up my cooler and pull out two Cokes, open my driver's door and go over to his door with an offering of something cold to drink. He could not accept the cold Coke to drink. Policy. Why was he there?

He told me he had a spotter pane keeping track of some speeders coming our way and he would be soon off to write tickets. The plane had a camera set up to read the speeders license plates.

'Good to hear!'

And I am sure it would be able to see deposit a body into a ravine. I did notice his log book with his last entry in it telling of being parked by a plum colored semi. There was no way I'd leave her there.

(In late 1995, this police officer actually remembered our conversation. He was taken back hearing I had a dead woman not 20 feet from him in my sleeper.)

As soon as smokey bear left me, I did too. At Blythe I turned north onto Hwy 45 heading toward Needles. Before entering the canyon, I saw a turn out large enough for me to park in off the south bound side. A few miles ahead I found a place to turn around and head back south to the turn out and park. Had gotten out and established where I'd carry her body after it became dark enough to force people to turn on their lights.

When it became dark enough for me, I carried her stiff body over to a log and placed her next to it. Ran back to my truck and got the hell out of there back to Interstate 10 East. At the next truck stop called Ken Giffon, tossed away the soiled bedding and bought new blankets. Murder was not just messy but expensive. About as much she would have cost me to pay her for the sex I got.

A couple weeks later I had a load of Washington Beef headed for Fresno, California. Heading down Hwy 99, I pulled into the rest area by Turlock hoping to find a parking spot. Sat there waiting to see if any semi moved out, leaving me a spot. No one was moving. A very pretty hooker climbed into my step to talk to me. I reached down to feel her small boobs.

'Come with me. I'll bring you back after we get done.'

'Can't do that,' she said and told me why. She worked with several other girls all wearing red tops. They had a code of conduct to keep each other safe. All business is done inside the rest area. Period!

If I were to get her to get in my truck, I needed to find a parking spot somewhere where there isn't any. So I parked in front of the parked trucks. They would have to get me to move before any of them could leave. As soon as I was parked, I opened my door and she stepped inside and headed to my sleeper. Followed quickly behind her and brabbed her by the neck. Was pushing down hard to force her unconscious. My intentions were to kidnap her and take her with me to Fresno. After my delivery I would be sitting all weekend with nothing to do. So why not provide me with some entertainment? A couple minutes into it, I let go and yes she was still alive when I heard a noise behind me. Two girl's faces were pressed hard up against my passenger door window.

'Had I been caught?' I thought to myself. 'I have to get out of here!'

Panic came to me fast and I slid into the driver's seat, released the brakes and put it in gear. Those faces jumped. Drove to the next exit and parked on the on ramp. Went back to secure my victim before driving toward Fresno. At Livington, I pulled in behind the Blueberry Hill Cafe. There is enough parking to hold maybe ten trucks. My spot was open for me. Parked, I went into the sleeper to have a close look at the woman I planned to have sex with all wekkend. I melled shit. I undid her pants top and discovered she had loaded up her bottom with dark crap. There would be no fucking that! Removed all of the tape and carried her to the middle of the dirt parking lot and left her face down in the powdered dirt that flowed under each step. I kicked her, stomped on her neck before I pulled a tumbleweed over her. Drove out the lot and made my delivery in Fresno and parked at Klein's truck stop all weekend with nothing to do except wonder what my victim was doing now. She was alive when I left her. But also believed I could have killed her when I stomped on her neck.

(Apparently, she had survivied and walked away. No body had been found in the parking lot where I put her. However, a few days after I had left the area, a Cynthia Lynn Rose had died of an overdose and her body was placed by a tree just 20 feet from where I had put my victim. The one coincidence was she too, wore a red top being she also was a hooker that wrked the Turlock rest area.)

On November 6th, 1992 I loaed at Harris Ranch Meats in Selma, California heading to two deliveries. One at the United Groceries in Medford, Oregon on November 7th at 6:00 AM. The load came off without a hitch. Continued to drive north on Interstate 5 to Exit 86 and stopped in at 'Heaven on Earth' bakery for a cinnamon roll. My next unloading destination would be Waremart in Salem, Oregon. Had all day to get just what would take four hours to drive. Too much time to kill. Stopped at Ricehills at Exit 161 and later at a truck stop at Exit 101. (Fat Harvey's.)

The kidnapping part was not working. Too much to go wrong. My victims had a will to live. Maybe she shit herself as a deterant to being sexually assulted. It worked!

No way was I going to dive me into her feces filled pants. Had left her there fully dressed. The other Jane Doe just found it crazy to be tied up. And she almost got away. I began to form a plan for the night. Yes, I was going to kill her! And I already knew who she was. I had paid for sex from her before a couple times up at Exit 286 off of Interstate 5 in Wilsonville, Oregon.

Laurie Ann Pentland.

I would drive past Salem and park at the Burns Brothers ruck stop and call her over to me. Pay her to have sex and then kill her. That simple.

At about 7:00 pm I pulled into the Burns Brother truck stop while it was raining. Parked in the third row close to the west side of the yard and went in to JB's Lounge, yes the JB's Lounge Laverne Pavlinac said she had gone to Wilsonville to pick up Sosnovske in her confessions to Detective John Ingram of Multnomah County. Purely coincidence.

For about an hour or so I had coffee and a piece of Pie à la Mode. Seen several trucker I knew. Hell, over the road we come to see lots of drivers and hear lots of crazy stories. Part of being a real truck driver is complaining about everything. It occupies our time to listen in. you never know what you might learn.

Out in my semi m at near 9:00 pm I turned on my CB radio to listen for her to call. I certainly didn't have to wait long for it.

'Any one out there want some horizontal company?'

I knew it was her by her voice.

'I'm in the third row. I'll walk out to meet you,' I said to her and heard lots of other truckers telling all that will listen: 'You'll get AIDS!'

It didn't take long before I saw her dressed in her full raincoat walking between two trailers. I voiced an, 'Over here!' to her and she came to me. 'I remember you.'

'I'm parked over here.'

Ad we walked to my truck and got in. the cab was deliberately dark to keep prying eyes off of us, off of our transactions. In the sleeper, we closed the curtain and turned on the dome light.

'Thirty right?'

'That's right.'

'Here,' and she puts it in her front pocket.

Our clothes come off and we fall together to at first hold each other tight in a hug.

'I missed you,' I told her.

Pentland was not the prettiest of girls. What she lacked in sex appeal, she made it up in how she conducted herself. We acted like lovers and I entered her and she moved with me to get me off. Stayed in her to hopefully get her off. Thirty dollars gave me an hour with her. A full hour! I had been with other hookers who felt my time was up the moment I orgasmed. Either two or twenty minutes didn't make it an hour. If I called them on it, I'm the asshole!

The rain was really coming down when our hour was over. She got dressed and into her rain gear. I had gotten my thirty dollars worth and looked down at her and smiled.

'I'm going to strangle you now.'

And to my surprise she said, 'Go for it.'

I put my fist into her neck and pushed down hard. She didn't resist at first because I believe she believed I was joking around. By the time she began to struggle, it was too late. She began to nod off. I kept it up as I looked at my watch to time it to at least four minutes. I could smell her urine.

'Can I have your money?'

She never said 'No' and I pulled out all of her pockets to get almost three hundred dollars. Who says crime doesn't pay?

I had to think. No point in being in a hurry. I had all night to find a place to put her. November 8th, 1992.

I thought of putting her in an empty trailer on the back row. But decided against it. Decided to drive down to Salem and look for her resting place as I drove. As it turned out, I was driving the road past the GI Joe's store just before Waremart and saw her place in the back lot of Salem's GI Joe's store. Pulled in and made a sweeping turn in a circle and parked next to the chain link fence. There were several small piles of leaves along the fence. Felt I should make one big pile with her under it. But first I needed to walk around to check for cameras and security guards. Not seeing any, I pulled her body from my sleeper and let her fall against the fence next to some blackberry vines. Picked up those small piles of leaves and covered her up.

At that time, I was missing a small white plastic flashlight. I looked everywhere for it and found it under her body. Almost left my fingerprints.

Pulled out of the lot and drove the two hundred yards to the holding area of Waremart warehouse. In the morning my load came off and I left Waremart and cruised past the GI Joe's yard and could see the large pile of leaves still intact.

Two weeks later, at the Burns Brothers truck stop in Wilsonville I saw a photo of Pentland every five feet in the store.

'Have you seen her?'

I wanted to take one, but felt that is what they hoped for.

Had spent several hours at Burns Brothers and every time I looked up, I felt my victim was staring back at me.

And she was.

A poster every few feet.

Haunting!

Again and again I kept fighting the 'wanting' to take a poster with me. The sooner I got out of there, the better to control my urges. I wanted to take a poster to my truck so I could stare at her and masturbate over and over what I had done to her. I just felt people, not just her, were watching for any reaction by a person at seeing those haunting eyes staring at them. Pentland's body would be recovered shortly after that day and the posters were taken down.

I had entered 1992 as a plain murderer of one person and here it was in November I had killed three and became what the law calls a 'serial killer'. Yes just three. I never counted my Turlock victim as a kill. Not at first. What would change that is the unknown part of her story. She was alive and breathing when I placed her face down in the open parking lot. Then I stomped on her behind her head- neck area hard. The unknown part was did that stomping kill her? And there became a paradox when someone else used the Blueberry Hill Cafe's rear parking lot to get rid of their victim called Cynthia Lynn Rose. It all comes down to timing in the end. The end?

(After my arrest and I was connected to the Happy Face letter that talked about leaving a victim behind the Cafe in Livington, a connection went to Cynthia Lynn Rose because that was the only body found in the area close to where I said it was. Because I wasn't sure if my stomp on my victim killed her or not, I would assume like everyone else that it was Cynthia I killed. So I talked about her being my victim not knowing she wasn't. My confusion only helped to create more confusion with everyone else including detectives working the case. Later in 2010 I found out everyone's mistake.)

I had gone two and a half years without killing again. Thought I would never kill again. What changed? The Jane Doe came to me and I kept thinking of all I didn't do and could have done to Taunja Bennett before I killed her. And I had too much time to do everything to someone else and because no one knew who I was, no one had seen her get into my closed off room, like when Taunja entered my home, my lair, my trap, I could do to her what I hadn't done to Taunja. And possibly when I got done, two more people will claim my next victims as theirs too, just like Pavlinac and Sosnovske had done.

Each failure to achieve what I wanted out of my victims created more wanting to perfect the perfect day and night of fulfilling my sexual fantasies. But some how as I went forward each different victim presented different problems to cover. I was stumbling along trying to make sense of who I had become. I was a serial killer.

Back in 1991 while I looked after Eldon Schwilke in Spokane, my grandmother Margerie Bellamy in Chilliwack passed away leaving me- well all of us- a sum of $5,000.00. I sold off my pick up and camper and bought a 1984 Oldsmobile Ciera Wagon. Put in a custom stereo system and moved forward. A far better ride than a truck.

While driving for A & G Trucking. It sat there in their parking lot with the other driver's cars. Christmas was fast approaching us and I just didn't have time to get my children the trampoline they had asked for. Why? I was always helping my boss out of a problem situation. Anthony would ask a favor and tell me he 'owed me one'. That same day all of the bailing out of his problems would be paid back. Three days before Christmas 1992 he asked me to do him another favor in taking over another load from a problem driver that had stumbled. My projected time to get into my car to drive to Spokane would be late Christams Eve. No time to shop at all. Every store would be closed by then. I felt it was time all of those 'I owe you's were cashed in. I called up A & G Trucking and asked for Anthony and Gina's son-in-law working there to go to Shopco and buy me the trampoline for my kids and have it there so my children could have a Christmas from Dad.

What did Craig say? He had no time to do it. Basically he told me to fuck off. He wasn't my Christmas helper. When I called back and asked to talk to Anthony, he got on the line and I let him have it, not allowing Anthony to respond.

'This is bullshit Anthony! Pure bullshit! Here I am doing you a favor and all I am asking is for a favor in return and you would think that all of those 'I owe you's would fucking count! But hell no! I ask for one favor, one little thing for you to do and I am told to fuck myself. Well fuck you and your company. I'll do your load. I'll finish this trip. When I get there, I'm gone and you'll never see or hear from me again!'

Click!

I hung up.

I knew he would not expect that from me at all. He certainly had to find out what I had been talking about. What favor? I had envisioned Craig getting an ear full. After I unloaded at Associated Grocers in Seattle I called to tell A & G my load came off without a hitch and I'll be heading back to Wiley City yard. Anthony came on the line to tell me my trampoline was sitting with a dolly to help move it in the back room. He was sorry it had come to this and thanked me for doing him his troubled load.

(I bet now Anthony and Gina wished they had never hired me to drive for them in 1992.)

Back at the yard, the first problem was all of our pay checks had not been placed where we pick them up. (No cell phones.) had to find a pay phone and call up Craig to open their office to get them for us.

I found my trampoline where it was supposed to be and loaded it into my wagon. One other driver had a problem. His pickup truck had a flat tire and his spare was flat too. He lived in Wenatchee, Washington and needed to get home to see his family.

'Get in!' I told him, 'I'll take you home on my way to Spokane.'

He put in my car the presents he had for his family and we headed north on Hwy 97. I drove the canyon between Selah and Ellensburg. Not over Interstate 82. as we drove, I gave a tour to him about the area.

'Did you know I won the Grizzly Bear Pizza Rover Race on the Yakima River for three years?'

back in 1976 I had been training to enter the 22 mile long river race sponsored by the Grizzly Bear Pizza Restaurant in north Yakima.

For the previous three years a man in Kayak won it. I bought a six man rubber raft and outfitted it with paddles. Several months I met criticism from my wife and family telling me I had no chance in winning. So why try? On the day of the race, I couldn't get help from Rose or my father. Asked them to drive up with their vehicle and park it at the finishing line, ride up with me to the starting line and drive my pickup truck back to the finishing line so I could load up my boat after the race.

Rose said 'No' then I asked my father and he said 'No' as well. And jumped in to complain I'm wasting my time. I told him I'll just leave my keys in my pickup. If it is there when I get to it I'll drive it home, if someone steals it, oh well!

The race was being covered by a local radio station promoting the annual river race and float down the 22 miles and stopping at the boat launching area about the Rosa Dam. A TV crew also would be there monitoring results for our local communities.

I remember the Kayak owner coming to me with a question for me.

'How are you going to race?'

He told me he was going to paddle for 45 minutes, rest for 15 minutes, and paddle for 45 minutes to the end. I told him I was going to paddle all the way down. We all were ready in the water when the starting pistol popped. At the halfway mark, we were tied. 15 miles into the race I was ahead by a lot. I looked over at the road and saw my pickup being driven to the finishing line and my father's pickup close behind it. When I rowed up to the finishing line, I was leading by over half a mile. There in front of me was my wife with a smile on her face and she showed some leg. Father was standing in front of the TV camera bragging to the Yakima audience about how proud he was of his son Keith for his hard work in achieving the win. (Before the race I had no sponsors.) There was my father telling all that we had three sponsors who have been behind me all of the way. Larson Fruit Company, Helms Hardware, and of course, the Silver Spur Mobile Home Park.

At the race and float banquet that night at the Grizzly Bear Pizza Restaurant I was given my prize, $50 and all of the pizza I could eat. Of course my whole family showed up to enjoy the banquet and news coverage.

In 1977 my wife tried to convince me to allow her to ride along. Had to explain it is called a race for a reason. Not a ferry boat ride. I won it again but not by half a mile. The guy trained harder. In 1978, Rose climbed on board and like I thought would happen, she complained all the way to the winning finishing line about being wet. Because I had won the last three years, I believe the race was canceled. Why? The guy in the Kayak owned the Grizzly Bear Pizza Restaurant and didn't like to lose.

It was close to 11:pm when we pulled in front of his home in Wenatchee. His wife offered coffee and I had a cup and filled my thermos. At 6:00 AM I set in my car outside the home of my ex wife and children. When I saw faces glued to a window looking out at me, I went to their front door and walked in to greet them.

'Daddy's home!'

They didn't care about presents. They were glad to see me. Rose had coffee for me and I sat there on the sofa with all three trying to be the one to sit in my lap.

'I have something out in the car,' then added, 'Just one gift for all three of you.'

at the back of my car, I pulled out the dolly to load the large box onto it. Wheeled the box into their home. Jason realized what it was.

'Dad got us a trampoline!'

And of course it had to be put together in the back yard. Piece by piece and yes I read the instructions. Took a good hour to put together. Then all three bounced on it and I went inside to sleep on a bed. I'd wake up about three hours later with all three of my children wrapped around me. For Christmas dinner, I took everyone, even Tom, her husband, to the Broadway truck stop for a full meal experience. A day later I was back driving for A & G.

in February 1993, A & G Trucking went into receivership and would come out of it two weeks later as a smaller trucking company called Pacific North Trucking. Back in October 1992, Anthony sold me number 19 tractor in a lease option to purchase deal. Basically it saved him paying taxes on wages. I was a contractor. But when A & G folded, my tractor #19 was seized by collectors. Now, if I could raise $25,000.00 I could buy my truck back. Dad would not load the money to me. He hated me being a truck driver because of his experience in 1987. so for a time I lost out and would be just a driver like before.

For two weeks we were not working and I drove my car to Portland, Oregon to visit my girlfriend Seanna Webster. She stood five foot nothing and weighed ninety pounds. No hips, small breasts, with a chipmunk face, she looked like the olympic gymnast Kerri Strug. We met on the dance floor of Jubitz truck stop and I invited her to go with me to deliver at Waremart in Salem. We fucked like rabbits. Her mother looked after her two young children while she spent time with me. I was to keep calling in to see when our new company had clearance to start hauling product.

A couple days of being with her was enough. I called in to find that they were looking for someone to fly down to Yuma, Arizona to rescue a load and a driver that was sick. Not for our company but for for Gene Tripp trucking, our competitor in Yakima. What I didn't know was Anthony told his dispatcher not to send me. When I was asked to go, of course I couldn't say no. We truckers have to look out for each other. I drove back to Yakima and parked my car. The dispatcher took me to the Yakima airport. Flown to Portland, Oregon to catch a larger plane to Sacramento to switch planes to Los Angeles LAX and be put into a smaller plane to Yuma. My father being a snowbird living in Yuma, picked me up at the airport and drove me to the Texaco truck stop where the yellow Peterbilt 379 tractor was hooked to a fully loaded 48 foot refer. Spent a little time with dad before leaving with the rig.

I knocked on the door and a familiar face stared back at me. Dwight wasn't sick! He had over loaded his trailer with lettuce and decided to pretend he was sick. Six thousand pounds overweight! Looking at his bills, I knew the warehouse foreman and called him on the phone. He could take it off, but not accept the product back because it was too old to re-sell it. Oh well!

Dwight acted sick for his boss when he called in. he was also a lease to purchase driver. Beautiful rig! Maybe that is why Anthony didn't want me to drive a Gene Tripp company semi. Afraid I would jump ship.

Knowing I was over loaded made it simple for me to choose my-our routes home. Drove up Hwy 95 to Blythe, California and up to Needle past the place I had put my second victim. Turned back toward Barstow and up to Las Vegas, Nevada. Picked up Hwy 95 again in Vegas and drove north to Reno.

We fueled in Reno at a Pacific Pride fueling station. I called home and Anthony answered. He was pissed to hear I was on the load. Really pissed to hear it was not about being sick.

Drove up Hwy 395 toward Susanville, California up 395 to the Hwy 31 to La Pine, Oregon. North on Hwy 97 past Bend and Madras Oregon, crossing the Columbia River at Bigg's Junction. Climbed the hill to Hwy 14 heading east and north on the Horse Heavens Road taking me to Prosser, Washington, avoiding two scales.

Had left Yakima, Arizona at about 9:00 pm and drove into Gene Tripp's yard in Yakima at 7:00 AM a day and a half later. When I told Gene about the over loaded trailer, he said he had known it. He would have had me deliver the load to Seattle. Told him that would have been easier to get to than Yakima. He paid me just $200 to deliver Dwight back to him. Anthony sent his son-in-law to pick me up. We were back in business.

So a friend of Anthony Silva's had trucks in his fleet. Loyd had heard I was buying #19 and gave me the same deal with #22, the exact same semi as #19. both bought at the same time in 1989. a plum colored Peterbilt 359 series. 400 Cat motor, 15 speed transmission, 244 inch wheelbase and 48 inch sleeper with a varshield on top. Running 24.5 low pro tires. A really pretty hard to miss truck.

All in all it sounds good being an owner operator of my own truck. But as a lease purchase, I am at the mercy of the company handing out loads. The good paying loads going to their company trucks. The leasers get the rest. Sure, I kept busy. Busy moving cheap freight and deadheading hundreds of miles to cover the asses of the company.

It was late April, early May 1993 when the heavy rains pounded California. My boss had sent me to Salinas empty from Yakima to pick up a load of produce fro Seattle. Angry of being empty for over 700 miles, it didn't fit well with me knowing several of the company trucks were loaded and sent to Arizona. The heavy rains forced everyone to seek shelter where ever they could.

I pulled into Corning, California and parked behind the Petro truck stop building. By chance I got a parking spot close to the south entrance. Left my truck idling with clearance lights on, I ran into the building to find it was extremely crowded. Made my way over to the 'Iron Skillet' restaurant and looked about for an open seat. By chance, I saw several people leave a booth and ran over to it and sat down before the waitress had time to clear the dirty plates. Three other drivers came over and asked to join me.

'Okay.'

We introduced ourselves as our waitress cleared our table. I'm a people watcher and I carefully looked over the crowded restaurant to check out all that was happening. That is when I spotted her. My next victim. All that needed to happen was for her to want to get into my truck. People were staring at her, pointing fingers at her, telling every waitress to get rid of her. Why? She looked like a drowned rat that climbed out of the darkness and sat at the counter staring at plates of food walking by. Starving and no money to get anything. To people looking to sit down, she was the problem. The staff could not feed her. That would cause others to expect to be fed there. The homeless drug addict was out of the rain and caused a problem to customers for just being there to see.

I talked to the other drivers at my table. Told them we were about to get the best service in the place. They looked at me puzzled.

'In your dreams.'

Our waitress came over to take our orders. One by one she asked each man what they wanted. Then she looked at me.

'See that woman sitting at the counter?' I pointed to her and I could see my waitress looked perplexed. 'Let me buy her whatever she wants. Just don't tell her who paid for it. I don't want a lost puppy following me.' Then I gave her my order.

A broad smile came over her and she said, 'Thank you!'

The other drivers thought I had lost my senses.

'Just watch and wait. You'll see this place change as soon as people see her eating something.'

The waitress went to her to tell her a customer bought her a meal. To order anything she wanted. The wet woman looked around the room hoping to see who. Then ordered a soup and a sandwich. The waitress told the other waitresses and cooks what that nice man over at me had done. One by one each waitress came over to refill our coffee and to say, 'Thank you' to us all for helping them out. I kept an eye on my victim. My meal arrived and I ate it quickly. I wanted to be ready for when she got up and moved. As soon as she looked like she was done, and every body had quit pointing, I got up to pay for our meals.

She passed me in the hall and entered the restroom. I stood by other truckers in the lobby, noticing another driver watching her and watching me watch her. Could see the wanting in his eyes. He wanted her too. But I had the edge. Minutes later she walked out and over to the glass doors of the southern entrance staring out into the heavy rain coming down, dreading walking out into it to find another place to stay dry. I walked over and stood by her.

'You didn't have to buy just a soup and a sandwich. You could have ordered a steak.'

She just stood there waiting for my punchline.

'I'm heading to Salinas to get a load of produce. Have to be there by morning. I really hate this rain.'

'My sister lives in Sacramento.'

We both just stood there as she hoped I'd absorb her question. We were not in hurry. Didn't want her to feel rushed. After just a few minutes of silence I spoke up.

'I'm going past Sacramento. I guess I could give you a ride there. If you decide to ride along. I'll be leaving when you see my headlights come on. I have some paperwork to do that will take me a few minutes.'

Not waiting for an answer, I walked out to my truck and sat in the driver's seat making sure she saw me drawing lines in my logs. All the while I eyed her looking of at me. Turned on my headlights and shut off my inside light, put the truck into gear and started to move ahead. Trap set!

Her mind made up, she bolted from those glass doors and ran to my truck, got in and smiled at me.

'I have some things over there in that field.'

she waited for me to say something and didn't.

'Oh hell,' she said. 'I won't be needing it.'

We pulled out onto Interstate 5 going south. As we drove the heat on in my truck dried her hair. Under dry hair, she actually was very cute to look at. She became very talkative. Even flirting with me.

We drove south on I-5 to the Williams area rest area and I pulled in telling her I had to stop to pee. She stayed in the truck while I got out and let loose behind the cab. The heavy rain pelted my truck. Got back in and told her to move into sleeper. This wasn't her only rodeo. She knew to expect a sexual encounter with whomever gave her a ride.

I leaned down to kiss her and she said, 'I just don't want to get pregnant.'

She really got into this. Had taken off my clothes and upon seeing me, she grabbed a hold of Keith Jr and began giving a hand job, but too hard.

'Softer, not so hard.'

She just didn't know what I meant.

'Don't grab me so tightly.'

Think she hoped to get me off with just a hand job. Continued to pull her out of all of her clothes and we laid there together making out. She spread her legs and allowed me to enter her and we worked together to get me off. Like she had asked, I pulled out to keep my seeds from staying in her. After just a few minutes, I was hard again and entered her again. At this time, I didn't know her name. Didn't want to know. Knowing their names made it harder to kill them.

We had spent a good two hours there at the Williams rest area. Got dressed and just as she finished putting all of her clothes on, I leaned down and put my fist into her neck and pushed down hard for four minutes.

She hadn't seen it coming. Now what to do? I continued down I-5 to Santa Nella and turned west on Hwy 152 toward Gilroy, the garlic capital of maybe the world, depending on who you ask. Crested the pass all the while looking for her resting place. About a mile west of the summit on the right side is a wide turn out I could park in.

Had to make a walk around the area to see where to put her. Found a pile of boulders to the north of the lot next to the hillside. Returned to my truck and carried her body over to the boulders and tossed her behind them. As I tossed her, the yellow and black rubberized small flashlight snapped off of my wrist and went flying to somewhere. Returned to my semi just in time to see another semi park next to me. Before he could stop, I pulled back on to Hwy 152 and drove to the Shell truck stop at Gilroy next to Hwy 101. in the morning I bought new bedding because she had soiled my blankets.

(A truck driver would find her body a few weeks later, what was left of it that the coyotes hadn't eaten. The coroners report would say she died of an overdose.)

Early on in 1993, Senna Webster and I had broken up when I came to Portland's Jubitz truck stop to see her dancing and kissing on another truck driver. Confronting her, she blamed me for not calling first to let her know I'd be in town. Can't make this shit up!

One morning at the Burns Brothers truck stop in Troutdale I'd meet Julie Winningham and offer her a ride. She climbed into my rig and we made a run down to Irvine, California and back to Troutdale. Julie looked like Maggie, the woman on the sitcom called 'Northern Exposure', filmed in the small town of Roslyn, Washington. A real bitch at times like Roberta had been.

We had parked at Bakersfield when Julie looked at me and said, 'I just got to thinking. No one knows I'm with you. You could rape me and strangle me and no one would even know.'

That very night we spent in a motel and fucked like you know- rabbits. Didn't have to rape her. If anything, she raped me. Back in Troutdale, she got into her car and drove back over to Washington to live in a house. A few weks later I got a call. She needed a place to live. Cleared it with Jerry and Janet for Julie to use a spare bedroom. I heard it from Jerry. He was only allowing Julie to live there hoping to be able to fuck her. That may be all three would have a sex party. What ended up happening is Janet and Julie sat around getting high on marijuana eating up our money. Julie was asked to leave and I lost track of her.

About a month before I met Julie, my ex wife complained to the courts that her car, the 1984 Mercury Topaz was not working out. She tells the court she needed my Station Wagon. And the court agreed with her and I lost it to her. She did however not be allowed the Mercury Topaz and I got it back. It took me several hundred dollars to make the car as good as new. Rose just put gas in cars and drove. After Julie left Jerry's home, I turned the Mercury Topaz over to him to help pay for her stay there. Even paid to have the title changed over to Jerome Day. What thanks did I get? He claimed in his divorce of Janet that she was having an affair with me. And he tossed all of my property at his house into the trash. Gave the Indian sweater my mother knitten for me to a relative of his. A real asshole (Years after I came to prison, Jerry wrote me to tell me the car finally broke down after it went over 250,000 miles. He seemed angry that the car I gave him didn't last longer.) He had yelled at me on the phone to never speak to him again. But months later, that would all change.

Pacific North trucking didn't ;ast long. By April 1993 we were now leased to Ranger Transportation of Jacksonville, Florida. We all had to get our hazmat endorsement on our licenses to be able to haul bombs- military stuff. Shortly after killing my Jane Doe at Williams rest area, Ranger took over and our bos opened a Ranger outlet for loads to all points. My travels had me going through Nevada a lot. I'd stop in at the Stockman's Casino in Fallen, Nevada and met a nice woman named Karen Ruiz. She had once been married to a mexican guy. A local in Fallen. Out in my truck, she gave great head. Took her false teeth out and gave me a ol' Gummy. If you've never had a Gummy you don't know what you are missing out on.

I'm not sure exactly the date this episode happened. I had loaded up with military supplies from the depot in Umatilla, Oregon and dropped it off in the military base in Hawthorne,

Nevada. Made arrangemnets with Karen to meet her at Stockman's Casino at 9:00 AM to play nickel keno, along with her brother and his wife.

That morning I arrived at Fallen and found an ATM machine to cash in several hundred dollars to play keno. Nickels and live. Parked across the street pointing east next to the mobile home sales yard. Stockman's security cameras were pointed out in my direction. At about 6:30 AM I entered the casion and actually had breakfast in the company of the owner.

After breakfast I went to the nickel keno machines to play and wait for them to arrive. They came in at 9:00 AM and Karen sat across from me. Using my tracking number #1601, I bought into the live games every once in a while.

Are you familiar with keno?

Each ticket bought has the time and date purchased as well as my tracking number. I always get a tracking number to keep track of money I spend versus money I win. Good for taxes.

Karen and I were flirting all morning and playing keno when at about 12:30 pm we heard a page.

'Will the driver of the purple semi come to the front desk?'

'No what?'

No telling what it would be about. I left Karen there and walked to the front desk to see a cop standing there.

'What seems to be the problem?'

He pointed outside and I went out in front of him.

'Up against the wall! I need to search you!'

Two cop cars behind my trailer and one in front. All with flashing lights. He read me my rights and like in Corning, I talked to him. For the life of me I had no idea what was going on. I had no murders in Nevada.

He told me what I was being accused of. About an hour before, I had fueled my truck at a truck stop about 20 miles away and drove off without paying for the 100 gallons of fuel.

'I've been here all morning.'

He just looked at me, 'Really?'

'I can prove it to you! My truck doesn't have 100 gallons in its tank.'

We walked over and I pulled the fuel cap off and used a stick to dip the tank. It showed maybe eight inches deep.

He wasn't impressed by it and said, 'We have witnesses telling us it was your truck.'

'Here', I pulled open the hood and put my hand on the cold motor's turbo. 'If I had been driving in the last hour, I couldn't touch this without burning my hand.'

He had his witnesses and didn't want to hear my excuses.

'Who are your witnesses?' I asked.

We walk to the lead car and there are two girls in the back seat. Both yell at me, 'That's him! He's the one!'

Then it hits me to ask, 'Do you play keno?'

He admitted he loved to play keno.

'What time do they say I was at there ruck stop stealing fuel?'

He leaned in and asked them and their answer was right at 11:45 AM.

I pulled out my keno tickets, 'See, I'm here at 11:30 buying this one. I am here at 12 now buying this one. And the truck stop is 20 miles away? I'm not flying the Starship Enterprise here!'

He looks disappointed and rasies his right hand in the air and twirls his index in a circle and all of the flashing lights are turned off and the cops are gone. No apology, no nothing!

Behind me a large crowd had spilled out of Stockman's including Karen and the owner of the casino. I told him and them what they were accusing me of and he went to his security camera. The cop car that was in the lead had been parked behind my trailer at 11:00 AM. This was a set up to do something. My trailer has Floridaplates on it. Maybe a set up to take money from an out of state trucker. Your guess is as good as mine. Maybe when you readers drive through Fallen, Nevada, you can stop and ask the owner of the casino. I'm sure he filed a complaint against the police for this.

Karen would eventually move to a mobile home in the worlds largest mobile home park just a little north of Reno called Sun Valley or something like that. I'd continue to stop in to see her to get her world famous gummies. What a treat!

At the same time I dated Karen, I also dated a woman called 'Legs'. She worked as a keno runner for the Western Village casino by the 76 truck stop in Reno. Had taken her home once and kissed her a couple times, waiting for my chance to have her. But some other trucker took her with him. My loss.

And at the time I dated both of them, I also dated Adrian Meyer, a keno runner of the Oasis Casino in Mesquite, Nevada. I was looking for love in all the wrong places.

In the early spring of 1994, I met with my brother Brad, my accountant to see how I was doing owning my truck. He tells me I'm $6,000 in the hole! His advice was to pull the plug on it or get better paying freight. I chose to pull the plug.

The Letters

Again, I'm not sure exactly when I did this. It was either late 1993 or early 1994 when I was driving through Toppenish, Washington late at night around midnight. Decided to pull my semi into the parking lot in front of Hop Grower's Supplies clip plant, parking my truck's nose up to the doors. Got out and used my key to open it up and walk in to look over the press. Turned on the lights and compressor. Noticed there were no jectors around to put in one to be able to run the press.

The ejectors were aluminum machined pieces of metal with a chromium tip on them to be on a cylinder forced by air to push the clips off of the dies onto a conveyor belt and into boxes. Each cost about $200.00 to make one at a time, it would be into the thousands. Not having one there, I had always wanted to try to eliminate ejectors using just air. Took the cylinder apart, removing the guts of it and placed a copper tube where the ram came out, pointed it at the presses dies. That way when the can told the valve to send air to the cylinder to push it out and to bring it back in, the dies would get two shots of high presser air blasts.

Took me about 2 hours to put it all together and run the press one punch at a time until I saw it was working. Then I let the press run with every second a punch came down and air shot the clips to the conveyor. Made about ten boxes when I noticed a flashlight at the door. Had opened the large doors by a crack to be able to see if anyone was messing with my semi. The cops were here. Stopped the press and went to the door to talk to them.

'Are you supposed to be here?'

I gave them a short history lesson on the W shaped clip and who invented it. Showed them my key and explained I had an open invitation to come to check over the machines at any time.

'You can call Ken up to see if I'm telling the truth.'

They left satisfied I was. You can bet they wrote everything down just in case.

I ran the press until about seven that morning,, shut it down and drove over to Hop Grower's Supply.

'Ken, you can call up the machine shop to stop making ejectors. I got the press running on just air!'

He drove me back over to the plant and I used my key to get in. started up the press to show him it worked.

'Have a nice day!'

Ken called my father and told him the news. Dad drove down to see it run. He only changed the pressure on the air compressor to satisfy Ken that it will be okay. He told me later that I probably saved Ken ten thousand dollars a year changing it to air.

In March 1994 I sat in Selah talking with family and missing my children. Trucking just wasn't working. Sure I loved being over the road, but it came at a cost. And then there was the serial killer factor.

Victims were too easy to come my way. I remember once telling- no asking Jerry about murder.

'Hey Jerry! I'm killing people and I just don't know how to stop. It's taking over my life. What do you think I should do?'

And Jerry tells me to carry my heavy bag with me and hit it when I got the impulse to kill. He was on a good track, but honestly I believe he thought I was pulling his leg. Keith a serial killer? Nah!

Get better freight? I'd have to stay on the east coast. Certainly would have to stop using Ranger's New Yakima office for loads. They were used to stealing percentages off loads before giving it through Ranger and getting another percentage before us drivers got the load. And of course nothing had changed when good loads were available. Company trucks got them. I remember another driver hauling for A & G told me to get away from them. Branch out to get your own loads. Too much much!

Yes, I called up Ranger and told them I was no longer an owner and gave the truck back to Loyd. (Years later I regretted the decision. Should of at least give it another year or two. Besides, I gave away $10,000 of payments to the truck.)

with the money I had left, I bought a 1982 Chevrolet Malibu four door car and drove to Newberg, Oregon to live with Jerry Day in an apartment behind the 'Hoover House!' historic landmark. Jerry and I had re-connected as friends even though I had told his parents why he divorced his wife Janet. Not that she loved me, but because of their life style.

For the next few weeks I'd try to land a job running heavy eqipment. Had some very good offers and some not so good. My problem was I had been out of the construction business for a lon time. Everything changes and we all have to keep up with it. I had been trucking and new ways of doing things had lapped me. I was no longer the veteran on the job. I was certainly struggling. However, some welding jobs came along and that I could do.

While I sat at breakfast every morning reading the Oregonian Newspaper, I still wondered about those two crazy people in prison for my first murder. Perry Mason just didn't show up at their trial to solve it, proving they didn't do it. What could I do? Certainly I didn't want to go to jail. Maybe write a letter to the courthouse telling them they got it all wrong. Do it anonymously and give them details only the real killer could know.

(What I could not know, was all of the evidence I could come up with had been used in her trial. By design, to keep the real killer from proving Multnomah prosecutors knew Laverne and Sosnovske were actually innocent.)

In writing a letter to the court, I made the same mistake that Pavlinac did when she called the cops to tell them Sosnovske was Bennett's killer. I went to the local phone book and looked up the address to the courthouse. Being in Washington county, I sent the letter to the Washington County courthouse. Not to Multnomah county where it needed to go.

And just like Pavlinac's call to the Clackamas Sheriff's Office, my letter to the Washington County courthouse was re-directed to the proper prosecutor at Multnomah county, Michael Schrunk.

What did District Attorney Michael Schrunk do? He showed it to ADA Jim McIntrye and Keith Meisenheimer and all three tossed it into a file as a hoax. Granted, if Sosnovske and Pavlinac were not in custody and no one had been arrested, the information would have been taken seriously. And again had the case been open, I would never have sent the letter. This was not a cat and mouse game. Just letting the court know a mistake had been made.

Do any of you remember the Paul Harvey news broadcasts? In the letter to the Washington County courthouse, I wanted confirmation they read it by posting a response on Paul Harvey's noon hour show over the radio. Have been an avid listener to Paul Harvey since 1980.

'Good morning Americans! Stand by for news!'

Not hearing it on Paul Harvey news, I wondered why. Maybe it wasn't being taken seriously. Staring down into the newspaper looking for a job, it hit me. Reach out to everyone by writing a letter to the Oregonian Newspaper.

A strange feeling came over me. Have you ever had that feeling you get knowing if you did something it could be bad? A dread feeling! That sending this letter could turn out really bad? As I sat there holding the drop box lid open, I had that feeling. The hair on the back of my neck tingled or even stood up in fear. Should I or shouldn't I? I felt the same way in 1988 when I stood over a river and 50 feet below me as I leaned over ready to dive into the cold water below. Letting go would be the hardest part. I dropped the letter in the box. Then drove back to Newberg.

'What was in the letter?' you ask. Well, thank you for asking. To be honest, I don't remember all that I said in the letter. I didn't want to put stuff in it so Lt. Tragg could arrest me. I needed to cover points in the Bennett case to push Multnomah prosecutors to have another look into it. And I also needed to add power to the search by providing locations where to find four more bodies, proving I was *'dead* serious', pardon the pun. Mostly an exaggeration of material to talk about things that could not be true and believed to be true about a sexual sadist terrorizing the United States. Told them I drove trucks. The body north of Blythe, California, the body found behind GI Joes in Salem, Oregon, the body found behind the Blueberry Hill Cafe in Livingston, California and the body found in the rock pile north of Hwy 152 going to Gilroy, California. There were a lot of filler material to throw off who I could be.

Days went by and I just didn't hear Paul Harvey talk about it and my money was running out. Had to go back to work and construction in Portland just wasn't doing it for me. I would hire on to Systems Transportation in Spokane, Washington driving flatbed trailers in all 48 lower states and some provinces in Canada.

I would leave Newberg before any of the editorials came out in the Oregonian Newspaper, written by reporter Phil Stanford. He believed the killer was real! He gave the killer the name of 'The Happy Face Killer' because of a smiley face on the letter. One smiley face on one letter and I'm the Happy Face Killer! Go figure!

So the letter landed on Phil Standford's desk and immediately he took copies of it to be sure he had a copy that the police couldn't take. As it happened, Multnomah county seized the letter I sent as evidence. They wanted to bury it in a file so not to reopen the case.

Multnomah prosecutors would tell the many press requests to fuck off. The Bennett case was closed and they had the right people in prison. Every week Phil Stanford reached out to the Oregonian readers asking to help solve these cases. And soon the DA's office responded by asking the Oregonian's boss to terminate the many editorials Phil Stanford was printing. At first it fell on deaf ears. Stories like this sold newspapers. The Happy Face Killer was out there! Lions, tigers and bears!- oh my!

Then a woman from Bend, Oregon called Stanford to say her estranged ex husband was the Happy Face Killer. No shit! Another ding bat woman wanted to get rid of the man in her life by using police to do it. The next editorials in the newspaper explored her claims and it caused a frenzy over at Multnomah county district attorney's office. 'Something had to be done!'

DA Michael Schrunk put Det. John Ingram and Det. Al Carson on it. To go to Bend, Oregon to solve not the Bennett case, but to solve a serial killer's cases. Now think about it? Multnomah county was sending men over into Deschutes county to solve cases not in their jurisdiction if we are to believe they were not there to re-open the Bennett case. They showed up in Deschutes county and tailed the man his ex wife said was the killer. After a couple weeks they came to the conclusion she was just like Laverne, trying to be rid of her man. Of course, their report said other stuff.

I believe the letter scared them at Multnomah county. They feared the killer could be caught by another jurisdiction and could maybe prove they arrested the wrong people. They were there to cover their asses. If he proven to be the HFK, they would have killed him on the trip home to the county jail. Case closed!

I know what you're thinking. Why didn't anyone from the other four cases the HFK talked about, go over to Bend to try to solve their cases? Because the Multnomah county DA told them they would be handling the investigation to see if her claims were real. So fuck off!

Phil Stanford kept writing his editorials and it caused lots of people to talk, to ask questions. Phil had to be forced to stop. Pressure came to the Oregonian from the paper's owners, the LA Times Newspaper. Stop printing them! Stop looking into the Bennett case or you'll be fired! Pretty strong! Stanford ignored the order and he was fired.

Every time I drove into the Portland area, I'd hear over the radio about another Ted Bundy driving a truck and killing women all over the United States. And there I was parked at the Burns Brothers truck stop in Troutdale talking to 'Ma', an older lady working the cash register of the B & B restaurant. I've always liked her. Even did some flirting with her and her daughter that also worked there. She was really scared to go out to her parked car alone when she got off of work at 10:00 pm.

'Will you walk me to my car Keith?'

Told her to wave me over and I'd be 'Happy' to walk her over to her car. She held onto my arm as I escorted her to her car.

'My truck is over there. Why not come with me and I'll do my best to curl your toes.'

One night I thought she was going to take me up on it. Normally a laugh and she'd look up at me and smile, let go of my arm and start her car. I'd stay there until it warmed up and she put it into gear. We waved each other a goodbye. We can laugh at this now.

I was protecting her from me. (Years later while I'm in prison here at OSP, Ma's son was doing time here and had her on the phone, handed it to me and we laughed over those times.)

not really sure exactly when I took a load of aluminum coils of tread bright to a building in Tampa, Florida. Could be late July early August 1994. I got unloaded by 7:30 AM eastern standard time. My watch said 3:30 AM. We log our log books to the time zone we live in. not change time zones every time we cross them. That would be 'time travel'! Imagine standing over the line and jumping forward and back yelling eleven-o-clock, twelve-o-clock, eleven-o-clock, twelve-o-clock. Like magic! But it would sure screw up a log book. I drove over to the 76 truck stop off of Interstate 75 by Tampa, Florida. I remember the last time I had been to Florida. Back in 1993 I hauled a load of pears to the Publix warehouse in Lakeland. Unloaded and drove to the 76 off I-75 in Tampa. The only parking spot I could find was right up front next to the frontage road. At about ten that night, I spotted a woman walking to the parking lot and she had to pass by my trailer. Got out and escorted the African-American hooker into my sleeper. She was beautiful with her nappy hair and great body dressed in spandex top to bottom.

We sat down and she stares at me and says, 'You're not a serial killer, are ya?'

True fucking story!

At hearing her question I laughed at her. She seemed to be distressed over my response.

'No darling,' I told her, 'I'm not a serial killer tonight.'

We got down to business. Whatever she wanted I was ready to pay it. $20.00! Hell, I tossed her $30, wondering where she was going to put it. Her spandex fit extremely tightly on her. She took off a shoe and placed it under the shoe's sole. Turned off the dome light and we fumbled in the dark taking each other's clothes off and all the while kissed and made out. Every sexual undertaking I had with an African-American woman had been wonderful.

After our sex, I hated to see her get dressed and let her walk out of my life. Almost asked her to see of she wanted to go trucking with me. Had I taken her home, my father, the prick would not accept her color into our family. I have never seen what the problem is.

She was standing out in the entrance of the parking lot of the 76 truck stop, dressed in flower pattern dress that showed off her fabulous figure. On the luggage tote beside her was three pieces of blue samsonite suitcases. There were truck drivers walking up to her trying to get her to go with them. I had parked next to the restaurant and my truck's front end pointing out to her.

I just had to ask and walked out to talk to her.

'Where do you need to go?'

She tells me she is heading to Lake Tahoe, Nevada.

So I tell her, 'I'm out of Washington state. I'm over there and waiting to hear from my boss where I'll be going and why. I'm sure I will be able to get you to at least Nevada. Lake Tahoe is a little out of our route. Hopefully I'll be leaving here in an hour. If you want to ride with me, I'll be in the truck stop.'

And I pointed to my tractor. Turned around not waiting for an answer. Didn't want to sound pushy.

She stood there making up her mind while I walked off to the restaurant. Remember back then we had phones at every table in the restaurants. No cell phones. Sat down and ordered ice tea and called my boss, my dispatcher from Safeco. Systems bought out Safeco trucking.

'Nothing yet Keith, call me back in an hour.'

And that is how it went. For a couple more hours.

About an hour after talking to her out in the hot sun, I looked up to see her standing them staring down at me.

'I thought you said we would be leaving in an hour?'

And so I asked her to have a seat and drink some ice tea. Told her about trucking and how it worked. As soon as I have a load to go to, we will be off. But until then, sit down and relax. She's a pretty girl with shoulder length hair that is shaggy- curly- unkempt. Could smell her body odor. Too much walking in the hot sun. finally another call mead, we had a load to go to in Cairo, Georgia to pick up conduit pipe going to Boise, Idaho and Spokane. The boss gave me directions to the plant so I didn't have to call later to get it.

At the truck, I placed her three pieces in the lockable side doors under the sleeper's bed. We got in and she looked at all the extra room we had in the cab and sleeper.

In awe, she said, 'Hey, can we go back to Miami to pick up the rest of my stuff?'

'No Susanna, we have to get going. We have to get to Cairo before the plant closes at midnight.'

She looked disappointed not to hear we would go back to Miami. Even if I had enough time, no way! Dropping her off at say Wells, Nevada, she would then be stuck with all of the extra stuff she added to carry the rest of the way to Lake Tahoe. We pulled onto I-75 North. Drove about 80 miles to another 76 truck stop to fuel up.

Systems ran off of a 'trender' credit card system when it came time to fuel. We carried a book full of places we could use the card. Pulled into the fueling island and filled it up. Told her we will be showering here and even eating our meal. Got her a shower key and towel and pointed her to a stall to use. Told her to meet me in the restaurant as quick as she washed herself. She ordered spaghetti all you can eat and tucked away almost three plates of it.

We were the last truck to be loaded of the Cairo, Georgia plant. After I secured my load, I went into the driver's lounge to get her. I called her.

She let out a blood curdling scream! And she kept screaming until she saw it was me.

'We have to get going.'

It was right at midnight eastern time when we left the building. They shut off the light after we left.

Looking over a map, I decided to back drive twenty miles to a road heading back to Florida's Interstate 10 West. I wanted to cruise on an interstate, not puddle jump cars on small two lane roads in Georgia and Alabama. Just get it up to 60 mph and set it on cruise control.

It was about 3:00 AM eastern time when I decided to pull into a rest area so when I pee, the woman with me had a place she could feel comfortable to pee. Driving with Roberta taught me to do this. Pulling over to pee on the side of the road got me some punches in my thigh and bad looks...always provide the pussy a place to sit down and pee. I pulled into Exit 18 and followed signs over to the rest area.

The only parking space for me to park in was behind the rest area's security guard. In all of the rest areas in Florida I've been to, there is always a security guard there to chase away panhandles and hookers. In this one, he drove a small pickup with a canopy on it.

I leaned back and spoke to Susanna, 'We are at a rest area. If you need to use the restroom, I'll walk you in.'

She wiped the sleep from her eyes and moved to her passenger seat. I get out and walked over to her door and she jumped down to me.

'Who is that?'

'He's security. All Florida rest areas have them.'

I did my business and waited for her to come out. Then we went back to the truck. She sat in the seat as I got into mine. Keith Junior was telling me to make a move. No mess. I pulled her from her seat and pushed her into the sleeper. Helped her out of her dress and layed down with her. Her body shined in the light from outside. The security man had no clue what I was doing. He sat in his pickup oblivious to us. I kissed her and like Taunja, she never kissed back. Her lips remained closed. Went down to lick her nipples and then I heard her say something.

'Get this over with and let me out of this truck!'

I climbed on top of her and I was hoping she would spread her legs, but she kept them tightly together. If I wanted to fuck her, I'd have to force the issue. I wasn't into forcing her to fuck. I had gotten what I wanted. A look at her breasts and touched her lips. She would live with me forever in my mind allowing me to masturbate to the memory of her.

'Get dressed!'

She pulled on her dress and put her shoes on. Could hear her mumbling to herself. Something about not trusting men. Dressed, I pushed her back down and on top of her I kissed at her some more and felt her body with my hands. She didn't kiss back. Put my fist into her throat and pushed the life out of her.

I walked up to the security man and asked him if he could move so I could get going west. He got out of my way and I drove back along the road to the interstate. A small all night store to my right with several cop cars parked there, I pulled over and grabbed my thermos to get it filled with coffee. Spent a few minutes talking to the locals and got into my truck and went searching for a place to put her. The sun would be coming up soon.

At Exit 11, I pulled off of the I-10 and parked on the on ramp as far up as I could on its shoulder. Got out and looked for her resting place. Before taking her out of my sleeper, I placed two 14 inch long plastic ties around her neck. One would not fit. Had to use two to go completely around her neck and pulled tight. Why? She had eaten a lot of damn spaghetti.

The sun was coming up when I pulled onto Westbound I-10. At Exit 10 is a Texaco truck stop I would normally stop at. Not tonight! Felt a need to keep moving to be past the Alabama weigh station before it opened. If it opened on Saturday. Past Alabama, I drove maybe another hundred miles before finding a truck stop to park at to sleep. When I woke up, I went through her bags to see what I could keep. I would keep her radio boombox and her luggage tote and toss everything else away. She had pieces of bark and moss along with tarot cards. All of her clothes were soiled. Walked over to a dumpster and tossed all three suitcases away, being sure to empty them first. Eventually, I'd give the radio to Stephanie, the daughter of my girlfriend in Mesquite, Nevada. And toss the luggage tote in the trash.

All I kept from my victims are the memories of them being killed by me. It is enough to lay in bed and thank about what I could have done to each and every one of them.

Every time I came a calling to Andy Meier in Mesquite, Nevada, she asked me to get a job to live with them in a mobile home. Adrian 'Andy' Meier worked as a keno runner at the Oasis Casino. I once gave her a thousand dollars after hitting a jackpot. A nice woman with almost red hair cut short. She lived with her mother and daughter. Right after I killed Susanna in Florida, I quit Systems and moved in with them. Had gotten a job driving heavy equipment for the local construction company building a new golf course and housing plots in a canyon north of town.

My sleeping area would be on a couch with Andy. The L shaped bed had me on one end, and Andy on the other. For room and board, I paid $600.00 a month to help out. Yes Andy is beautiful and all that, but I fell into a mess living with these three girls. I bought a washer and dryer to keep my clothes clean, only to be told I couldn't use it because my greasy clothes were too dirty. Had to use the laundry in town. My car left a few oil drops on their driveway and her mother had a fit over that. And they had no car!

At night, well that is a whole other issue. Mother ran around in a see through nighty, even woke me up a few times by leaning over me and letting little boobs stare me in the face. One morning I woke up to find her sucking my dick! Yes, I let her finish, I had to. It was her home. She must have thought I was her dead husband came back to life. Several times I woke up to Andy and we got to kissing and she had me eat her pussy. I'd lick her and rub my nose into it as I licked her. She never allowed me to fuck her. A hand job here and there would have to do until we were married. Like that was going to happen while mom was alive!

We were sitting on her couch one evening before I moved in. Mother talked about when two men robbed them. She feared they would rape Andy.

So I asked, 'Weren't you afraid they would rape you? You're a beautiful woman.'

And she said in a smile, 'I hoped they would. I haven't had sex in a long long time.'

She asked me what my intentions were with her daughter. Told her I might want to get married at some point.

And she barked back, 'Hell no! You're not white enough to marry into our family!'

Strange family! I could lick Andy's pussy, have Mother suck me off and get hand jobs and I wasn't good enough to marry.

And then twelve year old Stephanie joined in to make me want to leave. She, like my own daughter Carrie, liked me to carry her on my shoulders. One morning she wanted to go next door to a park and wanted me to carry her. I picked her up and put her on my shoulders and noticed she wasn't wearing underwear. As I walked over to the park, I felt her wet pussy rubbing up on my neck. Felt something dripping down my neck and she was grinding up against me. She knew exactly what she was doing. She is twelve! I felt I better get out of there before I killed all three of them.

Andy quit keno running and hired into Oasis's new bingo hall. I spent lots of time with her playing bingo. Old ladies would speak their mind every time I called 'Bingo!'

'He wins all of the time!'

Told my boss I had to go and stopped to say goodbye to Andy while I played bingo. My car was packed. Before I left Mesquite that day, I won like $1,600.00 playing bingo. Bought new tires for my car and drove back to Spokane to work for Systems again. Andy and I would part company a few weeks later.

At the Peterbilt plant in Denton, Texas, I had a tarped load of frame rails from Dana Corporation being delivered there. The wind was blowing hard as I pulled the tarps and rolled them up. In another Systems' truck, a woman named 'Huggy Bear' sat there watching me struggle with my tarps, finally the forklift came and pulled off my load. Was about to leave when Huggy Bear came over asking me to help her remove her tarps.

'Go ask some other driver who gives a shit! You didn't help me. I'm not helping you.'

I drove north on Interstate 35 to our regular fueling 76 truck stop. I was sitting at a booth after I had showered and called my boss when I saw at least five other Systems trucks pull in. he told me all of us were to go to Houston, Texas to pick up the same kind of load. Three 50 foot long pipes to haul to Tacoma, Washington. Huggy Bear came in and sat at my table. She introduced herself. I told her I don't call people by any nicknames. She wouldn't tell me her real name. She talked to me and not the other drivers who helped her with her load. They probably thought she would suck their dicks or something for helping. I had put her in her place.

'We all are heading to Houston to the same place. Let's convoy down there.'

'I don't convoy.' I told her.

'We are all leaving in about ten minutes.'

'Bad idea!' Looking at my watch.

They had no idea what mess they would be driving into going south into the Fortworth-Dallas area at 7:30 PM. Wall to wall traffic all the way. They all convoyed to Houston and I went to bed. Waited until almost 10:30 PM before I headed south. By then the traffic flowed all the way at the speed limit or faster. I pulled into an old truck stop several miles north of Houston. The stop could accommodate maybe forty semis. They drove to the large truck stop that holds two hundred semis. Too many problems with those places. Us older drivers love the older truck stops. Better fuel and better service.

At a magazine rack I saw what I was looking for, True Detective Crime Magazines! On a cover of a New York based magazine I saw, 'Does Oregon have another Zodiac Killer?' By Frank Hughes. I opened the magazine and there staring back at me was my letter to the Oregonian Newspaper. They were calling me the Happy Face Killer because of a smiley face on the letter.

I bought the magazine and several others. As I read the story, they talked about the Bennett case. How those two injected themselves into being arrested and later convicted. I don't remember putting the smiley face on the letter. Maybe I did. And maybe this reporter

Phil Stanford needed a name and he put it on the letter. In any event, I was the Happy Face Killer named by the reporter Phil Stanford!

In the article, I saw lots of mistakes in evidence. I decided to write a letter to the New York based editor to clear up issues. Of course I added the location to my Florida victim as proof I was the Happy Face Killer. Calling Florida my 56th victim. Okay I lied! I told other lies too! Just can't remember them all. Sent the letter from Houston and waited to see maybe an update to the story in future Detective magazines.

(To this very day as I write this, May 29th 2024, I have not seen that letter I wrote to New York come out anywhere. They got it I am sure of it. How else were they able to connect me to the Florida case before I told them I was there?)

In the morning, I arrived at the pipe plant first and the forklift driver was there waiting to get busy. I placed three pieces of lumber 4x4s eight feet long on my trailer. One in the center of my load and one over the center of my driving axles and my trailer axles. Tossed three chains next to the lumber before he placed the three fifty foot long pieces of pipe on it. I used nails to secure the wood to the trailer's deck, he took just a few minutes to place the pipe evenly on my 48 foot flatbed. Maybe ten minutes to stretch the chains as belly wraps on the pipe and was just getting done putting several straps over my load when all five of the other drivers arrived. They wanted to use my hammer and nails and I said, 'No, get your own.'

Everyone left to find wood and tools leaving Huggy Bear behind. The forklift driver came over and wanted to get her loaded, so I helped her to do what I had done. Showed her how to use two chain binders to stretch a chain tight. She didn't need to be 200 pounds to do it. We were both leaving when the others showed up with tools and lumber. I didn't have the heart to tell them the forklift driver supplied it to us.

Huggy Bear took the lead as we drove north out of the Houston area. Several miles up the road she yells over the CB radio, 'I have to stop up here to pee.' and at the next truck stop exit she pulls off of the Interstate. She notices I didn't pull in behind her and kept going.

'Hey, where are you going?'

'I don't have to pee.'

Had made it to the Amarillo 76 truck stop, fueled up, showered and ate and was sitting in my sleeper when Huggy Bear showed up next to me. She went inside and as soon as she was out of sight, I drove on to Tacoma, arriving there to get unloaded on Friday. Heard later, the other five got there on Monday, three days later. That is trucking!

Keith Hunter Jesperson
OSP 11620304
16th January 2024

Friday the 13th

Angela Subrize came to me willingly at the Ridpath Hotel in Spokane, Washington one night. Told me she was an exotic dancer, meaning she takes her clothes off so men can look up her vagina and hope to put something in it. I happened to be invited to enjoy a sexual experience by allowing her to sleep in room 425 with me. But how did I get to her? How was it, I came to being at the Ridpath Hotel? There were a lot of turns left and right to put me there to watch her walk off of the street and land just six feet away in a bar. Allowing me to convince her to come with me to my room.

There I was in System's yard of Lake Station, Indiana. The morning of January 11th, 1995. My boss there arranged for me and another driver to be at the Castle Metals yard in north Chicago by 7:00 pm that evening for a 9:00 pm loading time. We were to haul two loads of Castle Metals steel to their Los Angeles Castle Metals yard. We were there signing in and getting our bills of loading signed on time. I signed the stack of papers before getting loaded as they required us to do. Their steel going to their other yard. Simple! They load it, we secure it and truck it across the country.

I don't get paid for loading my trailer. I was getting 25 cents a mile to drive it there. If I tarp my load, I could get a little extra. If I fail to tarp a load and I'm caught, I could lose fifty dollars or more. Even get fired! System's has a snitch policy. If I see a trailer not tarped and call it in on the other driver, I could get fifty dollars. If I reported an unauthorized passenger, I could get one hundred dollars. Rules! In all of the time I drove for Systems I've never called to report a violation on another driver. Had to tell other drivers to mind their business or face the wrath of Keith.

If a load didn't require to be loaded like these steel loads, either my boss would tell me not to tarp it or the shipper told me and I'd tell my boss. We pulled over to the staging yard and waited to be called in to the very large building. While we waited, we caught up on sleep and looked over our log books.

At 10:00 pm a knock on a door woke me to see a worker tell the other driver to follow him into the building. At 3:00 AM a knock on my door by the same man had me follow him into the building. He had me drive all the way to the last bay and park within the yellow painted loading area to my left. I made it look easy placing my semi and trailer well within the yellow painted area to load. Behind me was the other Systems semi, the man that loads us is the one that had us drive into the place. Three lanes of traffic. The center lane to drive along. Loading lanes on either side to park in. at least six bays long. Huge building!

The man comes to me and tells me, ;You'll have to move over six more inches or I'm not going to be able to load you.'

He's fucking with me right?

'I'm not moving over,' I say.

And he barks back, 'I'm going on break and you better have moved over or I will not load you!'

He leaves for their break room and I turn to see the other driver wide awake sitting in his cab. Walking past his cab and see there is nothing on his trailer.

'What the fuck?'

he gets out of his cab and tells me the guy had him in the second bay on the right, then over to the third bay to the left and finally to where he was. I look down at some soapstone writings on steel on the dock at our feet reading LA Castle Metals.

'He's fucking with the both of us. This is bullshit!'

what I wanted to do to this man was to punch him in the nose. To fuck him up! Saw a spud wrench sitting there and would have loved to poke him in the heart and kill him. Trouble is he has no heart. If he did, he wouldn't fuck with us drivers. The real issue here is he believes all truck drivers are the same. That all we are capable of doing is to sit on our asses and drive. Period! He saw us as being beneath him. He had control issues. If he had been a cop, he would have been a bad cop. Pulling people over just to fuck with them. And if someone pulls a gun and shoots him, he is the victim. If I punched him in the nose, he is the victim. And I hoped he made a fist so I could light him up. I was still in shape. Ran 4 miles a day and worked out on my heavy bag. Granted the last time I fought anyone was in 1982 at the Golden Gloves that I won my division in. that was thirteen years ago. Had we gone at it, his fellow employees would have had to pull me off of him. And then of course I'd go to jail and he'd be the victim. No, to make the prick change you have to hit him where it hurts, his ego. Challenge his orders to move. Call him on his bluff. Make him be responsible for his actions.

The prick came out after his break knowing I hadn't moved because he had been watching me from the break room.

'Move over six inches or I'm not going to load you!'

'That's not going to happen. Load me where I'm parked.'

'No, move over...'

'Open the door so I can leave.'

'No, I'm not opening the door.'

'Where is a phone at?' I ask.

'What for?' He seemed puzzled.

'So I can call the police to report you are kidnapping me holding me against my will.'

'I'll just load you there!'

'Oh no, we are past that! Open the door!'

Reluctantly he pushes the button and the door opens. I drive out of the building and over to the office. Because my name is on the paperwork, I rip all of them up and toss them at the office manager.

'You people need to change your attitude!'

I left Castle Metals and drove back to Lake Station, Indiana and parked in Systems yard and went to sleep.

As it turns out, the prick panics and loads the other Systems trailer in record time. 15 minutes later, that driver drives back to Lake Station and parks next to me. The prick did a lot of back peddling after I had driven off. Questioning what had just happened to his control. He pointed to me leaving as my fault, not his. He hoped this would go away quietly. Not!

In the morning, both of us were called into the office to sit in on a conference call on speaker phone with our big boss in Spokane and Castle Metal's big boss. We both told them exactly what happened. I made a statement to Castle Metals CEO

'We get paid to drive and get products to where it is supposed to go on time. If we are messed with at our plant for hours, it is your fault why we are late. We are providing you with a service. I know sometimes things can't be avoided and there will be delays. But can't we all just work together for a common goal to get the job done?'

(I can only imagine the prick's boss calling him in to have a talk. The first thing out of his mouth is '6 inches! All of this bullshit over 6 fucking inches! Half the width of a tire! Go empty out your locker, you're fired!)

(That prick will certainly remember that learning curve the rest of his life. And I'm sure people at Castle Metals will read this book and remember it. That the prick faced a serial killer and lost!)

By mid-morning on January 12th, 1995 I had been given a two day load of steel going to Denver, Colorado and San Francisco, California. I had to get going and stay at it to make my first drop in Denver by Friday.

It was almost noon when I left Lake Station, Indiana. At almost 8:00 AM Friday morning the 13th of January 1995 I had just passed Sterling, Colorado on Interstate 76 when I heard a loud explosion.

BANG!

I looked in my mirror to see the rear left inside tire fly apart. Pieces flew every where. Pulled over and stopped, the tire, what was left of it burst into flames!

'What the hell going on!?'

Grabbed a fire extinguisher and pulled the trigger. The fire went out and immediately started back up again. Crawled under the trailer to see the broke drum white hot. I knew then I'd need lots of water to stop it. Had to separate the truck from the trailer and got busy lowering the landing gear, pulling the fifth wheel release and disconnecting the airlines and electrical connector. Pulled the burning tractor ahead of the trailer by at least 100 feet and shut it off. Got out and watched it burn.

It surreal to watch how the fire consumed one tire, then two, three and then four. I was sure police were called and then the Sterling Fire Department because I heard sirens blaring far off and coming closer. Traffic stopped in both ways. The firemen put over 500 gallons of water on the fire to stop it. A highway patrol officer called my boss for me to give him an update. Was told another Systems driver would show up soon to get the trailer to make the delivery. To wait for him. A wrecker showed up and took the semi to Denver Peterbilt after I removed my suitcase and CB radio.

The other driver showed up and made the observation that the rest area was ahead of us, not behind us. At Sapp Brothers truck stop he called the boss to explain the rest area was ahead of me.

(Why is that important? Most brake drum fires happen when a driver leaves a rest area with a locked up brake. How does that happen? Because we drive through water and when stopped, the water freezes the brake pads to the drums. If we have a frozen drum, use a hammer to vibrate the drum and free it from it's grip. What had happened to me was something else. As it turns out, the automobile slack adjuster broke and Denver Peterbilt said it was mechanical error, not driver error.)

we made the Denver drop and were instructed to drive me to our fuel stop just south of Las Vegas at Boomtown and drop me off. We arrived in Las Vegas on the 14th of January. I got a motel room and waited overnight for another team of drivers to pick me up and deliver me to Systems Fontana yard off of Cherry Ave on the 16th of January.

The Fontana boss told me to drive a semi that was planned to be returned to Spokane Peterbilt and pick up a trailer and head to California Steel up Cherry Ave to load a couple steel coils to be delivered to Spokane.

Leaving southern California over I-15 to Hwy 58 west to Mojave and then Bakersfield and north on Hwy 99 to Sacramento to Interstate 5 north to Weed and north on Hwy 97 to Hwy 14 east to Interstate 82 to Pasco, Washington and north on Hwy 395 to Ritzville and east on Interstate 90 to Spokane, arriving to deliver the two coils on the morning of January 19th, a Thursday to unload.

By 10:00 AM, I had a sit down with Systems big boss to discuss Castle Metals and the good that was done standing up to the prick. He tells me Denver Peterbilt had my truck fixed and I was scheduled to return ASAP to get it. He would be sending me and several other drivers to Ridpath Hotel for the evening. To be sure to catch the shuttle at 6:00 pm.

Normally I would drive my car to Spokane to see my kids. But my ex wife didn't want me to disrupt my children's lives on a school night. So I decided to take the shuttle to the Ridpath Hotel at six and rest for my journey back to Denver in the morning. I was given room 425, went up and settled in. I decided to go down to the ground floor bar to have a cold one. I could see the other drivers that had come with me sitting in the Hotel's restaurant. I really don't like to talk shop when I'm not over the road.

Looking out onto the sidewalk, I could do a lot of people watching. Could watch people checking in the hotel as well. Lots of airline pilots and stewardess. I saw her walk in to sit her luggage at a chair outside the hall by the check in counter and walk into the bar, not talking to the staff. She sat at a table not six feet from me. I could smell her perfume. She ordered a beer. No one had joined her, so I made my move to her.

'Mind if I sit here?'

She pointed to the chair across from her table.

'I see you haven't checked in yet. Why don't we share a room? My boss set me up in a room already. It has a big bed, big enough we both can be comfortable. Maybe buy pizza and a six pack to go. What do you say?'

She took her time to study me and then said, 'Promise me you're not going to hurt me?'

That question told me a lot. She is in the business of being with men.

'I promise we will have a good time and I will not hurt you.'

She then tells me, 'Best offer I've had since I've arrived here in Spokane.'

We got up and went to room 425. Passing the restaurant carrying her luggage, I saw the other drivers taking notice of me.

Dropped off her suitcases and went back down to the lobby and out the door to cross the street to the pizza parlor to order her pineapple and Canadian bacon pizza (my favorite too) and a six pack of Budweiser to go. Then back up to room 425 to eat and talk and then she tells me she is an exotic dancer trying to make a living. Came to Spokane with another girl. When she wasn't paying attention, the other girl split, leaving her there wondering what to do next. Walked into Ridpath and I came to her rescue. We both got into the shower first before eating pizza and me going down on her. She seemed very proud of telling me she was clean shaven down there. I took her hint and did my best to lick her where it counts as my nose rubbed her where it needed to be. Then came everything else we could think of. She certainly made an impression on me. She was selling herself to me, allowing me to enter her again and again. Rescue me!

The six 'o clock wake up call came too soon. Didn't want to leave her. But I had to. I tossed what money I had on the desk, about $35.00 and a note with my information how to reach me through my boss at Systems. (Had I not left the note, she would have survived me. Another one night stand to get away.)

At about ten that morning, I climbed into another System's semi to be taken to Denver's Peterbilt. We drove to Montana and fueled at Park City. After our meal and shower, it was my turn to drive. He told me to wake him up when I got tired. At around 7:00 AM on Saturday January 21st 1995, I woke up the driver as we were pulling into the truck stop at Cheyenne, Wyoming. After coffee and breakfast, he took over and we went to Denver's Peterbilt so I could pick up my tractor. We were shown the burned parts taken off of my truck and asked me several questions. I could remember hitting the brakes hard back when I entered I-76 from I-80 when a car cut me off. That must have been when the adjuster screwed up. But that was like 80 miles before my tire went bang. It's the little things that will stop us.

I drove over to Sapp Brother's truck stop to pick up the empty trailer left by the driver that picked me up and called to dispatch to give me a message. Drive to Pueblo, Colorado to pick up 44,000 pounds of railroad rail destined for Seattle on Monday morning.

'Oh by the way, Angela called and left you this phone number to call as soon as you can.'

I tried her number and she didn't pick up.

Made it to Pueblo and the place that loaded me with rail. Hauling railroad rail can be tricky. Brake real hard and if not properly secured, it can slide into the cab and kill me. Back in 1982 when I drove for Bighorn Trucking of Lethbridge, Alberta, a semi hauling gas pipe came to a railroad crossing on his way to Calgary. He didn't see the train was backing up over the roadway until it was too late and slammed on his brakes, jackknifing his rig. The pipe slid out and went into the trains caboose, spearing the man inside, killing him.

We set the rails on my trailer. Made sure to add chains over the nose of the two tiers of rail to make sure it couldn't slide. Plus added lots of chains and straps. No such thing as overkill when securing a load.

It was near 7:00 pm when I drove into the truck stop at Cheyenne, Wyoming. While I sat eating supper, I used the booth's phone to call up Angela. She asked me where I was. She told me her father lives in Fort Collins, Colorado. Any chance I could pick her up and take her to see him? I explained the no-rider policy with Systems.

'Oh please!'

'Okay, I'll give you safe passage to Fort Collins, Colorado to see you father.'

I made sure she gave me directions to the place she was staying at.

'When will you be here?'

'Monday morning at around 1:00 AM.'

'Monday! Why can't you pick me up sooner? Like tomorrow?'

'Listen Angela, I'm not flying the Starship Enterprise. I can't just ask Scotty to beam you up. It will take time to get there.'

had been awake since six Friday morning and it was now Saturday night. I stayed up and picked Angela up at 12:30 AM Monday and delivered the rail to Seattle by nine Monday morning. Dispatch gave me a load of cedar to be delivered to Pennsylvania as soon as I could get it there legally. Yeah right!

Everything takes time. Time to load. Time to tarp the load. And time to eat and get cleaned up. We pulled into Exit 34 on Interstate 90, Bends truck stop to have supper and have my thermos filled. A snow storm threatened the pass up ahead and I decided to keep ahead of the storm, driving until 2:00 AM on Tuesday morning, poking in the truck stop at La Grande, Oregon on Interstate 84. Only sleep was on my mind being up for 4 days. She must have thought I had died, sleeping until almost three that afternoon. We had a meal and most of the next hour I adjusted my log book. We could move, but not very far. By late January 25th, we were at Twin Falls, Idaho parked at a truck stop north of the Interstate. There is no making up sleep. The body uses what it needs and moves on. I was ready for round two with Angela inside the sleeper.

On Thursday January 26th, we were parked at Fort Bridger, Wyoming and sat in the diner having our meal.

'Have you called your father? To let him know we are coming?'

She said no.

'Do you want me to call him?'

She nodded yes and gave me his phone number. I dialed the number, paying for it with my father's AT & T calling card #728-172-0396-2222. She talked to dad and the conversation seemed a bit angry. We retired to the truck and slept. The snow storm had caught up to us. Blizzard conditions made travel slow. Late int the afternoon of January 27th, we were at Sinclair, Wyoming and suggested she made another call to her father in Fort Collins to say we will be there soon. Again the conversation was hostile.

We continued on and at Laramie before Elk Mountain, she needed to use the restroom and I pulled into the Petro truck stop. She ran in while I turned around and waited. She came back and I said, 'Hwy 30 is here. I normally drive to Fort Collins down 30 the back way, saving lots of miles.'

'I don't want to see him. Keep driving.'

We pulled back onto the interstate and climbed to the top of Elk Pass and headed to Cheyenne's Burns Brothers truck stop at Exit 377. we had outrun the snow! Last chance to go to Fort Collins.

'Last chance Angela. Fort Collins is down I-25. We still can get there from here.'

'Will you wait for me there?'

'Wait? No, I have to keep going.'

'Then I don't want to go.'

And there it was, the end of safe passage for her. All bets are off now!

It now comes down to how much longer I wanted her in the truck with me. To stay ahead of the pending blizzard, back on the interstate to Nebraska. Then I saw a rest area sign ahead on a curve. My semi hit a patch of black ice and I almost lost it on the curve to the left. Straightening it up, my semi pointed into the rest area and we parked there. Enough fun tonight. Angela made the bed and we piled into it and had round three.

When it came to pillow talk, we knew it was still early. I knew there was a Burger King not far from the rest area at Exit 58 or was it 59? We got dressed. Time to cut my losses. She stepped out of the sleeper fully dressed and I pushed her into the floor.

'You promised not to hurt me!' she yelled.

My hand went to her neck to hold her down and I said, 'Okay, I lied. Sue me. Oh, wait you won't be able to because you'll be dead. Guess what? I'm a serial killer.'

My fist pushing into her neck, she could only stare back up at me in horror. The deed was done.

'Shit!' I said out loud.

I used my dad's credit card to call her dad's place. Not once, but twice. I had to give serious thought to what to do with her body. But for now, Burger King!

Across from the large Elk in front of the Cabela's sporting goods store is the Burger King. I bought two Whoppers and sat in the truck and had a nice conversation with Angela.

'These sure are good Angela,' I laughed, 'Wish you could have tasted them.'

And then it hit me! I remembered the movie *Vacation* where Chevy Chase had tied his dog leash to the trailer hitch on his car. Forget the dog and drove off dragging the animal to death, to nothing but a leash. Some cop pulled him over and said something along the lines of poor animal never had a chance, he was running as fast as he could until he couldn't.

I pulled out my map and decided to do it past the next weigh station. Pulled into the rest area at mile marker 198. Parked at the far east part of the area away from the other trucks where very little lights were. Went out with a length of rope to tie it to my trailer and estimated where her body would be between the rear tires so no one could possibly see it there as I drove in the dark. Went back into the sleeper with a shorter rope to tie each end around each of her ankles. I taped her arms up front of her with her hands in a cross pattern. All I needed to do was to wait for the right time to pull it off.

In Nebraska at around 3:00 AM, traffic bunched up into packs of vehicles every three miles or so. All speeding along together. My plan was to slide in behind a pack and get up to cruising speed, which was slower than they were moving. Slowly the pack would leave me and the one coming up to me would take so long to do so. By then pull over and let them by, pull over and cut the rope and leave what ever was left on the shoulder. What could go wrong? Well, for one thing, Nebraska cops liked to sit in the mediums with headlights on to see what was going by. That would be fucked up!

When I felt the timing was right, I opened the sleeper from outside and grabbed the loop of rope tied to her ankles and pulled her body out and it landed with a thud. Dragged her to the middle of my trailer and positioned her face down between the tires. Tied the rope to the loop and went back into my cab to wait for the moment to pull in behind the next group of cars. As I drove out onto the interstate, I could actually feel the truck pull differently as her body dragged on the rough pavement tearing pieces of her off.

One mile, then two, then I saw the approaching pack climbing on me. At twelve miles I pulled off the road as the others passed.

Another truck driver asked, 'Are you okay?'

'I just need to pull over,' I said, ' just need to get rid of some excess baggage is all.'

I came to a full stop and jumped out. I had about 3 minutes to pull it off. Using my side-cutter pliers, I cut the rope to the trailer and pulled what was left of her to the tall grass on the shoulder. Ran back to my driver's seat and was moving ahead when the next group caught me. Not far up ahead, I saw a sign for the Grand Island exit to the 76 truck stop. Pulled in and parked. I then went to sleep.

Saturday morning January 28th 1995 I sat in the restaurant thinking I better take another route on my log books to show I wasn't even on I-84, I mean I-80. 84 turns into 80 east of Salt Lake City, Utah. Of course I didn't go to Salt Lake City, I-84 goes past Ogden, Nevada and meets I-80 coming from Nevada. I logged me dropping down to Denver and heading east on I-70 to Kansas City, Kansas to our fuel stop to wait for my log book to catch up with me.

Later that day, I'd drive east to Lincoln, Nebraska and south on I-35 to I-70 and east to Kansas City, there at Kansas City, I went through all of Angela's things. One thing caught my attention. Her key ring had about twenty keys from motels. Key 425 from the Ridpath was on it. She had been a busy girl.

'What are you asking me?'

'What was left of Angela after twelve miles?'

'I'm going to tell you what. If you ever want to lose weight, get dragged behind my truck. A sure fire weight reduction plan! She had lost 60% of her body weight. Ground off her arms, her face to her ears, her whole chest cavity was missing. Ground her down to her crotch area. Had I driven her another twelve miles, my guess she would only have her ankles left.'

(Even though I had done this to keep people from identifying her, it didn't work! When Angela was young she had broken her hip and it had been pinned together. The pin in her hip had a serial number on it, checking out medical issues, it didn't take long after her body was found to identify her.)

CHECKMATE

My memory is failing me. Can't remember parts of my life way back when. Kind of strange I can be talking to someone and something they say will generate a story from me. Have no real idea when or where, but it is a true story. Then, sitting somewhere, it will come to me where and when, but that someone is long gone. Does it matter? Getting old sucks!

Jerry Day divorced his wife shortly after Julie Winningham drove out of life in late 1993. He told me Julie one day drove away my semi, never to bring it back home. That was on par for the course with her. A free ride to everywhere.

But what about Janet? Where is she? Jerry put her and their two children on a train to Indiana to see Janet's mother. When they got off of the train, a carrier was waiting for her to hand her divorce papers. And there they stayed in the little town of Ireland, Indiana. When I lived with Jerry in Newberg, he didn't trust me to know her address. I did know the town. In February 1995, I parked my trailer down south at a truck stop and bobtailed to the small town. Stopped at the only bar in town and the bartender pointed to a house a block away.

'There'

I drove and parked out front, walked to the front door and peered inside to see Roland and Crystal along with a friend at the dining room table. Knocked and Crystal answered the door. They were both surprised to see me. I heard an earful from Roland about his father Jerry. Roland had another father before Jerry came into the picture. He, Jerry, was not happy about Janet having had a son already and kind of resented him. Personally, I thought there was some abuse going on. Not for Crystal though. She was his baby. And then the way he sent them away really soured it for them.

Crystal said, 'Boy will mom be surprised! She's at work. Follow me over to her job and let me go in first.'

We drove maybe ten miles east and parked at a restaurant. Crystal went inside to say, 'Boy do I have a big surprise for you.'

And then I walked in.

After she got off work, we went on a drive in her car. No sex. I didn't expect it. We just talked about Jerry and problems. Back at the restaurant she and I kissed goodbye. She stayed parked by my semi as it warmed up. Almost thought she would come to me. Our lives had turned in different directions. The swinger life had been Jerry's idea. His drinking would be his downfall. She had her suitcases packed and in her car for years. Remember once telling Jerry that if she left him, she could come with me. That I'd make sure she would be well looked after. That would be the last time I saw her and her children.

My boss had been called by Bonnie at the Department of Transportation office in Cle Elum, Washington. She was concerned about an order long over due of picnic tables for rest areas along Washington states highways. He told her he had his driver Keith Jesperson picking them up that very Wednesday March 1st, 1995 at the plant in Iowa Falls, Iowa.

'I know Keith,' she said, 'He's the only driver to ask me to give him a fix-it ticket.'

Bonnie knew what time I left the plant in Iowa and when I'd be arriving there in Cle Elum. No way could I drive the route on paper legally. And she actually was the weigh master to the Cle Elum weigh station on I-90; the one who wrote driver's tickets for doing what I was doing.

I had left Iowa Falls at noon with a three drop load of recycled plastic picnic tables destined for Washington state. In the early hours of Friday morning at Spokane, I tried to get another driver to take the load to deliver it because I was out of hours and my truck needed to be serviced. But no one would help me. At around six in the morning I arrived in Cle Elum and saw Bonnie waiting for me. She got the forklift and removed her part of the load. Even called ahead to Ballard, to let them know I would be there around ten. She didn't ask. She knew my log books would look legal even though she knew they couldn't be. At around three that afternoon all of my products had been unloaded.

'I'm out of hours,' I told dispatch.

'Where do you want me to go?'

I had to think about it. I was closer to Portland than Spokane.

'Send me to Troutdale, I'll sit it out there until my book is legal.'

I had another driving motive for going to the Portland area. Cribbage! If I pushed my days off far enough down the week, I could play at least three clubs and the following weekend was the Barker City tournament. Pulled into Troutdale late that night and spent the night in my sleeper. At noon Saturday March 4th, I checked into a room in the Burns Brother motel. Not often do I get a motel room.

All of the motel rooms were booked for Sunday March 5th because of a custom collector's car show. I would have liked to have a second night in a room. Had I had a room though, I would never had met Julie Winningham when I checked out at eleven in the morning.

She was standing with a man and woman talking in the hallway I had to go down to get to the lobby. First, I ducked into the men's restroom to talk it over in my head what to do. Picked a booth and sat there deciding my line of actions with Julie.

In 1993 after spending a lot of money on her before she left me, I vowed the next time we met that I would kill her! But like my second murder, I had too much time to kill, pardon on the pun. Really thought I could convince her to ride with me to Hwy 14 and east all the way to the scale house near I-82 on the ruse I needed to switch trailers with another driver and deliver it to Portland.

Then along the way I'd fuck her one last time, before killing her and I would tie her body under my trailer and lose her into tiny pieces being eaten by the road. That would take up like just six to ten hours. Then what? Why not just take her to bed in the packing lot and keep on having her all week until I really have to leave?

I regret not killing her right away.

I choose to go out to see her and get into a conversation about being there. We did go out to the truck and got reacquainted in bed. And then I heard her problem. Julie always had problems. The woman I'm not paying money to fuck is generally the most expensive to be with. A very needy person will add up a large bill of goods quickly! Would have been cheaper to offer her money for sex. At least I would know what I was paying for. And she would not follow me home....

After sex, into the store for a carton of cigarettes. Not just a pack. She had to have the good ones. Her car was out gas and she needed to eat something like steak and eggs. And why not drive over to the Jubitz truck stop to play pool and maybe dance and of course drink a lot of alcohol? Maybe even score an ounce of weed? No, not an ounce, I'll get an eighth! Her pussy was gold plated when it is all over!

We did spend time at Jubitz not dancing but playing pool and she drank like a fish while we played. Every once in a while, she would come over to me and rub my dick through my jeans to keep me thinking about sex more. As we walked to the truck she said, 'We should get married.' stood there waiting for an answer. I felt it was a loaded question. Say no, no sex. Say yes, we'll fuck like rabbits. Hell, I am going to kill her anyways.

'Yes, maybe we should.'

It is not like we were really going to get married. She was drunk and I hoped she wouldn't remember. I would hear it all in the morning about the trouble she was in. she needed to see her lawyer early Monday. A few weeks back, she had been in an accident while she was impaired. Handed the cop her driver's license and if she got someone to drive her car she could leave. Well a so-called friend just happened by and Julie got her to drive her car and her from the wreck. A few blocks away, Julie kicked her friend out of the car and drove herself into another crash a mile down the road. The same cop shows up and Julie hands him her spare copy of her license. Two DWI's within about 20 minutes time.

Drove her over to Camas, Washington to talk to her lawyer. Her lawyer told me that Julie told her that I'll be paying all of her fines being we were engaged to be married. We were just fucking!

After meeting her lawyer, we stopped at a local bar restaurant for brunch and to use the restroom. Julie found another friend and while I was peeing in the restroom, they hatched a plan. Julie would sell her the crumbled up 1976 AMC Spirit to her and her friend will drive Julie to wherever Julie wants to go. Crazy!

'We have to go,' Julie said.

All three of us drove back over to Troutdale so Julie could give her car away to this new blonde beauty. This is a bad idea! I told her so. She seemed to think it will work out. Besides, she was also told she she will be able to stay in one of the woman's spare bedrooms. Sight unseen. I didn't want to get involved, but Julie had me write out a bill of sale to them both to sign. And I really screwed up when I signed as a witness. My real name! And then Julie sprung it on me!

'My car needs gas. It's empty.'

'What do I get out of this?'

'What do you want?' says her friend.

'How about you fuck me before you really fuck me?'

She started to take her clothes off. Well okay then! Julie watched as I boned her friend. A sign of a real fiance! I emptied my tank into her before I filled her tank of gas. Both Julie and her friend drove off to look at the room she would be renting, I drove to Multnomah Falls to jog the paths. We were supposed to meet up later.

On Tuesday morning March 7th, I called dispatch and asked that he have me loaded heading east on Friday. Julie had gone missing for the moment. Maybe fucking her friend had pushed her over me. I drove to Gresham's Bogey's restaurant and played the cribbage club that night. I had fun playing with everyone I knew. After which I drove over to Camas's

KFC parking lot to find Julie there pissed off. Her friend had stolen her car and had hidden it some where in town. I heard it all! She gave her the car. Even signed the bill of sale and didn't like the room and decided then not to let her car go. But it was too late and my fault for making out a legal bill of sale. My fault! Sleeping with her was at any time going to erupt into an argument. Thought I could defuse the whole mess by fucking her.

'Is that all you think about?'

I just don't think I had the right answer to anything she said that night. Fucking did take her mind off her car trouble for about an hour.

'Now what?' I ask.

'Tomorrow,' she said, 'we have to go find me a place to live while you're trucking.'

'What about court on Thursday?'

She waved me off and we went to sleep.

A breakfast Wednesday morning March 8th, we bought a newspaper to look it over. Julie checked out hotels and studio apartments. Places to live she will never see or be around to use. I had made up my mind that later after I played cribbage at Round Table Pizza off of 122nd Street, across from K-Mart, I'd meet her for the last time and kill her. All of her car problems were a pain to deal with. She would make her rounds around Camas and Washougal all day to see if she could find her car. Her friend's car now. And meet me at Camas's KFC parking lot around midnight.

Julie was pretty wasted when she opened my door around 2:00 AM. The pizza I bought was cold. It didn't take much effort to get her out of her clothes. She only had on shorts and a t-shirt. She didn't say no when I climbed on to give it to her one more time. I think the idea of having court that morning was holding her emotions down a bit. Maybe feared she would get jail time.

'I'm going to be a really good mom to your children. Can't wait to meet them.'

All the while she was really getting into fucking me. And then she cut loose. Diarrhea shot out over me and her. Shit went everywhere!

That drunken bitch!

'I'm so sorry!' she cried out.

What a fucking mess! I got my load off and so did she, yuk! I met her mother Snooky once when Snooky was just as drunk as Julie. What a pair? No way would I ever marry a drunk. It was time!

I put my fist into her neck and pushed. She had already shit herself. Might as well get it over with. I was just about finished when a local cop drove by. Used tape to secure her and cleaned up enough to drive out to Hwy 14 east over the county line to a wide parking spot. Pulled off the tape and finished the deed. What a fucking mess!

At about that time, a Clark county sheriff's car drove by slowly.

I let paranoia come over me. Felt a need to be rid of her body as quickly as possible. Didn't want to be in possession of dead Julie. I got out and crossed the guard rail and walked twenty feet and spotted a pile of garbage. Felt it was a fitting place to put the shit covered Julie. Went back to the sleeper and carried her over to the drop off and tossed her naked body onto the other pieces of trash. Drove back to Troutdale to get a shower. Sitting across the river, I thought I should go back to pick her up and take her down Hwy 14 and do what I had first thought about. But I talked myself out of that.

Back over at Troutdale, I went to sleep after cleaning as much shit as I could find of hers sticking to just about everything. The whole cab stunk of sex and feces and urine. Later on Thursday, I travelled over to a DMV to get my driver's license renewed. My 40th birthday was coming up fast. Every five years a must. And later that night I went to Dad's restaurant over by the St. John's bridge to play cribbage at another club.

On Friday March 10th, I was sent to Corvallis, Oregon to pick up a load of lumber for Pennsylvania. It was close to six that afternoon when I was parked at the Burns Brothers in Troutdale's fueling island topping off my tanks and staring across the area where Julie laid.

'Maybe I should go over there to move her some where else? Maybe drag her into nothing?' I asked myself.

But the draw of playing cribbage at the Baker City tournament pulled on me too much. I drove east. Met a woman at the tournament. We seemed to hit it off. I actually gave her Julie's coat. She climbed into my cab and we did try a little touching, but not sex. She felt uncomfortable. Lived in Boise, Idaho. Offered to drive her home.

(A few years ago on a TV show, she talked about getting the coat and denied getting into my truck.)

Since I basically had all seventy hours to run across America, I did so almost non-stop except to adjust my book to fit fueling stops. Made my delivery on time and called in for my next load. (My last load.)

Ever get those feelings that something is not right? That something is going on and you just can't put your finger on it? Dispatch gave me a wide load out of a steel yard in Washington, Pennsylvania to be delivered to a mine north of Deming, New Mexico. A wide load nine feet wide. Three inches wider than my trailer rails on both sides. There was several other Systems semis there getting loaded. When I walked over to them, they just waved me off. Not the normal reaction. Normally, we talked shop. But no there. As if they were told not to talk to me. Or was it my reputation?

On Friday March 17th, I stopped at the 76 truck stop in Little Rock, Arkansas and called up my daughter Carrie in Spokane to wish her a happy birthday, her 12th. Had sent her a hundred dollar bill.

'When am I going to see you again dad?'

'As soon as I can get there Carrie.'

Had called from the front of the Jimmy Dolen dance club, which I was a member. Spent several hours at the club having a grand ole time! Pulled into the 76 truck stop at Texarkana on March 18th, 1995 and met two women that I ended up kissing and spending time with. Had actually called dispatch to claim I had the trots and couldn't leave the truck stop for 24 hours. Had walked into the store to see this tall slender woman dressed in black leather jacket and slacks trying to buy something she didn't have enough money to buy. I stepped up and paid the extra two dollars. We got to talking. Even had coffee in the restaurant. She owned a new freightliner and her husband didn't like to drive. We walked about being a team. She gave me her pager number to call. Walked her back to her truck and kissed her while my left hand was in her crotch.

'We'll play tomorrow when I get back.'

We had breakfast early the next morning before she went home to her husband. From behind I thought I was looking at Roberta Ellis all dressed in leather. Yummy!

Was doing laundry that morning the 19th of March when a woman came to me asking for a ride to De Kalb, Texas, the home of Hoss, Dan Blocker of Bonanza. She came with me to my semi and got in. she climbed into my sleeper. Part of me wanted to wait for Black Leather to come back! But this one was willing and able to engage in love making to secure a ride to her home.

She tells me her story. She is married to a man 36 years older and they live in a mobile home not far from town with a couple children. They also raise mountain lions. Yeah right! So I drive her west out of Texarkana to De Kalb, Texas, drop my trailer in a lot where others had dropped theirs. We drive bobtail to her home. We are beside it when she opens the door and her daughter sees her and yells, 'Mommy! Mommy!' and runs up to my truck. She grabs her kid and shuts the door yelling at me to go.

'Let's get the hell out of here!'

'I'm not doing this.' I tell her. 'This is kidnapping!'

I could see her man shaking his fist at us, at me and I drive up to the stop sign and stop.

'Get out! I'm not taking you anywhere!'

They both get out and walk back home. I get back to my trailer and was about to leave when she drives up in a car alone.

'I want to show you my cats.'

She drives me to store and I buy a couple Mickey's malt liquor bottles in the barrel mouth type. We then drove to an open field with three chain link pens out in the middle. Got out and walked to the pens and they really had a mountain lion or cougar depending who you ask. She pulls a chicken out of a box and tosses it into the first pen and her pussy cat eats the shit out of it! She does the same thing with the others. Then we go for a drive in the country to show me more sites to see. Introduces me to people she knows. I thought she was going to park and we do the round two, but it didn't happen. Brought me back to the semi and went home. Seen all of her pussies.

It takes a long time to cross Texas. I pulled into the 76 truck stop in El Paso at about six Tuesday morning March 21st and called my boss. Even there, the other drivers for Systems didn't want to talk. They just walked away quickly. I would take a True Detective magazine into the restroom to read. Think the main story was about Susan Smith, the woman who claimed someone car jacked her and took her kids. Only to find out she sent her vehicle into a lake with her kids still in it. When I exited the restroom an alarm sounded. But they could never find the magazine. It was just an oversight.

I called in to my dispatch and he told me I'd have to stop and buy a permit to haul the wide load into New Mexico. I told him I knew how to get around the port of entry and then he told me not to do that. That was one of those moments that hit me weird. Bosses always want to save money. And here he was telling me to spend it. Why? I got the money to but it and decided to do what he wanted me to do. I crossed the port of entry north of EL Paso and went into the building to get my permit. As I was leaving, one officer asked me my name. They never do that. Another point. That was weird! He wanted to know my name. Why? The permit is for the truck no matter who drives it. At top of the hill going west out of Las Cruces, New Mexico is a small truck stop on the south side. Also the Las Cruces fairgrounds. I always look over things as I go. Nothing was going on except someone was installing irrigation to the front lawn. Close to Deming is the exit to head up the road to the mine I was taking the steel plate to. I followed the instructions up the two lane road. About ten miles to go I started hearing about two unmarked police cars parked on the north side of the road about five miles from them mine, just ahead. I drove past them and stared over at them. Weird! They were staring back at me.

At the mine, I was guided to the unload area and as soon as my tarps and straps and chains were off, a lift pulled it all off. Quickly! Again, weird! There were stacks of the same size sheets everywhere. Normally it took a lot longer to get unloaded. Because the wind was blowing hard, I just strapped down my tarps and would tackle it later when there isn't wind. Drove out of the mine and parked at a nearby store and called in.

'Do you have a load for me?'

'Not yet.'

'Where you want me to head to?'

'Don't know yet.'

'What do you want me to do?'

'Drive to Deming and call me.'

I'm a firm believer that if you don't understand something, slow it down. Make the problem come to me.

So all day there had been things taking place I just didn't understand. So I went to sleep for several hours. No point in getting into a hurry to go no where and Deming is no where. It was close to five that afternoon when I decided to head to Deming. Those cop cars were still there but not for long.

As soon as I went past them, they pulled in behind me. Heard it over the CB. And just about a mile before hitting the interstate to Deming, one by one they passed me. The second one got along side of me, he looked up at me, then sped off back to Las Crusas. I turned right and drove to Deming. At the truck stop I called dispatch and was told to call in the morning.

After dark, things really got weirder when I decided to go for a run through town and to go to the McDonald's to get a couple burgers. A Ford red colored Bronco followed me everywhere. Call me paranoid! Or was it a kid dragging the avenue and I made too much of it? The shower felt good to get that evening.

In the morning before the wind began to blow, I pulled out my tarps and folded them up. Went to have another shower and was told they were out of service. Weird! All of them? So I drove over to the truck wash and it was closed. The red colored Ford Bronco was parked by the truck wash entrance. Weird! Went into the restroom and washed with a cloth. In the restaurant I noticed several men in regular clothes that looked like cops because of their hair and how they held their arms out. As if they were used to be carrying a belt full of guns and stuff. Maybe I was being really paranoid. But things were acting weird all day yesterday and now!

I called in and my boss told me to be at the Las Crusas fairgounds by noon Las Crusas time.

'But there isn't anything going on there?' I said.

And he gave me the man's name I'd be meeting there.

'He's a detective from Las Crusas. I'm sure of it.'

There was silence over the phone.

'I don't think so. What makes you want to say he is?'

'I read the detective magazines. I'm sure he's sheriff of Las Crusas.'

'I don't think so!'

And there it was! What difference would it make if he was a cop? I'm getting a load of something. Cops have toys too. I felt a need to clean out my cab of everything Julie and the others. Make damn sure I was clean.

'I could be wrong,' I thought. 'But better safe than sorry.'

at about eleven Las Crusas time I pulled into the small truck stop to wait until noon. As I left Deming, as soon as I was on the interstate, the truck wash opened up for business. Over the radio they called and I damn near turned back to get in line. That certainly would have been a tell telling me I was being looked at seriously. As it was, I cleaned out everything I thought was there and before emptying my trash, I used my binoculars to spy the cop car on the overpass to see him spying on me with his.

Noon came and I pulled into the fairgrounds and behind me came guess who? Yes! Mr. Ford Bronco, red all over. The man got out and sure enough it was the detective I remembered. He pointed to the smaller gate to my left.

'Can you pull in there?'

'No problem.'

As I drove past the gate, he followed, then passed me and stopped in front of a hut to our right. Got out and told me it is right over here. We walked around the hut and all of a sudden I'm walking up to no less than six guns pointing at me. There was cops from the truck stop and the one guy in the car that looked up at me.

'Up against the wall!'

Another said, 'You are being held for questioning in an ongoing homicide investigation.'

Another started to read my rights.

'Homicide?' I thought. 'Which one?'

I was sure they would tell me something soon enough. When the one finished reading me my rights he asked, 'Do you want to talk to us?'

I had been thinking that one of these days something like this was bound to happen. In the Daun Slagle case it worked well to just talk to them. In the end, the case went away. Asking for a lawyer, I thought, was a sign of guilt. In this case, had I asked for a lawyer and got one, I might have avoided all of the other cases. But like in the Slagle case I told them, 'I'll talk to you.'

'Have you ever been arrested before?'

Should I or shouldn't I tell them about the Daun Slagle case? Certainly they had looked me up on their computers and knew I had. Better to be honest here.

'Yes, I got caught shoplifting when I was thirteen. Also I had been arrested in Shasta, California in the Slagle case that eventually was dismissed in April 1992.'

They put me in a car and headed to the Las Crusas sheriff's office just down the street from the truck stop. Put me in a room with a view of the parking lot. Cops were going over my truck and trailer looking for what they were looking for.

'Who died?' I asked.

'Julie Winningham.'

'That was quick' I said to myself.

'Julie's dead! How?' I said out loud, trying to look surprised. Had to act innocent and speak of her in the present. Not the past. That is hard to do when I'm the killer.

'We think you did it.'

'Did what?'

'Strangle her.'

'I didn't do her in. did you talk to those drug addicts she hangs with?'

'We did and they a;; point at you.'

'Me? They probably don't even know my name. Julie calls me Chris.'

'We didn't get your name from them. You're right about that. We got your name from the bill of sale you wrote as a witness.'

So there it was, my mistake in getting involved by writing down my name. For the next six hours I denied killing her. They took my blood and hair and asked me to take a lie detector test, but didn't have time to set it up. Deny! Deny! Deny! And then the door opened, they gave me their business cards, gave me a copy of the affidavit, they had to do what they did and let me go.

March 22nd, 1995.

I drove down the street to the truck stop and parked. Took the affidavit with me into the restaurant to read. And there it was in black and white.

Everyone Julie knew had pointed at me as the most likely to have killed her. Sooner or later I would be in custody. What to do? Why not kill myself? Just end it? That is what I decided to do.

Not being a drug addict, I didn't know over the counter sleeping pills will not kill you. I took 77 of them and said goodbye to my kids and passed out. Only to wake up and stumble into the truck stop to pee with only one boot on. Then when I came back to my truck owned by Prime INC, why?, well in the darkness, it looked like my old 1989 plum colored Pete pulling a refer. Boy was I surprised when Prime's driver came out of his sleeper yelling at me.

'What are you doing in my truck?'

And I was arguing with him that it was mine. Well, the cops took my keys and told me to pick them up when I wasn't so doped up. Told them I had taken a few sleeping pills after learning my fiance had been killed. Even told the sheriff I had been in his holding all day. Those pills just fucked me up.

In the morning, my boss told me to head over toward Phoenix, Arizona. Had to tell him the cops took my tarps. Why? Because they believed I carried Julie's dead body into the woods wrapped in the tarps. The 200 pound tarps!

Drove to a truck stop called 44D about 60 miles from Wilcox, Arizona and decided to try it again, only this time half as many pills. Before I ate them, I wrote a suicide note- letter to my brother Brad in Selah. It basically said I've been a killer for five years, killing eight people. Sorry for how I turned out.

I dropped the letter into the mail drop box. Woke up Friday March 24th with a headache. Looked up at the snow on the mountains and decided to take a hike to snow line and let the cold do me in. but as I hiked, I noticed I was being followed by a man on horseback. My luck, I'd wake up to a warm fire he built.

Maybe it was sign.

I turned around and decided to let the legal system kill me. I drove back to the truck stop and called Detective Rick Buckner of Clark county sheriffs, Washington state and confessed to him over the phone.

An hour later, Sheriffs from Wilcox came to me and I walked over to them and told them who I was. By eleven at night I was in a cell under suicide watch. The following morning a bus load of us were taken to the Bisbee county jail. As my head cleared I realized I really fucked up. I could have traveled to Canada being a Canadian citizen and stayed free. As soon as I sobered up, I thought of the suicide note to Brad. What an idiot I was for using drugs! And not very good drugs at that. All because I had been feeling sorry for myself and my paranoia took over.

On Monday March 27th 1995, a court appointed lawyer took me to the side to explain to me the worst thing to do is to tell cops anything. Best to keep quiet. We were there to not fight extradition back to Vancouver, Washington. Not sure exactly what day Det. Buckner arrived to fly me to Portland and to drive over to Vancouver.

There were the two cops from Clark county there to drive me to Tuscan, Arizona. Fly me to Phoenix to change planes and fly me to Portland. One took a car to the Clark county jail.

At this time I kept thinking I needed to call Brad up to tell him to destroy the note. Probably would have been best not to call him. But I did. He said he destroyed it.

On April 4th, 1995 I'd meet my attorney Thomas Phelan and I'd be in court to hear the charges against me. Rape, kidnapping, murder. The basic umbrella cover charges. Just toss everything at the suspect and see what sticks.

I would celebrate my 40th birthday on April 6th 1995 sitting in the Clark county jail's 'C' block reserved for those suspects accused of crimes against women and children, cell number 9. There were about thirty of us in the pod. It didn't take me long to realize I was in school learning how the law really worked. The cases of all in different stages of their course of actions. One thing became apparent. Time slowly moved ahead, Phelan had told me he would keep in touch with me. A month later on May 11th 1995 he had me in a room and he tossed down a copy of my suicide note to Brad.

'Is there any truth to that?'

'Yes.'

'Well, it seems Det. Buckner has made a match to your handwriting. Are you the press called Happy Face Killer?'

Told him about reading about it in a Detective magazine back in November 1994. He explained how it would be best to settle those eight cases. Do my last case first. Second to last second and so on and so on. No preceding cases to show a pattern of crimes. And also told me chances are the DA's will never do it that way. To prepare for cases going in every direction at the same time.

'Tell me about them?'

I started with Bennett, telling him every detail I knew about it. Then I went down every case telling him the absolute truth. My #2, #3, #4, #5, #6, #7, and of course #8. The one he was most concerned with, Julie Winningham. As of this note taking, my Angela Subrize case is a Nebraska case. (These notes would become very important in dealing with the Bennett case. Prosecutors would require Phelan to show them these notes.)

'What do you want to do with them?'

I told him, 'I want to solve them all. Get them all behind me as soon as possible.'

his one main concern was to not allow them to give me the death penalty. He would work very hard to set up a deal in each case to spare my life.

'When you tell your stories Keith, don't speak of premeditation. Come up with something to blame the victims for. But not to be cruel. Just not so harsh.

This was checkmate!

Columbia River

I-84

I-205

Vancouver

Julie's last RB place
X county line
can't Clark county

Topaz
Hwy 14

Washougal   Camas

Saving Face

Chapter Fifteen: Saving Face

While Det. Buckner and company were transporting me from Bisbee to Vancouver by planes and cars. He kept bragging about all of the infamous people he had in the very handcuffs on me. He told me they were looking around for more bodies I could still have out there hidden. That had me thinking about the note to family I sent to explain my death. And then he tells me he was the one to arrest Westley Allan Dodd, the child serial killer.

'No you weren't,' I said. 'He was caught by a 16 year old boy outside the movie theater and held there until the local police department snapped handcuffs on him. You were just there to transport him to your county jail.'

'How the fuck would you know that?'

'I was living across the river in Portland when it happened. Read it in the newspapers every day.'

Westley would tell everyone that if he were to ever get out, he would do it again. They put him on death-row in Washington State, held in Walla-Walla, the Walls. Westley didn't right his case. He fast tracked his own death by not appealing the death sentence and it took a short few years to hang him. When his time to be killed came, he walked to the hanging, not kicking and screaming like most did. For how he handled himself in death he is well respected for how he faced it. And here was Det. Buckner trying to take credit for his capture. Typical!

My attorney Thomas Phelan would come to me to tell me my father was one piece of work. A real grade A piece of shit! Les Jesperson had vowed to help police gather up information to help kill his own son to save face for the Jesperson family. He had turned in 'the letter' as he called it, the suicide note to my brother Brad, to the police and offered up his help on what else they needed.

'So Keith, watch what you say to your father. He is not helping us.'

We Jespersons have always known that Les Jesperson looks after only Les Jesperson. As long as what goes on benefits him, it must be okay.

Buckner was one of those cops that sought the recognition of every slap on his back proving he was a super cop. He had the suicide note and had taken the time to compare it to the 1994 letter sent to reporter Phil Stanford. He believed he had the Happy Face Killer locked up in his Clark county jail cell, Keith Jesperson. It was like Christmas to him. He could not wait to tell the world what he had done. He contacted reporter Bruce Westfall of Vancouver's 'The Colombian Newspaper'.

From day one, every detail to come their way claiming the Bennett case had been solved using the wrong people to convict was thrown out as a bunch of bullshit. At the top of their lungs they screamed, 'We have the right two people in prison! A jury of her peers convicted her and he plead guilty! Put it to rest people!' they sat there in their jobs cruising along feeling good with themselves that they had done the right thing. Oblivious to what was about to happen to their sweet deal. And why would they care what was going on over in Clark county, they had the right people in prison? Right?

They did care! Why would Michael Schrunk send his detectives over to Bend, Oregon out of his jurisdiction to see if the man could have been the real killer? He was worried that maybe the real killer would turn his case upside down and he had to stop it! They knew deep down they had fucked up. They were fully aware that their job had always been to seek the truth and if the truth isn't told, release the factually innocent. Their job is not to get a conviction by any means to get it even if it means to put people in prison who were not involved. The real issue to this whole Bennett case was they knew how the system worked and they used it against two nut cases to solve another unsolvable case just because they could.

It had become just a numbers game to them. 'The truth is what I say it is!' there they sat over at Multnomah county, Oregon and they would be very pissed off to learn that Det. Rick Buckner went to the press instead of them to have a go at Mr. Jesperson before the world knew of Buckner's findings. And why would Buckner? I was his ticket to stardom! He didn't like to share his findings with anyone. Like most police organizations, they don't share.

In our pod, we have a TV set on to watch shows like 'Northern Exposure' and 'Star Trek'. We also watched the news. One TV for over thirty people who looked for entertainment to keep them from drowning in their own misery.

Sometime in June of 1995, 'Breaking News' came on our TV and they began talking about the Happy Face Killer, could it be Keith Jesperson sitting in the Clark county jail?

It was mesmerizing to watch. My secret was out. I looked over the dorm at the other men watching the news and one by one they saw a photo of me on the TV and looked over at me to see me- the serial killer suspect. Life in 'C' pod will change.

You can bet those involved in the Bennett case cover up in Multnomah county stood up and took notes. They now faced a real dilemma. The real killer sat across the river being guarded by Det. Rick Buckner and they didn't have direct access to question him, me. You damn right they were pissed off! And when the press came to them, they double downed their commitment to their case.

'We have the right people!'

I sat in my cell, careful who I talked to. My lawyer came to me to tell me not to respond to any press requests. Do not talk to anyone about your cases! People will be planted in here to gather information. Every inmate is a potential rat! Loose lips sink ships! I filed each request in a box to use later, should I feel a need to. Phil Stanford asked for my help to help him solve the real Bennett case.

I was just a student in the school of law that was being taught in Clark county by the many inmates who have gone through this shit over and over again. A wealth of information! Each seasoned inmate came to me to talk about what I faced with eight possible convictions of murder. Just one conviction was enough. Overkill! I could be in court for years to get all cases settled. What a waste of time. How many times can they kill a man in prison? How much time is too much time to do?

Jimmy Strodes was facing rape charges and the prosecutor offered him a deal of eleven years to plead guilty. But Jimmy says he will prove they lied about his case. He went to court and at the end of his trial, the jury found him guilty and the judge gave him twenty-seven years. He said he proved them to have lied, but it made no difference. He admits guilt to us and wished he had taken the eleven year deal.

John Mastros was accused of allowing two fourteen year old girls to suck his dick. He tells us he didn't get it as many times as they said he did. He wanted to prove them to be lying. 'But Mastros,' I asked, 'you allowed them to suck your dick at least once. You're guily!' and in the end, he was sentenced to 42 years.

Every case in there had similar outcomes. A pattern was developing. We had watched TV and these people were glued to the news of me. They just couldn't get enough. To stop it, one day I poured a cup of water down the back of the TV before it came on. When the cops turned on the power smoke and sparks exploded and the TV went dead. Problem solved!

A big man named Ken Lee Monsebroten A.K.A 'Duke', because he looked like John Wayne the actor, came to my cell to have a talk. He tells me the best prison to do my time is where I'm at now, the Oregon State Penitentiary in Salem.

'Serial killers walk the yard. You have Randy Woodfield, the I-5 Killer, and Jerome Brudos that made lamp shades out of his victim's skin. If you can make it happen, get to that prison!'

He then tells me about the famous lawyer Gerry Spence out of Wyoming.

'If you just had a case in Wyoming, you might get him to defend your cases, all of them!'

The writing was on the wall. I was going to go down hard and I needed to come up with a plan.

'Hey, Duke, has anyone looking at what I'm looking at just come clean and confess to everything?'

'Hell no Keith! But that is exactly what the public is craving for. For us to take responsibility for what we have done. To stop hiding behind our rights and letting lawyers do our talking for us. If you were to do it, you'll be the only one.'

Sure, Duke was a wealth of information and had access to what I needed. But also he was the enemy. He was talking to me to come up with a deal he could pitch to the prosecutor to get his 'rape with a knife' reduced so he could get out some day.

'Duke, I have a body you are going to have to solve your own problems. Just help me with mine and who knows, one day you might be going home.'

I needed to get press releases out to the media confessing I was the Happy Face Killer and the real killer of Bennett. Felt that if I could free Pavlinac and Sosnovske, no prosecutor would want to take me to trial and deal me out. I would no longer be a suspect in all of my cases. I will solve myself. I would be fucking Det. Buckner out of his glory of doing it. My deal with Duke would turn my Nebraska case, Angela Subrize, into a Wyoming case. I'd tell Duke a lie to convince him she died at Exit 377, the Burns Brothers truck stop in Wyoming. I'd expect him to create his own lies to try to help prosecutors. He didn't disappoint me!

You may not know this, but all mail and phone calls are monitored in jails. Duke was to get my mail past the cops to the streets. He would recruit people to help. How was he able to do that? Such a scandal!

He tells the whole pod he is writing a book about me and our experiences. He is offering 10% of the profits to anyone to help our cause. He recruits everyone to help. Each gets 10%. as one leaves to go to prison, his replacement gets his 10%. and these guys keep Duke in coffee and other store items. Actually promising 300% of the book for their their help.

I'd be busy writing out seven confessions and put them into envelopes, each addressed to a media source. Put all seven envelopes into a 10x13 envelope to be passed to an inmate's lawyer to be placed in a mail drop box outside the county jail.

The blast of media coverage about me to the public in June 1995 stirred up interest in all cases connected to the Happy Face Killer letter of 1994. many of her jurisdictions stood up to take notice and to investigate cases to see if they could connect the dots. The Oregon crime lab went at the evidence full on. By August 17th, 1995 they had confirmed what everyone hoped for, that Keith Jesperson was in fact the writer of the 1994 letter to the Oregonian. This information was shared to all secretly. All prosecutors were trying to get in line to prosecute me. And not in the order my attorney hoped for.

On September 1th, 1995, my plan went into drive mode when inmate Alan handed off my 10x13 envelope to his lawyer addressed to Alan's wife in St. Johns, Oregon. The lawyer dropped it in the mail drop box outside of the Clark county jail.

On Friday September 15th, Marion county investigators were at the Clark county jail with their request for my DNA and hair samples to try to solve me as Laurie Ann Pentland's killer. Buckner stood guard as my lawyer and I had a small conference. We were hearing Det. Buckner bragging about his book he's writing how he proved who Jesperson was. Phelan laughed when I told him what I had done and what was about to hit the fan. My lawyer was glad I had done this. Why? It helped him not to have to explain to everyone who I was in court. It freed his hands. By chance, the nurse could not find a vein and we went to the local Salem Hospital to draw my blood.

'It's at eleven o' clock and down deep.' I told her and she slid it in.

I had sold my plasma for years. Given blood to the Red Cross. Telling a nurse where to dig for it was better than several tries to find it.

We were walking back to the car, me, Det. Buckner, Marion county's investor, and my attorney, Tom Phelan. We exited the hospital as I shuffled along in my legs irons, wearing my orange county clothes. We turned the corner towards the parking lot. I stopped. And they kept walking to the cars. I just stood there at the corner of the building and saw several nurses on break sitting to my left 20 yards away. They were watching it all unfold. All three were almost to their cars about 50 yards away when I yelled out, 'Hey guys! Are you missing me!'

I had turned and staged me in a running pose going the other way. 'Oh shit!'

They come back to me. Tom is laughing. Buckner looked around. 'Good thing no body saw this.'

I pointed to the nurses who witnessed the whole thing.

Saturday afternoon September 16th, Alan talks to his wife on the phone and she tells him the 10x13 envelope had arrived. She placed all seven envelopes into a drop box as told.

I had written an eight confessional and handed it to Duke to show to Det. Buckner on Sunday night September 17th. Why? I wanted Buckner to be able to confirm the confessions were mine to the press when they would be asking. I also needed Buckner to be on my side. He would be guarding me when the wolves from Multnomah came to play.

Duke had been called out to see Buckner and he gave me a thumbs up when I saw him leave the pod. He would be selling his pitch to make a deal using the Angela Subrize case to do it. Winner winner chicken dinner!

On Monday September 18th, nothing happened. The calm before the storm. Phelan asked me if it was still a go. I had told him I called my sister on Sunday to tell her I was the press called Happy Face Killer. Not to call my lawyer to ask silly questions. Tom appreciated that.

Very early morning at around 4:00 AM I'm woke up by several Clark county guards.all wanting to shake my hand for coming clean. About time! They gave me the morning newspaper that had most of my confession in it. Shit had hit the fan big time! All day we got media requests to be interviewed. I took a few.

Then on Wednesday September 20th, Judge Richards Harris had me in court and we argued over the 'gag order' he was placing on me. On me! Not the police or other inmates. On just me! Why? Even though I told him there would be no trial, he argued to say we are moving forward as if there would be a trial. He was making sure it would be a fair trial without the case decided in the press.

'I will not be happy until I'm in the prison cell that John Sosnovske was in!'

Phelan and I had a talk. He had been over to see Multnomah county district attorney Michael Schrunk. Schrunk told him he had two unsolved murders he could make as mine if I left the Bennett case alone. They seemed to think I was after a body count. I was after justice! To solve the Bennett case was the key stone to my whole plan.

I told Phelan to go back over to see Multnomah county to ask for a deal to talk to me about solving the Bennett case. Sort of a twist. Before I prove I killed her, before they have charged me with a crime of murder, they would have to be in written deal to do life in prison. Why? Because should I be able to prove I killed Bennett, all of the evidence provided would be on hand and they would not have to deal. Everyone's hands had to be tied to a deal to solve this case. (I would hear later that Michael Schrunk had gone to a judge to try to get the judge to issue a gag order on me to stop talking about the Bennett case. But because I had not been charged with a crime, the court was not in a position to grant such an order.)

On Friday September 22nd, Tom argued with Multnomah county and reluctantly came back with a deal to do 30 years should I be able to prove I killed Bennett. Of course, they were going to fight me all of the way.

In the press, and you can go to the press releases on file to prove this to be true, Multnomah claimed to everyone Jesperson is lying! They even reached out to other cases in the 1994 letter for support. Is he a liar? Merced county prosecutors and detectives yelled in support of Multnomah county's claim. Cynthia Lynn Rose had died of an overdose! She wasn't strangled like Jesperson said. He is lying! Santa Clara county, California yelled with Multnomah to claim my victim there also died of an overdose. Jesperson is lying. But Marion county? They wanted me to be telling the truth. Their whole case depended on me being on their side to solve the Pentland case. Riverside county, California was keeping to themselves.

The reporter Phil Stanford wrote me to hopefully get me to help him. But the gag order would be my hold out for the time being. However, I turned Phil onto Duke,, a former clerk at the Oregon State Penitentiary when Michael Francke was killed over at Salem's dome building. Francke had been investigating corruption at Oregon's prison system. He had found lots to report on and people's heads would roll. Something had to be done. A furniture warehouse had burned down and when the first fire marshal investigated it, he was about to report the building had been empty. So the powers to be found a corrupt fire marshal to sign off on it to say the warehouse had been full of furniture for insurance benefits of course. The real furniture had been sold off. The assistant district attorney for Marion county, Oregon met with a guy named Timothy Natividad to discuss the problem. Scott McAlister paid $10,000 to Natividad to get his group called 'Salem Three Murder Incorporated' to confront Michael Franke. Natividad, Devron Anderson and little Mike went to the dome building and in a scuffle stabbed Franke to death. Franke's briefcase was taken with all of the evidence of corruption. Later at Natividad's duplex home, his live in girlfriend, an assistant district attorney of Marion county, shot and killed him. She, of course, was not charged. Assistant DA McAlister had been told to leave town and is/was selling auto parts out east somewhere. To solve the murder of Franke, they got jail house snitches to testify it was a drug addict named Frank Gable who killed Michael Franke. Gable went to prison. And the department of corrections for Oregon went back to business as usual.

Duke got a lawyer named George Kolin to help with transferring mail to Phil. Not too surprising, Duke sold them both into his book deal too.

On Monday September 25th, 1995, I was to meet the people I had to deal with from Multnomah county. Included in the mix was Det. Chris Peterson. Why? Chris Peterson's son worked as a guard at the Clark county jail. He had a reason to be there with his son and no one would question this. I believe he was added just to have access through his son to me. You can make up your own mind about this special arrangement. I told my story. How I cut the fly area off her jeans and burned it in my fireplace. How I tossed away her tape player onto Interstate 84 over the Sandy River. How I tossed her purse and Oregon ID card into bushes along the Sandy River road. That really peaked their attention. But most of what I told them, they already knew. They asked me questions and I didn't know the answers and so I made mistakes guessing. Phelan took me aside to tell me to just tell them what I could remember. Don't guess! Had no one been arrested, what I told them would have convicted me and put me into prison for life. Maybe even death! It was plain to see these people were angry I was messing with their conviction.

On Saturday, September 30th, I broke the 'gag order' and called Phil Stanford several times on the phone. He then worked as a reporter for the Willamette Weekly. I complained about how hard it was to climb up such a hostile crowd to tell the truth. Unknowing or maybe he did it on purpose, he let me know about facts in the case I didn't know about like a red handled knife found by Taunja's body. I had to be careful with what he said because that could screw up all I wanted to accomplish.

Because I had violated the order, Clark county took desperate measures to make sure I had no access to a phone. Not directly anyway. I was placed into a cell inside the medical unit. They would lock me in there all day. Only allow me to be out to use the bath tub after 10:00 pm. By then, I really needed a break from the crew in 'C' pod. And the staff was angry because while I was in 'C' pod, it had quieted down a lot. You know what? Tossing a noise maker off of the second tier does wonders for moral. Almost did it twice. Guards stopped me before I could drop the kid. To punish me, they kept me locked in my cell for three days. It was worth it.

On October 2nd, 1995 my lawyer came to see me. We left with Buckner to drive over to the Multnomah county sheriff's station on the corner of 122nd Street and Glease Avenue, across from Jody's strip club. We walked into the old building in the rain. Everyone had a coat on but me. All of this wet weather would give me a sore throat later in the week. We were brought into their work station and I was told to sit down in a cubicle. The cubicle was staged. They had photos of Pavlinac pointing to the ravine. Papers about the case were open on the desk. I knew what was up. I lowered my head and pretended to not notice and napped. Not going to work boys!

We all piled out of the building into a nine passenger white Dodge van and the driver was to follow my instructions. We drive to the turn off to Everett Street and parked outside the home of 18434 NE Everett Street. I laid out the floor plan. Asked to go inside. They knew it was the murder house. Had they used that chemical to check for old blood? Luminal? All they could do is to argue with me on whether or not I had painted the living room. Certainly it had been over five years since I killed her in the house, someone must have by now repainted it. But why care? Only Roberta could tell them if I had or not.

I knew by their questions that they had already talked to her. I remembered telling her about something happening in the home when I was taken off the truck of Rock Island, Illinois in January 1991. and she had seen the mattress was in the living room when we returned from Ellensburg in late February 1990. I was certain they had talked to Roberta. Of course I had not painted the room. What difference would it make anyways?

Then we went over to the B & I Tavern and we parked outside and again I went into detail about the floor plan to the building. No real point to this. So we drove up to the Vista House and before the driver started down, a towel was placed over the odometer to keep me from reading how far we had to travel. Slowly we headed down the steep road. When the road turned northwest and came along the ravine I yelled.

'Stop! We are here!'

Did he stop? Hell no! He kept driving down to the switch back and all the way to the next waterfall turn out.

'Let's go back'

'Are you sure it isn't further down the road?'

'Turn around. It is back there!'

we turned back and when we were beside the ravine, I yelled again to stop. He continued to drive another 50 yards. We all got out in the rain and slowly I waddled over to the place I dragged her body into. Started to walk off of the road to walk down into the ravine and I heard, 'Stop! Don't go down there!'

'It's down here about 90 feet.'

Let the games begin! Right?

'Are you sure it isn't this one over here?' The cop had walked on down the road to the next one and to the next one. 'Maybe it is this one down here.'

'It is this one I'm standing at!' I looked over at Buckner and he had his hand on his gun. Some shit could be in the mix. I looked over at Phelan and he said, "Keith play along. We all know you know where you put her.'

'Jesperson which one is your best guess. A, B, or C?' He pointed to each one as he spoke.

'A is my best guess' I played along.

We all got back into the van. Time to show them where I put her purse and photo ID card. They had tipped their hand. No way could I tell them where to look without someone to watch over them to be sure it wasn't destroyed.

'Will I be able to walk down and pick it up? I already knew the answer before they even answered it.

'No, we'll have the explorer scouts come in to document it. It all has to be done legally.'

I just couldn't trust these cops and prosecutors to do the right thing on their own. I needed help and I knew who would help me.

We drove back to the Sandy River Road by the way of I-84 West to Troutdale. Started to drive south and when I saw the Y in the road I remembered the deep ravine opposite to the road coming down the hill.

'Stop!' I yelled.

And he stopped so quickly we all almost were tossed from our seats.

'Here!' I pointed.

We all got out and walked with me to the deep blackberry vines going everywhere ravine. Purely a nest of thorns. I held back my laughter as I pointed down into the thickest jungle to trek, 'Down there.'

Peterson looked around and stared up the roads towards the real place I put it. He began to walk up hill and I followed.

'Are you sure it isn't up here?'

'I'm positive! I know it isn't as far as that old tree stump up there under the telephone line.'

We went back to the van and went back to their office. Buckner took us to get burgers and curly fries at the local Burgerville before dropping me off in my medical cell. I knew they would return to the blackberries to see if they could find it on their own.

Back in my cell, I needed help to secure the actual place to look for the purse. I had recruited Dale Thompson in the medical unit. He was accused of murder based on a conversation at a bar in Camas. He was innocent of it. The real killer, John Lamb, would eventually clear him. But for now I needed his help because I didn't have access to the phone that he did. I got busy writing a letter to Phil Stanford telling him where the purse was and telling him to accept a collect phone call from Dale on Wednesday October 11th to get confirmation he got the letter so I could call over Det. Peterson to go to the new search area while Stanford covered it to be sure the evidence was not destroyed by Multnomah police.

Dale would send my letter to Phil in a letter he sent to his girlfriend with instructions to mail the envelope to Stanford. Fingers crossed! On October 5th Dale talked to his girlfriend and she mailed the letter.

Okay, I believed it was time to ruin my case in Clark county. Why? Phelan had every intention of taking my Julie Winningham murder trial full circle through a lengthy trial. He gets paid his full price if he does this. Told me he could possibly get me murder II. But murder II is still a life sentence. Where is the win here? Phelan would have defended a serial killer in court. A large point in his career. But at what cost to what I wanted?

The only reason for a trial is for discovery. If the court had it all, there would be no point to a trial. I felt a need to tie my lawyer's hands in the case. No trial! Just a plea and goodbye: Gag order. I made a request to talk to Buckner later.

At 11:00 pm on October 5th, Buckner had me in his cubical to talk over everything about the Winningham case. He brought me the article written by Stanford in the Willamette Weekly out that very day called 'Phone Calls From a Serial Killer'. We talked until I was returned to my cell at 6:00 AM on October 6th, the day I was scheduled to go over to the Oregon State Police office for Multnomah county off of I-205.

At about 9:00 AM, Buckner drove me and Phelan over to the state police station. I was to take a lie detector exam. Like I had hoped, everyone there had band-aids all over their arms and faces due to the thorns in the blackberry infested ravine. By now, talking all night and being cold and wet on the drive had me with a sore throat. Told the polygrapher I had a cold. He said it didn't matter.

Normally, lie detector tests are given to prove people are lying about the crimes. Here I was trying to say I did the crime. It was the police who wanted me to not be the killer. Does it make a difference? The polygrapher stopped the test to say my sore throat was the problem. Ruled as inconclusive.

Buckner had given all I had given to his boss, the prosecutor. The prosecutor called Phelan on his cell phone(yes, he had a walkie-talkie type phone) and told him to gloat over what I had done. Phelan turned to me.

'What do you want me to do now?'

'Plead me guilty in our case in Clark county and put off sentencing until I'm sentenced in Oregon.'

'Why?' he asked.

'I want to do all of my prison time in OSP in Salem. The best place to do my time anywhere.'

'But we haven't even proven you killed Bennett. How can you be so sure?'

'Don't worry Tom, I got it covered.'

On October 7th, 1995 explorer scouts converged on the area I had said to look and found nothing. Det. Chris Peterson had done good. He kept them within the boundaries I had laid down. On Sunday October 8th, Phelan told me the news.

'They found nothing Keith.'

'Don't worry Tom, they will.'

My lawyer is an officer of the court. He has an obligation to tell the DA everything to keep both sides of a case in the know. What Tom didn't know, he couldn't tell. I had to keep him in the dark and spring things on him. To keep the court guessing.

On Wednesday October 11th, Dale was talking to Phil Stanford over the phone while I listened through the heavy door to hear that he will be camped out on the site I described in my letter. If anyone is looking, he will document it. He was aware I would be telling them to search it soon. I got word to Det. Peterson by way of his son that I needed to talk to him.

On Friday October 13th, Det. Peterson pulled me out to talk to him in a room.

'I lied to you hwere I put her purse.'

'Where is it?'

'I have given the location to Phil Stanford and he might be looking for it himself. Now that would be something if he actually found it.'

'Tell me where Keith!'

'Remember when I told you not to go south of the large old dead tree stump under the telephone lines?'

'Ya, what about it?'

'Forty feet south and forty feet from the road. From the old tree stump.'

Peterson didn't wait for an escort to take me back to my cell. He just left me and left the door open. He needed to secure the search area to keep Phil from looking. And he would also know Phil would be watching.

On Saturday October 14th, 1995, the explorer scouts ripped into the new search area while Phil Stanford looked on. Fifteen minutes later success! They found the goods and couldn't destroy them!

On Sunday October 15th, I got a call from Phelan to tell me 'Good job'. He also had news. Multnomah was now going to claim I had been in on the murder along with those two. He also told me that I would be in court on Monday to plead guilty to killing Julie. Sentencing to be set back until I'm sentenced in Oregon. I had to get busy. The gag order would be coming off. Time to send a message.

On October 16th 1995, I plead guilty to killing Julie and handed a press release to Phelan to take to the pricks over at the Multnomah DA's office. It was well written. I addressed their new story that was bullshit. Told them I was about to rain down daily press releases to force them to let those people go. Phelan delivered the press release. He came back with their offer. If I didn't do any more press, they will work with me to solve everything and let those two out of prison. Tom was adamant to say that when people are cornered they do crazy things. Best to accept this. And we did.

Tom took over my answer and just like that, they located Roberta in just fifteen minutes and she told them about things I didn't tell her. They got her to lie to them to build a case to convict me for doing the Bennett murder by my lonesome. What is important here is I was in a very unique situation. Celled in Clark county across the river from Portland. We were all in the same pres zone. Had they rejected the deal to solve me, I could have yelled all I wanted to the press and Multnomah county people would have to listen to it. Why? I was in a deal already to a life sentence. So no gag order could be implemented on me. With them actually considering telling everyone that Pavlinac, Sosnovske and Jesperson were all involved in the case would certainly blow up in their faces with all of their press releases telling he world I was lying. I could have hit them with a real shit storm of bad press. Part of me wanted to tell them to eat shit and die. But Tom and I were also thinking of how they would react being cornered. Best let sleeping dogs lay. Sit back and let them come up with a solution to their problem. And I'm sure they knew that if they went back on the deal, I would jump on top and never look back as I pushed the press to force them to solve it. A problem they had created!

One problem to solve was to prove I didn't know those two people, to separate us from their convictions so there would be no doubt we were strangers to each other. On October 20th, Multnomah scheduled me and Laverne to meet at the Portland's field office of the FBI to do polygraph tests. They gave me the same questions asked of me on October 6th by Oregon State Police. Laverne was asked if she knew or have she ever met me. We both passed. John Sosnovske would not be tested. Why? I'm betting they feared he would fail the test because he failed the test back in 1990 when asked if he killed Bennett.

Then my lawyer Tom Phelan came to me to ask permission to show the prosecutor Jim McIntyre the notes he took down back on May 11th to prove I told him everything back then before I talked to reporter Phil Stanford over the phone. They record phone calls in county jails and had a copy of our phone conversations of September 30th between Phil and me. With all of the compelling evidence, the team converged to Marion county on October

25th, 1995 to ask if Judge Lipscomb would set both Laverne Pavlinac and John Sosnovske free.

This was a stalling point to how fast we were moving. They needed to slow it down to come up with a solution to avoid a new trial. Why? A new trial would ask Laverne where she got all of the material and information to convict her from. They could not let her testify where and who gave it to her to use. So a new trial would be out of the question. Imagine had they had a new trial and she spilled the beans? Heads would roll, cops and DAs would be fired, or worse, lose their positions. And open up Multnomah county to several multi-million dollar settlements to hopefully save face.

Judge Lipscomb told all to wait for his ruling. He sent everyone home to look how to solve this dilemma. Then on November 2nd, 1995 I was in Multnomah county courthouse to plead guilty to killing Taunja Ann Bennett on January 21st, 1990. I was sentenced to a thirty year with a twenty year minimum sentence. One of Pavlinac's family sat behind me whispering, 'Thank you.'.

Just because the Bennett case had been solved doesn't mean the other cases were not being covered. On November 8th, 1995, three years to the day I had killed Laura Pentland in Wilsonville, Oregon and dropped her body off in Marion county, I was taken to Marion county to seal the deal to solve the case. Tom had done a good job to get a life sentence in writing for my complete cooperation in solving it. Would pass a lie detector test. A good thing they never asked me if I had premeditated my decision to kill her or to question my reason why I killed her. I told a lie to say she tried to double charge me. Blame the victim!

Now Marion county told me they would be prosecuting me in their courtroom. I did argue with them to inform them it matters where she was killed not so much as where the body was found. They told me it doesn't work like that. If it doesn't, why then did they have Pavlinac change her story putting Bennett's death as happening in Multnomah county? Said they would check into that.

A major storm had torn the valley apart in late November. What better time to let them go when other major news articles are covering up pages of newspapers. On Monday following Thanksgiving, November 27th, 1995, Judge Lipscomb held a meeting to release both Laverne Pavlinac and John Sosnovske from prison. Both had a solution on how it could happen. Because Laverne was reported to wear a wire to entrap Sosnovske, Sosnovske's civil rights were violated and he could be set free. (But they never had her wear a wire to entrap John. They knew he was innocent and would never admit to Pavlinac any crime.)

Because Pavlinac had gone through a trial, releasing her would be harder. Under Oregon's law against cruel and unusual punishment, because she was factually innocent, but convicted of it legally, she could be set free. And still have a conviction to murder on her record. (Laverne would have to sign off on it. No mention of the money she could have asked for to sign it.)

In the press, Multnomah told the press it was all Pavlinac's fault. Had she not injected herself into the case, none of this would have happened. That part was true. But also, had the detectives done their job correctly, she would have been eliminated as a suspect early on. And the debate goes on and on.

And then on December 15th, 1995, I was taken to the Washington county courthouse to plead guilty to killing Laura Pentland back on November 8th, 1992. I would receive a 37 and a half year sentence to follow my 30 years in Multnomah county. Apparently it mattered where she died because Washington county caught wind of it and wanted to have me there. To get me, Washington county had to pay Marion county for their complete investigation into her death. And accept the deal made with Jesperson's attorney. They had to pay to play. At the end of the court talk, the pimp of Pentland was there to yell at me. A hooker too. Had she showed up that night instead of Pentland, she would have died. Just wanted to kill someone that night.

On a side note here, I wore orange from Clark county. Thought it would be cute to write the words: "Detective Rick Buckner is Gay. Just ask Bruce Westfall of the Colombian" on the back of my top. I was able to get it over there because it was on the inside. At using a restroom before court, I turned the shirt inside out, exposing it. With cameras rolling, I entered the courtroom. Minutes later, a detective saw what I had written and escorted me into a hallway to switch it back. Back in Clark county, Det. Buckner had me sign it and he probably still has it.

Then on the 19th of December 1995, I was in front of Judge Harris to get my sentence for killing Julie. We figured it to be around thirty years. He handed down 34 and a half years to run right behind Oregon time. Being it was near Christmas and the judge wore a beard, I told him, 'I was hoping to be able to be home with my children for a week's furlough. But I don't think Santa will be granting me that wish. Well Santa, reach into your bag of goodies and give me what I've got coming, sir!'

It had been quite a ride since I went public on September 19th, 1995 to tell all I was the Happy Face Killer. In the next ninety days I was able to be conviction in two Oregon counties and convicted in Washington state as well. Also able to get two people, two innocent people released from prison. I dare anyone to beat that! Can I go to bed now? I'm tired.

Killer Kit

Chapter Sixteen: Killer Kit

While I was there in Clark county, I managed to come up with a joke that grew feet. I called the joke the "Self Start Serial Killer Kit". Just an advertisement for a kit that doesn't exist. Something Billy Swift would sell on TV with the same energy used in infomercials. Don't ask me why I came up with this, frankly I just don't know. Maybe it was what questions I was being asked by everyone. But this is the first time I written it in 25 years, but this is what it looked like:

THIS IS THE OFFER YOU ALL HAVE BEEN DYING FOR! THE SELF START SERIAL KILLER KIT!

GET RID OF THAT UNWANTED FAMILY MEMEBER

BE THE ONLY SERIAL KILLER ON YOUR BLOCK

OPEN UP THAT JOB AT WORK

THIN OUT THE HERD AT THE RESTAURANTS

CLEAN UP YOUR TOWN

THE SELF START SERIAL KILLER KIT!

YOU GET A FULL-SIZED JULIE WINNINGHAM LOOK-A-LIKE DOLL WITH AN EXTRA STRONG SPRING BACK NECK SO YOU WILL SOON HAVE THE STRENGTH TO SQUEEZE THE SHIT OUT OF ANYONE! EACH OPENING ON YOUR DOLL IS FULLY FUNCTIONAL! YES, YOUR PLAYMATE IS YOURS IN REAL LIFE AND DEATH SITUATIONS. YOU GET A DVD FULL OF EASY TO FOLLOW INSTRUCTIONS.

SEND $99.95 TO WAYLAID INDUSTRIAL, 666 CEMETERY LANE, SUITE 13, BATTLEGROUND WASHINGTON 98ICU

LOCATED IN THE BASEMENT OF THROTTLE AND CHOKES CASKETS RENTALS. BUY TWO AND GET ONE FREE WASTE-AWAY TOW LINE SO YOU CAN WATCH YOUR VICTIMS WASTE AWAY BEFORE YOUR VERY EYES.

I just wondered how many people bought into this joke and sent the money to the address. So after I made it up, I sent a copy to Sandra London in Florida. She had a website on the internet carried by her carrier America online. She posted it and the Leeza talk show saw it and it started to snowball. My lawyer Tom Phelan had heard about it and wasn't impressed. He told me to kill it. But the genie was out of the bottle. Sandra London was the woman that befriended Danny Rolling, the Gainesville Ripper. You must have seen Danny sing to her in court proposing to London. I did on the TV and it was embarrassing to watch.

Once she got her feet in my door, I could not get rid of her. She became just like my father, trying to pull me down. Even asked me to be my police agent in my Angela Subrize case in Wyoming. As if I needed help talking to the legal system. She became a joke on the web. And the Leeza talk show exposed her and her website full of murder memorabilia. The Killer Kit created her persona as 'Squeaky Love' in a battle to take down her page. The governor of Wyoming saw it and decided to make it his duty to be re-elected using the platform to bring me to his state to kill me for killing Angela. But first kill Sandra London's website.

James Geringer, governor of Wyoming, met with AOL founder and decided to debate Sandra London and Larry Flynt of Hustler magazine on the live Larry King talk show. Of course London told all she was defending me, the Happy Face Killer, in this debate. In the fight over freedom of speech, freedom of expression, it was finalized by the founder of AOL shutting down Squeaky Love's website.

However, because of all the press in this debate, several carriers offered London a free ride for her to post her site on their platform. Nothing changed!

There were so many stupid things happened to me once I ended up in jail and then in prison, it is hard to tell this story to make perfect sense of it all. So I'll just wing it, try to follow the bouncing skull throughout this whole experience.

Ken Lee Monsebroten, AKA Duke, was a convicted serial rapist and made a deal with Clark county, Washington and Laramie county, Wyoming to kill me. He would testify in court if need be to get his 'rape with a knife' charge reduced to a simple 'sexual misconduct'. Allowing him to eventually be free! Although in 2003 after just three months of freedom, he passed away. His story about my case in Wyoming is a lie. And I helped to create this story by giving him Wyoming and not Nebraska as where I killed Angela Subrize. He told the story that I killed her at the Burns Brothers truck stop at Exit 377 and tied her body under my trailer and dragged it for 240 miles to Marker 210 in Nebraska. Easy to prove it could not have happened like that!

On January 12th, 1996, a legal team came to Clark county to interview me. They all asked all kinds of questions and told me they believed I raped her. They believed I was lying to them. They gave me a lie detector test and had a professor who teaches giving lie detector tests to be my tester to prove once and for all what I was. I passed the test, no I did not rape Angela. Yes I was telling them the truth. This really shut them down. Wyoming's legal team there had to go home to rethink how to get me.

Then Gov. James Geringer jumped on board with his re-election campaign. Kill Jesperson and his Self Start Serial Killer Kit! Remember in murder cases, there is no time limit in how many years it takes to prosecute them.

Take my case to Florida? In early 1996 Phelan was talking to Florida trying to make a deal when they sent their investigator Glen Barbaree to talk to me. Glen told me he had heard my story and yes I was guilty of killing a woman named Susanna, but what he really wanted to know was if I was the murderer of a black woman found near Tampa. He showed me photos of the crime scene and said, 'Just tell me if you did her so her family can get some sense of peace.'

I just couldn't confess to a crime that wasn't mine. And as it turns out, that murder would be solved when serial killer Sam Little confessed to it just a few years back in 2022. to confess to it would be like Pavlinac confessing to the Bennett murder all over again. Florida would kill the case calling it closed in 1996 because Jesperson was too much time already and the cost would be too much for Florida tax players to approve.

Then in around 2019, I get a visit by Det. Dennis Haley and Paul Moody wanting to re-think the case. What did she look like? Told them she looked like Nicole Kidman and they sent me photos of Kidman asking me to draw my victim. Laughing I did draw Nicole Kidman and sent it to them and they posted the drawing. "Have you seen her?" Go figure!

Fast forward to 2023 when I get crime writer Briar Lee Mitchell to tell Florida she will pay for DNA testing to see if they can backtrack her identity using different websites using DNA to research our heritage. This forces Florida to push forward on their own and in March 2023 identify who my victim is. Her family in Ohio isn't interested in publicity and will not attend a trial. In September 2023, Florida comes to me here at OSP to toss a murder II at me based on the story I told them. Then on April 4th, 2024, I spend just 6 minutes in front of a judge over a Zoom TV to pick up a life sentence of 25 years to run concurrent to my Oregon time for murder II.

In my lie to Florida, I told them when I pulled into the rest area of Exit 18, she began to scream as she panicked over being startled awake. That I killed her so the security guard would not report the incident to my boss. Blame the victim!

Along with Florida, Phelan had secured life sentences in writing for my 2nd murder, a woman we call Claudia, in Riverside county, California. They showed up here and set out many photos taken in the air over where I had put her body. In seconds, I showed them X marks the spot on several of the photos.

'It doesn't get any easier than that,' a cop said.

In 2019, my daughter Melissa goes on the Oprah talk show with Dr. Phil and her mother Rose and of all people Daun Slagle. Daun talks about her new lie telling the audience I had kicked her baby at my feet on the floor of my car. (But if that were true, why didn't the prosecutor charge me for child abuse?) The TV show sparked interest in solving me in the Riverside case. However they would need Oregon to help. They would recruit two staff members to type out a fast and speedy request to settle my Riverside case and try to get me to sign it, forcing Riverside to take me there to settle the case.

Pinkley Wertz and Lennex called me to an office telling me to sign it. Reading it, I signed it and and those two were high fiving each other yelling, 'You're going to die Jesperson!'. I told them both that I will be back at OSP in two months.

Riverside prosecutors had reached out to Phelan, but Phelan didn't respond. So they figured Phelan no longer looked after me and they could toss out the deal made in 1996 to a life sentence and take me to trial and kill me. How? By using what I had written in the Happy Face letter back in 1994 to Phil. Two weeks later, transport picked me up and drove me to Riverside.

We did stop at 'Heaven on Earth' bakery at Exit 86 on I-5 here in Oregon to allow me one of their famous cinnamon rolls drenched in real butter.

Once I arrived in the Riverside county jail, Phelan sent to me a copy of our written deal. Then in January 2010, I presented the paper to my attorney and we settled the case in just 20 minutes, I'd get another life sentence to run concurrent to my Oregon time. You can say Riverside prosecutors were not happy with how it played out. In February I was returned back to here at OSP. The next morning, I saw Pinkley and he was visibly pissed off I was back.

Along with Florida and Riverside county California, Phelan was working on Merced county, California to address the issues surrounding their original claims to back up Multnomah county to say I was a liar in their case too, the Cynthia Lynn Rose case. Because I had proven to be telling the truth in settling the Bennett case, Merced county felt an obligation to at least hear what I had to say. To get the chance, Merced county had to agree to a life sentence should I prove I was the one that killed Cynthia Lynn Rose. Just like the deal I made to solve the Bennett case. Let's be clear here, Merced county still believed Rose died of an overdose.

In the course of our meeting, one of the detectives said, 'This doesn't sound like our case with Cynthia Lynn Rose.' and as it would later turn out after going into my trucking records, I left the area at least two days before Cynthia had died and was later found just 20 feet from where I had claimed putting my victim behind the Blueberry Hill cafe in Livingston, California. And in 2009 while being transported to Riverside, a detective showed me a photo of a woman laying in a fetal position dressed in a red top, panties and sneakers.

'Tell me about her,' he asked.

'I don't know who that is. Who is she?'

'This is Cynthia Lynn Rose.'

'I put mine in the soft dirt in the middle of the parking lot. Your photo has her next to a tree on hard ground.'

when I returned home to OSP in February 2010, I mailed a letter to Phelan telling him of the photo. The Cynthia Lynn Rose case is not mine. My victim, as I have said was alive when I left her. To even seal this deal further, crime writer Ms. Briar Lee Mitchell went to what was once the back lot of the cafe with a set of cadaver dogs to see if they locate a place where a dead body had been. The 2023 search found nothing. Case closed! I'm thinking what might happen is someone reading this book will remember hearing my victim tell her story and come forward to once and for all say, my victim survived.

Remember there is another case that said my victim died of an overdose to support Multnomah county's claims that I lied. The woman I picked up in Corning in 1993 and killed at the Williams rest area and placed her body in the pile of rocks north of Hwy 152 heading for Gilroy. They decided to wait a long time before looking back into the case. Why?

They wanted my dealings in Oregon to be ancient history. In 2006, a new coroner is said he re-examined her report and called it a homicide. They believed me when I told them they probably found my yellow and black seven inch long flashlight at her body or close by. They did! Said I had sex with her, even though their findings couldn't prove sex happened at all.i told them she had told me she had recently stole from her sister and wanted to stay with me. Blame the victim!

In July 2007, I was taken to San Jose, California and given a life without parole sentence. The whole case was over in just 15 minutes. Then in April 2022, using DNA to backtrack heritages they were able to identify my Santa Clarita county victim as Patricia Skiple from

Oregon. This of course pushed me to push others to do the same for my other Jane Doe victims. And it also forced Florida to look as well. My Riverside county case is still trying.

WYOMING

Chapter Seventeen: Wyoming

Ken Lee Monsebroten would be sent to the correctional facility near Monroe, Washington where he would run into author Jim Fogle. Fogle wrote the book called 'Drugstore Cowboy' that was also made into a movie. Duke was still working on that book he started back in Clark county. Only now, he didn't owe 300% to those still in Clark county. He teamed up with Fogle to produce the book once my Wyoming case was done and he had helped to kill me. He introduced himself in the book as being convicted of petty crimes and misdemeanors. He's a serial rapist and snitch! But snitches can be manipulated because we know what they crave, what their end game is. I kept in contact with Duke to hear about all of the police agencies coming to him to ask about me. Hell, Tom Jensen of the Green River Task Force contacted him because my records had me in Seattle between 1983-1986 while I drove for Jerry's Steel Supply. They had been looking at truck drivers who came into town frequently. Now that I was a convicted serial killer, Tom Jensen wrote me a letter begging me to come clean and confess to being the Green River Killer.

A detective named Mike Kolsch talked to Duke and Duke sent him to me. I got a phone call from Kolsch asking if I'd be willing to talk to him in person about anything. He did have a specific case in Elko, Nevada he wanted to pin on me. I told Michael to be able to talk to me, his prosecutor had to give me a clean ride. No charges to be filed. Immunity from prosecution. A few days later, he calls and tells me I have been granted immunity and he was on his way to see me.

It was really early in the morning in early 1996 when Mike Kolsch flew in to Salem. I was taken downtown Salem to the office of the Oregon State Police. Chained to the floor. In walks two men, Detective Kolsch and his pilot. He began with a lie.

'I have to be completely honest with you Mr. Jesperson. I was halfway here and I forgot those immunity papers back on my desk. But don't fear, the deal is the same.'

I was not born yesterday. He could not provide me any deal that he claimed existed.

'I just can't remember a thing. I seemed to have left my brain back in my cell.' I fired back at him.

'Come on Mr. Jesperson. Talk to me. How many people have you killed?'

Like him, I lied, 'I have killed 166 people in 13 years, seven in Nevada.'

And there it was, a lie that would spread like wild fire on dry summer afternoon. He flew home and told everyone. Soon it was even used by me to help destroy my own credibility.

Oh what tangled web we weave!

They brought me to OSP in Febuary 1996. yes, I had a few fights to establish who I was in the prisons pecking order. While working in the kitchen, I had a man named Wayne Koker talk to me about his friend Jack Crescenzi doing life in an eastern Oregon prison for killing his wife. He wanted to help Jack by maybe getting me to say I killed Bobbi Crescenzi. Tried to explain to him it isn't easy proving guilt and getting people out of prison. The Bennett case was like advertisement to have a flood of people wanting to use me to get out of prison.

Credibility in prison sucks if you are a serial killer. Because I had it, all someone had to say is I told him some story and it is believed to be true. Not simply satisfied with my eight case, I was being bombarded by inmates and police and even Phil Stanford to produce more. I had a detective from southern Oregon's Jackson county come to see me.

He sat down, opened up his briefcase and said, 'I'm investigating you for the murder back in 1964.' I looked at him wondering where he got his brain.

'Are you suggesting that when I was just nine years old I drove my father's pickup truck all the way from Chilliwack, British Columbia, Canada, across the United States border to southern Oregon and back again before my dad realized I had taken his truck?'

He closed his briefcase and got up, not leaving me his business card and left.

Another detective came to ask me if back in 1976 did I kill a woman in Texas. And I wasn't even driving a truck back then. And I even got nuts like this Melinda Ramos Alston claiming I picked her up and attacked her at a time I couldn't have done so. I'm the boogeyman, a freshly convicted serial killer, convicted and sent to prison to be blamed for everything not nailed down! I'm not Henry Lee Lucas, the Texas serial killer who confessed to over 500 murders. No, just 166, 158 of them not known. If you believe that kind of shit!

Did I kill Bobbi Crescenzi? No! But if I said I did and I'm proven to be a liar, my credibility will be blown apart and even Duke's testimony being he is telling what I told him comes under question. If I lied about killing Bobbi I could have lied to Duke. And the only reason

Wyoming wanted me is because Duke made his deal to tell them a story. Okay, Wayne Koker give me all of the information to help me get your friend out of prison.

So here is the rub: Bobbi's body had never been found. If I were to prove I killed her, Jack needed to let me know where to find her body. He didn't want to do that, fearing it will backfire on him. Trust? He just could not trust me with where he put his wife. Believing that just saying, I killed her had to be enough. Okay, I'll try.

An investigator working for Jack Crescenzi named Sharon Brubaker provided me with what Mickael Koker couldn't. She even set it up for me to be filmed by NBC, channel 5 in Chicago's Dateline show. She sold the story to Dateline and we were to be filmed in October 1997. Me here at OSP and Jack over at Pendleton.

But in the middle of all of this, Gov. James Geringer of Wyoming had gotten into a pissing match with me over the Killer Kit. He was forcing prosecutors to come to Oregon to pull me out of before Dateline could film us. So to block Wyoming and get my Dateline show done, I filed a writ of Habeas Corpus to make sure Wyoming was doing everything legally. The show must go on!

In the middle of all of this I called James Geringer an idiot in an interview. Why? Because he was making the case political.

I told my defense team to make recordings of the idiot Geringer every time he spoke of his buddy ole pal Keith Jesperson. In one recording he was asked by the press, 'What about Jesperson?' He answered-and- I quote: 'I'm going to ring Jesperson to my fine state. I'm going to give Mr. Jesperson a fair trial and then I'm going to kill the bastard.'

Check, so much for a fair trial. I would be able to use it to squash the case if need be.

So, Marsha Bartell, produced the Dateline show. I told I killed 166 people. I told I killed Bobbi Crescenzi. She went to interview Jack and he told her he didn't do it. Then later in October I was to have a follow up interview over the phone with Marsha Bartell on October 21st, 1997.

she said, 'Why did you lie to us?'

'I didn't lie to you.'

'Yes you did Mr. Jesperson.'

'Tell me...prove it...how did I lie to you?'

Dateline is no joke. They do their research. Wayne Koker told all how he recruited me to lie for Jake.

'Why did you lie?'

'It will make a good story.'

'Why did you lie?'

'Are you going to use it?'

'Yes we are. Why did you lie?'

Then it was my final statement before I hung up the phone. 'I didn't kill anyone. Didn't kill Taunja Bennett. I'm innocent! This has all been a big frame up!'

'You killed Bennett! We are sure of that!'

CLICK!

I had my answer. A week later, I was being taken to the hole. Why? Because I had lied to prison staff, lied to Dateline and everyone else. Charged with it and was being punished for lying. Such a contradiction to how we inmates are perceived in here as liars, all of us! As I was being escorted to the hole the guard asked me, 'How does it feel being known as a liar?'

'It feels pretty damn good actually.'

'Why?'

'Would you rather be a murderer or a liar?'

'I see your point.'

Two weeks later before I was to be sent to Wyoming on con air, guess who comes to see me in the hole? Detective Al Corson. He had a proposal for me. Take back my confession so he could put Pavlinac and Sosnoske back into prison. To fuck even more with his head I agreed with him that I had lied. That Laverne and John were guilty. He promised to have my conviction over turned and the 30 year sentence dropped from my life. More on this later. We will get into the conspiracy theories on Corson.

A week after Corson visits me, I'm picked up by the US Marshall's office and transported via con air to Cheyenne, Wyoming. When they bring me back in June 1998 the bill is submitted to Wyoming for $136,000 to bring me to Wyoming and back to Oregon.

Dateline airs their show on me called 'True Lies' just after I got to Wyoming proving me to be a liar on national TV. The prosecutors know their case took a hit. And with what the governor said, we were offered a deal because apparently, we don't play fair. Who's playing here?

In court in June 1998, I tell the truth about killing Angela Subrize in Nebraska.

'Wait!' cries the judge. 'You killed her in Nebraska? Why are you here?'

'Ken Lee Monsebroten sir.'

The prosecutors tell how this case became a case solely on the testimony of a prison house rat, Duke AKA Monsebroten.

'So why are you pleading guilty in my court Mr. Jesperson?'

'The evidence proving I killed her in Nebraska will kill me in Nebraska. And just maybe you Wyoming jurors will not care if it is a Nebraska case and kill me here. Matters little to all of us where I'm convicted. Just that the case is over with a conviction.'

'So you are pleading guilty to avoid the death penalty?'

'Yes sir.'

He gives me a life sentence to follow my Washington state time and I'm on con air transport back to Oregon.

"And Duke has to rewrite his ending to his book with Fogle, not able to help Wyoming to kill me. Oh well!"

Back in 1997, NBC channel 5 in Chicago was on another kick about animal abuse. The head of Washington DC's humane society and another investigator came to chat about killing a cat. Why? I had witnessed news in Salem, Oregon about two local football players in high school who had killed a cat. A debate over the cat and their actions caused lots of editorials in the newspapers. I wrote a letter to the editor telling them I killed a cat and to look how I turned out. This put me again on the news and what I had to say meant something.

While we talked they asked me about Andrew Cunanan, the suspect gay killer, that would eventually kill Versace in Florida. My guess was spot on to him going to Florida. When the Dateline people checked out what I said a chill went down their spine.

(I'm guessing because I was so accurate in my assessment to Cunanan's travels, they didn't want to use what I had said, feeling public opinion would be outraged over hearing my prediction and no one did anything about it.)

Because Det. Corson came to me before I went to Wyoming for a possible death sentence, I had to rethink him. Corson had been duped! He was used to bring credibility to a case that had none. Det. John Ingram coached Laverne and when he was satisfied the story could be told by Pavlinac, Ingram calls Corson to listen to it. Corson to believe even Ingram was hearing it for the first time. I believe Corson would never imagine his co-worker John Ingram would do such a thing. So when he came to me in the hole, I went along with his belief that they were guilty based on Phil Stanford's phone calls. Then I added the material Phil gave me, the red handled knife. I put a world of hurt on Corson when I went along with his thinking. Corson went to his boss with his story and was told to never bring it up again or lose his position.

Chapter Eighteen: Life Inside

What is there to do in prison? Work, eat, and sleep. And here at OSP we have a lot more. How about a miniature golf course, real horse shoes to toss, real baseball bats to swing at balls, a weight training area and a track to run, to list it all is crazy! You'd think I was at a club med.

I would take up artwork to do in colored pencils. In 2002, activities put on an art show and it brought in the press. They took photos of my art and it made the front cover of their newspaper. How dare I be able to sell my art? Being pressured by the public, I was punished and told I could never use the smiley face ever again. It is not a rule, but just a direct order from here in OSP. I can't sell my art even today, but I can give it away to family and friends for donations. A fine line to follow.

In 2005, my daughter Melissa Moore showed up here to visit me with her husband and their two children Jake and Aspen. We had a nice visit. They never came back to see me. A short time later, Melissa goes on the Dr. Phil show to tell the world her father is the Happy Face Killer. She received lots of sympathy from the crowds watching and it effects her greatly. She helps to create a book called, 'Shattered Silence', to explain me. I've read this book and it has a lot of false stories in it. She soon followed the talk shows and even had her own shows about families of killers. She actually calls herself a crime consultant. All of this killer stuff made her husband leave her.

Melissa and Sam divorced and Melissa reunited with her childhood sweetheart Steve Kenoyer, the son of my best friend from high school. Even though they live just maybe seventy miles from me, they don't visit. Melissa is afraid I'll kill her for all the lies she has told about me over the years. Paranoia has taken over her life. Murdering my daughter Melissa is the furthest thing from my mind. Even though she has lied about me, she is still and forever will be loved by me.

My son Jason has spent the last 25 plus years in the U.S Military. I'm so proud of him. But we don't talk. Maybe some day we will.

My youngest daughter Carrie is a nurse in Spokane and we write to each other. She is married to a great guy name Bill and they have two boys. They have not visited, but maybe some day they will.

My ex wife Rose passed away in 2021 on my birthday April 6th. She would be 63 years old.

My father Les Jesperson passed away May 18th 2015, he was 87 years old. On the anniversary of Mt St. Helen's exploding. I had flown over the mountain a week before it blew in 1980. easy to remember.

In September 2011, crime writer Matthew William Phelps contacted me in hope I will be on his hit TV show. I ended up doing it. Season two and three as 'Raven'. The call in serial killer giving my best guess to a who done it scenario on unsolved cases. He would do a book that was mostly about him. He claims our relationship caused him to have anxiety and made him ill. Personally, I believe it is all bullshit. He is ill because I diagnosed his case with his sister in laws death. I told him I believe he is responsible for her death and the police should take another look at him as a suspect. She had come to him looking for money the night she died. Probably blackmailing him over sexual advances he made to her in his home. Phelps and I parted company. We had been friends for years and I helped him with his show. He will try to come back at some point. There is always something else to want.

I even had a call center job for six month in here. Made cold calls for different companies. Called my old school and almost messed up telling the IT director my last name. Called the Los Angeles county jail. We talked and he had no idea I was in prison. I called the Behavior Science building for the FBI in Quantico, Virginia. The serial killer profiler had no idea that a serial killer was trying to hook him up with Shoretel telephones. I had two phone calls my last day in OSP's call center that went to the White House. Seems like I got along really well with Obama's IT guy.

For the last 14 years I've been working in OSP's clothing room. Sort of run the place. I'm suffering from atrial fibrillation and I'm not taking my meds. Last December I spent five days in the hospital and almost died of cellulitis septic on my left leg. Had I waited 12 more hours, I might not be here writing this out now.

I have no cases in appeals, and I have no more time to do then I will live to see them. You can find out most about me on the blog Beyondthecrime.com.

<u>Defining Stupidity</u>

After everything you have read in this book, you may still have questions such as: What advice do I have for those who are thinking of murder? How can you not be a murderer's victim? And the ultimate 'why' about everything.

Almost 30 years behind bars and I have no real answers for people. Not what people have been told already. It always comes down to pluses and negatives. A tipping of the scales to what is important in our lives. What are you willing to lose? I lost everything when the doors closed behind me. I cried in my cell.

While I was killing I gave no thought to what my actions would do to my family. Why? Because getting caught never entered my mind. But sitting here in a 6X8 foot cell for the rest of my life hits home. What life I have left is defined by how I lived it outside these walls. I killed myself being a murderer. We only have one life to live and we have to make it a quality life. Not toss it off like trash. Am I boring you with my feeling sorry for myself? Boo-hoo! Getting caught as a serial killer will do that to you. Poor poor pitiful me.

I get it. You are not convinced. My advice is to not do it! And some of you will go ahead and become murderers regardless of what we convicted murderers tell you. Why? Because you believe you are special and not as stupid as us. You believe you'll do it right and not get caught or tell on yourself. You think you can commit the perfect murder.

I have heard people claim I believe I am cured of being a killer because I have said I will never kill again. That I have learned my lesson being in prison for the past 29 years. Cured? Are we calling murder a sickness now? Curable? I will tell you this, if released, I will not murder anyone. I value my freedom. If you value your freedoms, walk away from trouble. Do not engage in such a senseless act like murder.

Sitting in prison these past 29 years has taught me plenty. Crime shows like *CSI* and *Law and Order* have schooled me with ever changing technology proving the science of evidence is getting better. Killing is the easy part. Anyone can be a killer. Getting away with it is something else.

Reading my story in this book will explain who and what I am. The mistakes I made has robbed me of a good life full of family and friends that loved me. Robbed me of my freedoms. Do not let it rob you of yours. My advice: Don't do it! Trust me, it isn't worth it.

Who I am today is not what I was back then. I value life now.

Postscript Clutter

In recent events, the democrats have weaponized the justice system. It is no longer about the justice and the law. They charged and convicted former President Trump on 34 counts of who knows what. If they can do it to him, they can do it to anyone. ADA Jim McIntyre weponized the legal system to arrest and convict Laverne and John for a crime they at the time could not solve. Their only regret is they got caught. This is why they fought to keep them in prison. To not have to admit the legal system in America is flawed.

Mark Voss and Dion Costis were themselves prosecutors in Kirkland, Washington when the details oof the Bennett case were exposed. They were afraid of the shock wave coming their way due to the system being looked closely at so they switched sides to become defense lawyers and excitedd to be my lawyers when I went to Wyoming to face Governor Geringer. They worked with me to solve this Nebraska case in Wyoming, and I was not easy to work with. Why? Because I am a serial killer looking ahead of my situation. When a suspect is arrested for any crime, there are certain gimme's and certainties that will happen automatically. 1. Public opinion matters. 2. Because you were arrested you must have done something. 3. Because you were arrested and put in jail, you are a lair! That you will do and say anything to get out of the situation. 4. Some of your family will abandon you.

There are more obvious things to happen when arrested. But these four are automatic. Public opinion is fueled by press reports. Not in your favor, even one sided bias. These tip the scale of justice in favor of the police and prosecutors. Like at your arraignment when you are forced to appear to be a liar when the court will not allow you to plead guilty, it forces you to say 'not guilty'. Try to argue and the court will enter a plea for you as not guilty. Imagine being caught on video shooting someone and they take the smoking gun from you.

The court will still not let you plead guilty. Why? It is in our rights. 'You are innocent until proven guilty.' and when the public hears this crap they scream at the top of their lungs at the suspect for lying to them.

Most generally when police talk to suspects they rely on what we all have been taught by our parents growing up, you remember the talk don't you: 'Son/Daughter, if you come clean and tell me the truth, I'll go easy on you.'

they play on this to say, 'If you tell us the truth, 'they' will go easy on you. The thing is, the police tell you this to reference the 'they' in the talk is their bosses-prosecutors. Which is the wrong way for a suspect to look at it. The 'they' is your future jurors, civilians who have not been picked yet. Any lawyer will tell you the worst thing you can do is talk to the police. So who do you talk to to do the right thing? That is the dilemma. In a single case, talk to your lawyer and most will let the lawyer handle the case. But I can't do that. Allow one lawyer to take care of me in all of my cases in the multiple jurisdictions. See, I knew I was guilty and going to be found guilty regardless of any defense. My only hope that the story I want to tell to be heard is to take my fight to them. Force everyone to hear what I have to say before any trial is scheduled to begin. Have my future jurors reading mystery and debating over it as they sit and have coffee and bagels at Starbucks. My attorney Tom Phelan early on complained to me about telling the press I dragged Angela under my trailer for 12 miles down Interstate 80.

'They want to kill you Keith!'

And of course they do. But they will not be able to because they read it six months before court is to begin.

Why?

Because the only reason to have a trial is for the discovery of evidence. If all of the evidence is known by all, why have a trial to prove nothing? Imagine a prosecutor in his opening statement telling the court full of spectators and jurors, 'I'm going to prove to you everything that Mr. Jesperson told you in his press releases is true. There is no other evidence to counter his statements to everyone. But even though he has told you all what happened and has told you he is guilty of this murder, even though he has done what is the right thing to do, I want you to kill him anyways.'

No prosecutor in this century would dare to make the argument and that is why I have never been to a trial. All cases have gone to deals to life sentences and have taken mere minutes to seetle in court, not days, but minutes. Every lie detector test I've taken, I have passed. Why? Most times they test people who are lying and trying to say they are innocent. I take the test to prove I'm guilty and telling the truth based on the questions they ask. In the Bennett case, the prosecutors needed me to be proven a lair, that I didn't kill Bennett. This is why lie detector test results are not allowed as evidence in a court of law.

While in Wyoming, former prosecutor Marsha Clark of the OJ Simpson trial wanted me to be on her new show called 'Lie Detector'. My lawyers Mark Voss and Dion Custis would not sign off on me doing it. Ask them why?

When I was being flown from the con air intake center in Oklahoma we were on a Lear jet and about to take off when I addressed the guards guarding me, 'Just to let you know if these pilots get sick, I do know how to fly this plane'. The pilots turned and asked me a few questions and satisfied they went back and picked up a few extra guards. The more the merrier! Thanks for spending taxpayers money!

Some of you might have heard of me writing to other serial killers to inform them of what they are about to face in this flawed justice system of America. Why? It is obvious. I didn't know and had to learn watching other cases develop over time. No one really helped me. I write and tell them what to expect, who to trust, what not to do. And I tell them how I settled my cases.

I wrote to Wayne Adam Ford, the north California serial killer and he didn't write back, but his lawyer did thank me.

I wrote Angel Maturino Resendiz, the Texas railroad serial killer. He was prepared but didn't follow me on how to settle his cases. Could have been his access to the press issues. He wrote me right up until his death. Just weeks before he was to be executed, he had used a razor blade to cut himself. They stitched him up with over 220 stitches and two pints of blood just so they could kill him later. I still get letters from his family from time to time thanking me for being his friend.

There are at least six people I helped who have avoided the death sentence following my advice. When Ward Weaver murdered Ashley Pond and Miranda Gaddis, relatives in here asked me to write Weaver to help him stay off of death row so they could get him in general population to kill him. As it turned out I didn't have to. He took a deal, and got stabbed in the neck with a pair of barber's scissors while getting his hair cut. He didn't die. But the message was sent.

I wrote Christian Longo in Lincoln City, Oregon. He didn't follow my advice because the press intercepted the mail. He got a death sentence. Recently, Oregon refuses to carry out executions and he now is in general population.

Most recently, I have written Rex Heuermann, the suspect in the Long Island serial killer case in New York. He wrote me back and I made the mistake of sharing his letter with a man named Keith Ravere that posted it online for all to read. I told Rex to get ahead of it, hurry up and make a deal to do his time here at OSP. Solve all of his murders as quickly as possible to start in prison and quit doing hard time in county jail. Will he listen? It is too early yet to tell. I hope so. The worse he'll get is a life sentence in New York. But New York prisons are no joke. People die in them every single day almost.

Because of people like me writing to other inmates to give them advice and legal ways to deal with their cases, several states have stopped inmate to inmate writing from one state to another. From even one jail to another. Just one more way to tip the justice scale in favor of the police and prosecutors.

Most inmates in jail and prisons will vote Democrat because Democrats will help us get out of prison. No cash baits. Crimes down graded to misdemeanors or just a slap on the wrist and they are out to do it again and again. If I could vote I would vote for someone like Trump to take over and fix this county. Why? Lower fuel rates mean lower prices we inmates have to pay at the prison store.

Why did I them? Just thinning out the heard. Russell Obremski, a multiple killer here in Oregon was being interviewed and asked that very same question. His answer, 'It was a slow Saturday night.'

But if I could go back and do it all over again, what would I change? I certainly would not have killed anyone. Life is so short and so valuable. I completely understand that now.

What is my favorite color: purple.

Music? Male artist? Willie Nelson. I listen to Willis' Roadhouse all of the time. Met him in person back in 1987 in Mead, Washington. He parked his bus in my bosses yard and Burt Reynolds, Kris Kristofferson and Willie Nelson came out. He turned 91 on April 29, 2024, happy birthday Willie! Female artist? Taylor Swift, love her videos. Of course I also love Shania Twain!

My favorite movie actor is Dennis Quaid. Loved his Jim Morris portrayal of 'The Rookie' saw him first in 'Tough Enough' about backyard boxing tournaments. 'hey Dennis watch out for Gay Bob'. Favorite female actress? Sissy Spacek, loved her in Loretta Lynn's portrayal and of course in 'Carrie'. Because of her in 'Carrie' I named my youngest daughter Carrie. And of course my daughter tells me I named her that so she could be carried by me.

MORE POSTSCRIPT CLUTTER

After my arrest my father opened up his mind to let me know his true thoughts. He said I was just like my great uncle Charlie. Who? Never heard of a great Uncle Charlie. To satisfy my request for how I was just like him, I needed to know it all. So he sent me a file on Uncle Charlie.

Our family came from Denmark, crossed the Atlantic to New York and rode a covered wagon to San Francisco and up the west coast to Seattle on Fairfield Island south of Chilliwack, British Columbia, Canada. The whole family got their track of land. Charlie was ambitious and cleared his 640 acres quickly. He decided to raise beef cattle and not follow his siblings with their joint dairy farm. He even had his own home across the road from their expensive massive home.

Charlie wasn't the only one to break away. My grandfather Jesperson also didn't want to be a farmer. He became a blacksmith and operated a shop close by. In fact my grandfather would be the only one to marry and have a family. After what happened to his brother Charlie, he moved to Piapot, Saskatchewan and opened a blacksmith-machine shop. In Piapot, my father Les Jesperson and four siblings were born. They would leave Piapot and move back to Chilliwack during the dirty thirties, the dust bowl.

Now back to Charlie. Because Charlie became an outcast to his immediate family, they all started to call him crazy. And back in the 1920s calling someone crazy carried a lot of weight. Soon hearing his family calling him nuts, the town people pitched in and carried their torch calling Charlie crazy too. Just because he would not join in with what his family hand wanted, to use his land to pasture their dairy herd. Charlie fought back and it just made him even look out of control. With the whole town calling him crazy, his brothers and sister decided to call him on it. They contacted a shrink and told the good doctor to go talk to him to give them a current diagnosis. Charlie met the doctor with his gun, ordering him to leave. He yelled at him, 'They are doing this to take control of my land!' and that was exactly what the Jesperson family on Jesperson road were up to, trying to find a way to take away his 640 acres to absorb it into their dairy.

Well, the doctor returned with a constable RCMP to take Charlie into custody for evaluation. He was diagnosed with dementia, and paranoid schizophrenia. Charlie would be held in the Frozen Valley mental facility. Every six months, the quack doctor again said he was paranoid due to his claims that his family were out to steal his land. And that is exactly what they had done!

After seven years, Charlie had lost hope and decided to take his own life. Ho found a hammer and a long spike, placed the point of the spike into his forehead and hammered it in all the way. For the next 24 hours he walked around the facility until an orderly noticed it and pulled out the spike. Several hours later, Charlie died of the infection. Back in Chilliwack, there was hardly a bump in their activities on the farm. Out of sight, out of mind. It was almost an inconvenience to have to bury him in the family plot. And my own father was telling me I was just like my great uncle Charlie Jesperson.

When Fred died, the last surviving sibling of the Jespersons, instead of handing over the farm to the children of his brothers, he made sure none of it went to any Jesperson. Valued, the estate was worth over a hundred million dollars, half went to the Salvation Army, and the other half went to build a new wing on the Chilliwack hospital. All because my grand father broke away from the family business like Charlie had done.

Even More Postscript Clutter

My father went south for the winter. Those who traveled south are called 'snow birds'. Christmas 1993, I visited my father and step mother in Yumas, Arizona at the RV park they had parked their large RV. He was quick to ask me, 'Have you heard of the firecracker bandit?' I reached down behind my driver's seat and pulled out a gross of Blackcat firecrackers. 'Don't tell me!' he says to me, 'you're the firecracker bandit.'

'I just might be one of them.'

I went on to explain how it started. Pulling into rest areas to try to find parking spots to rest or sleep in, only to find Rvers were camping in rest areas full time. To try to make room, I used cigarettes as delayed timers to set off my crackers to make enough noise to get them to leave, opening up spots for us truckers one night. I chased Rvers down I-5 to the next rest areas. It got to be a past time of mine to keep them moving. My father told me that a couple of elderly people suffered heart problems because of being scared when the firecrackers startled them. That the police were looking for the bandit. As long as I had access to firecrackers, I'd set them off at rest areas to try to clear out Rvers. Only during winter months, and now you know who was the real firecracker bandit. Before anyone knew me as the Happy Face Killer. As Paul Harvey would say, 'Now you know the rest of the story!'

Tale of Two Tales

A Green River Task Force cop named Tom Jensen wanted me to confess to being the Green River Killer because he read a story shared with him by Duke called 'A Tale of Two Tails'. The story is online someplace, but maybe not. I keep thinking about the story. Should I write it out and have it here in this book? So, here is the story, the one I told Duke, and of course being the jail rat he was he ate it up and thought it was true, but he wasn't the only one to believe so.

In 1985 the Green River Killer was in high gear killing hookers he picked up along Hwy 99 between Tacoma and Seattle and depositing them in shallow graves or in the Green River. Some in an old housing area overlooking the end of the Seatac airport. Several other locations turned out to be where I parked my semi to rest along Hwy 18 and Interstate 90 at mile marker 38. Some investigators believed the killer was a truck driver like me. Others were not so sure because the victims were last seen getting into a dark colored pickup truck with a canopy. Often as I drove the area picking up steel products, I had been held up when the task force were busy removing dead women he had killed. The case terrorized the area. Everyone was on high alert.

It was late afternoon around 5:00 pm when I found myself in Tacoma and needed to get to Seattle to make my last pickup at Isaac Steel before they closed. A wreck on the north bound Interstate 5 had traffic backed up and using my CB radio, people told me to try Hwy 99 north. Sure, it had lights and heavy traffic, but certainly would allow me to get to Seattle soon enough.

At an intersection, I looked across and ahead to see a bus stop station. Waiting for my light to turn green, I spotted her when she walked out from behind the bus stop and stood at the edge of the road. Pretty! Long legs and slender body, deep inside me I craved for a bitch like her. I kept eyeing her when the light turned green and I let out the clutch, grabbing gears to gain speed in the old 1964 Kenworth pulling a 42 foot long flatbed. Then in an instant as I came to her there it shocked me to see her step off the curb and land directly in front of my bumper. I slammed on my brakes. But felt her body hit my bumper and roll over her. Panicked, I set the brakes and turned on my four-way flashers, exiting the cab to find her lifeless body behind my truck and under my trailer. No one was stopping! Every one was just in a hurry to be elsewhere. I gathered up her body and placed her in the passenger side of my cab, got in and continued up Hwy 99.

'Now what do I do?'

Being almost dark, no one had payed attention to what had happened and just maybe I could get away with her death. Looking as I drove north, I saw an open field to my right across from some large homes. The field was what I needed. Pulled off onto the shoulder, grabbed a flashlight and shovel and lifted her body over my shoulder and first checked to see if anyone was watching before jogging into the dark field.

At the southeast corner stood several large evergreen tress. I laid her down and began to dig a hole to bury her lifeless body.

'What a waste!' I said to myself as from time to time I stopped to looked at her gorgeous body.

Digging near the tress was a mistake. As I dug I ran into large roots I had to dig around. My hole didn't seem big enough for her. Thought I might have to break her legs to get her to fit. As I was looking the hole over, I heard a noise coming towards me and I froze and hid in the shadow of those tress to witness a strange sight. Another man was carrying what looks like a body and holding a shovel. To my surprise, he dropped her to the ground and started to dig a hole to hide his victim. Oblivious to me standing just twenty feet away.

As he dug his hole, I stood there motionless. 'Damn!' I said to myself, 'I'm running out of time, I have to get going.'

Holding my shovel like a club, I moved behind the man. I could just knock him out and then what? Dig another hole? But I felt why not just let him know he's not alone and we can take care of business and go off in different directions.

So to break the silence I yelled, 'Boo!' then shined my flashlight in his face, then shined over his dead body and over to where mine was laying. 'I'll get done digging my hole and I'll help you to dig yours.'

Slowly we went about doing what we needed to do. I kept my eyes on him to make sure he didn't move on me for any reason. I buried my victim and helped him finish his project. We talked after our initial explosive introductions and decided to go to the nearby restaurant to talk over what to do next.

About a mile north was a Denny's and we went inside. I found a phone and called Isacc Steel to find out they were open til midnight, giving me lots of time to get there. Then I sat in the booth with my new friend.

I told him how I had come to being out in the field burying my problem. He told me his story. Off work, he had stopped by a local bar and stayed too long. So he needed to sneak in to his garage without his wife catching him so to have an excuse he'd been in the garage working on his car and lost track of time. Well, he came over the back fence undiscovered, so he thought. All of a sudden the bitch started yelling at him, making all kinds of noise. He grabbed a shovel and hit her too hard and all went silent. So much for an uneventful homecoming. He just carried her across the highway when no one was coming and found me doing what needed to be done.

'You know something?' I asked. 'Our victims looked a lot a like.'

'I saw that too.' he said.

Before burying her, I stripped her of all her jewelry and set it on the table in front of him. A tear filled his eyes as he studied the pieces in his fingers.

'What's the matter?' I asked.

'You killed my other dog.'

Because two sisters were later discovered to be victims of the Green River Killer, Tom Jensen of the task force believed my tale of two tails fit his narrative of a killer and wrote me a letter begging me to confess to the murders.

One Last Story

Before We Go

You may be asking yourself why all this postscript clutter. Why didn't I just put it in the story itself? Well, I didn't want to bog the story down from what I wanted the overall message to be, that is why.

I am not the man I was.

I value life now. My heart has been altered by time. I just want to let it out, to air it out and put it all on the table. I don't know how much longer I have in this world, and since all my cases are settled, I can finally give a tell-all to my life without holding back. I admit my guilt, and there is no hiding from it. Maybe someone will learn something, maybe someone will appreciate me finally being honest and forthcoming with my whole story, only time will tell.

But here's one last story before we go, before you put the book down.

While driving for Jerry's Steel Supply in the mid 1980s I befriended the mechanic shop man working at the Huskey truck stop where Hwy 97 meets Interstate 90 at Ellensburg, Washington. Had taught Walt how to weld one night after seeing him struggle to weld on a semi. We became close friends. One night after returning from Seattle I stopped at the Huskey for coffee and to check in on my friend Walt. He was complaining about business being slow. Working on commissions to pay rent, he felt he would not make enough to cover it.

'Anything I can do?' I asked.

'What can you do, Keith?'

'Give me an hour Walt, I'll leave and get you something to do.'

I walked out to my semi, got in and drove back towards Seattle until I got to the exit at Elk Heights and crossed over I-90 and parked on the on ramp entering eastbound I-90. I walked to the back of my trailer and removed a case of roofing nails from my load and got the opened box next to me in the truck's cab. As I entered the interstate roadway, I tossed handfuls of nails onto the interstate. Continued to toss handfuls of nails until the box was empty. Running out just before getting back to Ellensburg.

Stopping at the Huskey, I found out I hadn't tossed the nails far enough because two of my tires were going flat with nails in them. Walt has a white bucket he tossed the items he pulled from tires into. He fixed my tires and added several nails to the bucket. All fixed up, I drove to Sunnyside to drop my trailer and pick up a loaded trailer for Seattle. Driving past Ellensburg on I-90 I noticed lots of cars, pickups and semis parked on the shoulder of East I-90. Several state dump trucks with magnet bars were driving up I-90 to gather what was left of those roofing nails. Interstate 90 between Elk Heights and Ellensburg on the eastbound lanes had been closed.

A few weeks later I stopped in and met Walt in his shop. Again he claimed business was slow.

'Do you want me to help you?'

'Hell no!' he yelled, 'I had one driver with eleven tires going flat!'

Looking down at his white bucket, I saw about 5 pounds of roofing nails.

Defining Stupidity

After everything you have read in this book, you have questions. What advice do I have for those who are thinking of murder? How can you not be a murderer's victim? An 'Why' about everything?

Almost 30 years behind bars and I have no real answers for people. No what people have been told already. always comes down to plus's and negatives. A tipping of the scales for what is important in our lives. What are you willing to lose? I lost everything when the doors closed behind me. I cried in my cell.

Afterword

Dr. Marie Lestrange, Crimson Cult Media and True Crime Researcher

As publishers of Happy Face: A Family of Monsters, we recognize the sensitive nature of this work and the concerns it may raise. Our decision to publish Keith Jesperson's recounting of events is rooted in its significant educational value for criminology students, law enforcement professionals, and researchers in the field of criminal psychology.

We approach this publication with the utmost respect for the victims and their families, with hopes that such a narrative will result in an increased understanding of the disturbed psyche of a serial killer. The book provides an (oft grammatically incorrect) and unfiltered opportunity for expert analysis, unveiling crucial context and insights that can aid in the prevention, detection, and rehabilitation efforts related to violent crimes.

In light of the upcoming television dramatization of these events, we believe this book offers a valuable, in-depth perspective that goes beyond entertainment. It serves as a primary source for those seeking to understand the complexities of criminal behavior, promoting critical thinking and media literacy.

We have taken steps to minimize potential distress, including consultations with victims' advocacy groups and the inclusion of support resources within the book. Our aim is to contribute to the public's understanding of criminal psychology while maintaining sensitivity to all those affected by these crimes.

This publication represents an opportunity to delve deeper into the psychological and sociological factors behind such behaviors, potentially aiding in their prevention. We believe that by responsibly examining even the darkest aspects of human nature, we can work towards a safer society.

Resources

National Organization for Victim Assistance (NOVA)
(703) 535-6682
https://trynova.org/
NOVA is one of the oldest and most respected victim advocacy organizations in the United States. They offer crisis intervention, advocacy, and trauma mitigation services.

National Center for Victims of Crime
855-4VICTIM (855-484-2846)
https://navaa.org
https://victimconnect.org/resources/
This organization provides a wide range of programs and services to victims of crime, including a helpline, advocacy, and resources for specific types of crimes.

Rape, Abuse & Incest National Network (RAINN)
Chat: online.rainn.org
800-656-HOPE (4673)
https://rainn.org/resources *RAINN is the largest anti-sexual violence organization in the US. They operate the National Sexual Assault Hotline and provide resources for survivors.*

Office for Victims of Crime (OVC)
Directory of Crime Victim Services
https://ovc.ojp.gov/directory-crime-victim-services/search
Part of the U.S. Department of Justice, OVC provides funding for victim services and training for professionals who work with victims.

National Domestic Violence Hotline
800.799.SAFE (7233)

Text BEGIN to 88788

https://www.thehotline.org/

This organization provides 24/7 support, resources, and advocacy for victims of domestic violence.

National Human Trafficking Hotline

Text INFO to 233733

888.373.7888

https://humantraffickinghotline.org/en

Operated by Polaris, this hotline offers support and resources for victims of human trafficking.

Forensic Psychology Study Questions

1. How might Jesperson's narrative style and content reflect common psychological traits associated with antisocial personality disorder or psychopathy?

2. What forensic evidence was likely crucial in linking Jesperson to his crimes, and how might modern forensic techniques have altered the investigation?

3. Analyze the psychological manipulation tactics Jesperson employed in his correspondence with various individuals, including the author and other writers.

4. How does Jesperson's description of the American justice system align with or differ from criminological theories about the effectiveness of the legal process in dealing with serial offenders?

5. What forensic psychological principles could be applied to assess the veracity of Jesperson's account, particularly regarding potential confabulation or intentional deception?

6. Analyze the cognitive distortions present in Jesperson's justifications for his crimes, and how these relate to common patterns observed in serial killers.

7. How might the concept of "serial killer culture" as defined by John Borowski impact the psychological study of serial killers and public perception of such crimes?

8. Discuss the ethical considerations in forensic psychology when publishing and

studying the unedited words of a convicted serial killer.

9. What insights does Jesperson's case provide into the psychology of false confessions, as exemplified by the Laverne Pavlinac and John Sosnovske case?

10. How might forensic linguists analyze Jesperson's writing style and content to gain insights into his personality and potential deception?

11. Examine the potential psychological motivations behind Jesperson's decision to share his story at this particular time in his life.

12. What psychological theories could explain Jesperson's apparent need for attention and recognition, as evidenced by his interactions with various media outlets?

13. How does Jesperson's case contribute to the ongoing debate in forensic psychology about the reliability of criminal autobiographies as sources of information?

14. Analyze the potential psychological impact on victims' families when serial killers like Jesperson continue to seek public attention through books and media appearances.

www.ingramcontent.com/pod-product-compliance
Lightning Source LLC
Chambersburg PA
CBHW020538030426
42337CB00013B/900